FREE MARKET

FREE MARKET

THE HISTORY OF
AN IDEA

JACOB SOLL

BASIC BOOKS

NEW YORK

Basic Books
Hachette Book Group
1290 Avenue of the Americas, New York, NY 10104
www.basicbooks.com

Printed in the United States of America

First Edition: September 2022

Published by Basic Books, an imprint of Perseus Books, LLC, a subsidiary of
Hachette Book Group, Inc. The Basic Books name and logo is a trademark of the
Hachette Book Group.

The Hachette Speakers Bureau provides a wide range of authors for speaking events.
To find out more, go to www.hachettespeakersbureau.com or call (866) 376-6591.

The publisher is not responsible for websites (or their content) that are not owned
by the publisher.

Library of Congress Cataloging-in-Publication Data
Names: Soll, Jacob, 1968– author.
Title: Free market : the history of an idea / Jacob Soll.
Description: First edition. | New York : Basic Books, [2022] | Includes bibliographical
    references and index.
Identifiers: LCCN 2021060264 | ISBN 9780465049707 (hardcover) |
    ISBN 9781541620230 (ebook)
Subjects: LCSH: Free enterprise—History. | Capitalism—History. |
    Economic history.
Classification: LCC HB95 .S65 2022 | DDC 306.3—dc23/eng/20211210
LC record available at https://lccn.loc.gov/2021060264

ISBNs: 9780465049707 (hardcover), 9781541620230 (ebook)

LSC-C

Printing 1, 2022

To Anthony Grafton
Mentor and Friend

CONTENTS

Contents

A NEW ORIGINS STORY
OF FREE MARKET THOUGHT

Few discoveries are more irritating than those which
expose the pedigree of ideas.

—LORD ACTON, CITED BY FRIEDRICH HAYEK
IN *THE ROAD TO SERFDOM*, CIRCA 1940

IN THE UNITED STATES the "free market" is perhaps the most
familiar of economic bywords. Since at least the Great Depression,
the term has been a staple of the nation's political discourse, used
both to praise and to criticize policy. An economic philosophy in-
tertwined with a number of powerful political ideologies, it has become nothing less than a Rorschach test. Many of us, when asked
what we think about free markets, have a strong emotional reaction
very much in line with our other personal convictions.

At the same time, not everyone agrees on what free markets are.
The French rationalist economist Léon Walras (1834–1910) famously
described the market as working in "general equilibrium," by which he
meant that the interaction of supply and demand created a balanced,
self-adjusting economic system that regulated prices and interest rates,

1

produced a constant flow of goods, and generated wealth without government intervention. In certain contexts, free markets can mean specific types of economic liberties or privileges: the right to pay lower tariffs in a free trade zone, say, or even to exercise an approved monopoly. Free markets have thus become synonymous with low taxes and limited government involvement in the economy. In most wealthy, industrial countries today, a free market economy is considered a basic component of social democracy, along with public education, transportation, retirement plans, public health systems, regulatory bodies, national banks, and the free exchange of ideas. More often than not, however, the market is free in the eye of the beholder.[1]

The most familiar modern definition of free market thought comes from the work of the Nobel Prize–winning economist Milton Friedman, who defined the idea as the absence of any and all government activity in economic affairs, or, more broadly still, the absence of the law interfering "with people's pursuit of happiness." Among Friedman's most famous observations is that "underlying most arguments against the free market is a lack of belief in freedom itself." Held as a universal model for all economic growth, the free market is seen by its proponents as effective at all times and in all places. Ideally, in Friedman's totalizing system, the market runs without any state intervention in response to private demand and supply, driven by the desires and choices of individuals, companies, and shareholders. Freeing up the market in this way, according to Friedman, ensures the efficient production and circulation of goods, wealth creation, and innovation.[2]

In the past thirty years, though, free markets have proven to be less a certainty than a puzzle. Leading figures from all sides of the political spectrum, at least for the sake of political rhetoric, have become critical of orthodox free-market doctrines. In the United States, in a startling reversal, the Republican Party now supports trade tariffs, while British Conservatives have left the free trade zone of the European Union, raising taxes and social spending in the process. It has been left to the head of China's authoritarian Communist Party, President Xi Jinping, of all people, to argue that the world must defend free trade and deregulated international markets. How exactly did we get to a point where the United States defends protectionism while China defends international open markets?[3]

To answer this question, we need to study the long history of free market thought, for the rise of free market ideology within authoritarian China is hardly the only example belying Friedman's claims. The simple fact is that his ideal free-market vision for America never came to pass. Since the 1980s and 1990s, America's middle class has been shrinking as China's grows. And while they may criticize government interference in the market, US finance and business interests feed on low interest rates, federal monetary policy, and state aid: twice since 2008, the US government has bailed out the financial system and various businesses, conveniently and deliberately sidestepping orthodox free-market thought, which clearly fails to account for periodic and devastating market failures.[4]

Friedman is no straw man, mind you. His orthodox free-market discourse still prevails in the boardrooms of most leading corporations, even those making huge profits from the US government, as well as in business schools—even publicly funded ones. Friedman's orthodoxy remains the credo of the US Chamber of Commerce. As a result, the United States and other democracies with liberal economies often fail to acknowledge that we are in an essentially abusive relationship with free market thought, looking to it for wealth creation and innovation while living and reliving endless cycles of deregulation, dangerous levels of debt, bankruptcies, frauds, and crashes followed by government bailouts, growing monopolies, wealth inequality, and political instability. And so we come back, again and again, for more of the same contradictory and self-canceling policies. Given the economic challenges that lie ahead of us as we move further into this pivotal new century, it is essential that we understand what the term "free market" means, what its history is, when free markets work, and when they do not.[5]

If Friedman is the favorite son of free market ideologues, the eighteenth-century Scottish philosopher Adam Smith is seen as the tradition's father. The modern conception of Adam Smith as a Friedmanesque champion of deregulation and unfettered free markets, however, is not particularly accurate. Misunderstood, misquoted, and reduced to clichés far removed from the eighteenth-century context in which he wrote, Smith's work nevertheless provides valuable lessons about how to approach economics. Until he wrote *The Wealth of Nations* in 1776, no one had provided such a wide-ranging and complex vision of economics and society as a vast, self-regulating system of wealth creation. Yet Smith also saw a significant role within the market for government and its institutions. The market functioned best, in his eyes, when virtuous, Stoic leaders—those versed in the Greek and Roman philosophy of the pursuit of happiness through self-knowledge and discipline—worked side by side with wealthy landowners to steer both politics and the market, putting the appropriate guideposts, incentives, and checks in place to keep the economy running.

Smith inhabited a very different social, philosophical, and religious universe from our own. It was a time of expanding empire and commerce, slavery, constitutional monarchy, elite parliamentarianism, and landowning oligarchy—all things, it should be noted, that he embraced with enthusiasm. Smith, a student of philosophy and history, saw parallels between Great Britain and the Roman Republic and Empire, which is one reason why he found the writings of the first-century BC Roman senator and philosopher Marcus Tullius Cicero so attractive. Smith was an eighteenth-century deist— and not necessarily a Christian—who fervently believed that God was an "architect" who designed a clockwork system of nature on earth, one that also mirrored the movement of the planets based on Isaac Newton's laws of gravity. While no statesman, he thought, "should attempt to direct private people in what manner they ought to employ their capitals," he also hoped that human economic life could mirror what he believed were the harmonious laws of nature. And for this to happen, man (and he meant man) had to adhere to ancient Stoic philosophy and discipline. Only in this way could society foster the good government and institutions that allowed individuals to create virtuous wealth.[6]

Smith did not think "greed was good." No Stoic philosopher did. Stoicism was based instead on the idea of self-improvement through moral discipline and civic duty. Smith's mission then was to understand how to make commercial society and its inherent greed fit *into* a moral system. The middling members of commercial society—"the butcher, the brewer, or the baker"—would be motivated in their daily lives by simple self-interest. Society had to find a way to harness this commercial self-interest and channel it toward the common good. Rather than ruthless commercial competition—which alarmed Smith, as he feared it would undermine society and the nation—he believed that morally trained, literate, and impartial leaders could turn society toward peaceful and efficient commercial cooperation.

Smith's hope that society would progress toward philosophical and ethical enlightenment mirroring the virtues of Republican Rome is difficult to fit into the libertarian corporate social Darwinism of Milton Friedman, let alone the pop economics of Ayn Rand, where only the strongest, most competitive entrepreneurs climb to the top of society. Indeed, it is hardly surprising that modern free-market thinkers rarely, if ever, mention that Smith was an admirer of Roman senatorial oligarchy, a man who harbored a deep distrust of merchants, industrialists, and corporations and who was himself a government bureaucrat (working, no less, as a tax collector). Worse yet, this so-called father of free market thought was a proud and radical teacher of the liberal arts who earned his bread as a university professor and administrator. Try to imagine the protagonist of Rand's 1943 novel *The Fountainhead*, the driven, impatient, modernist architect Howard Roark, tolerating Adam Smith's ideas of long tradition, duty, patient learning, genteel empathy, or pride in tax collection.[7]

So how did we get from oligarchic market-builders like Cicero and Smith—philosophers interested in building highly educated, philosophical, agrarian moral societies, and who believed the state was necessary for market freedom—to libertarian pro-business champions like Friedman? And how did modern free-market thought evolve into a rigid either/or philosophy that sees any state involvement in the economy as an existential threat to wealth creation and liberty? To answer these questions is the purpose of this book.

KEY TO UNLOCKING the free market puzzle is, paradoxically, someone who died forty years before Adam Smith was born, the very man who has long been seen by economists as Smith's antithesis: the famous chief minister of French king Louis XIV, Jean-Baptiste Colbert, who oversaw the French economy from the mid-1650s until his death in 1683. Colbert is credited with organizing and bringing good management to French royal and public finances, standardizing weights and measures, and building the commercial circulation systems of French roads, ports, and canals. He was responsible for creating the Paris police and an industrial inspection corps, as well as French industry, the French navy, and the Palace of Versailles. As the director of state research, he founded the royal library and archives and the French Royal Academy of Sciences. Viewing all of these endeavors as essential to the creation of functioning, fluid markets, Colbert emerged as the most successful large-scale market-builder of his time, using tariffs, subsidies, state monopolies, and political repression to achieve his goals.

One of Colbert's major aims in bringing the heavy hand of the state to bear on market-building was to develop French commerce to a point where it could compete freely with English commerce. He believed that "liberty of commerce," as he called it, came from symmetrical markets and balanced trade treaties. While Colbert saw international trade as a zero-sum game, and gold and treasure as limited, he also was certain that societies that focused on commerce and industry would be the most economically successful. France, when he took power, was a primarily agrarian nation. Making economic development his mission, he favored industry, innovation, and trade over agriculture in the belief they provided a path to a freer, more smoothly circulating economy that would make France a rich and glorious nation.

Colbert intrigued Adam Smith. In *The Wealth of Nations*, Smith coined the term "mercantile system" to describe Colbert's focus on trade and industry over agriculture. Smith was not in full opposition to Colbert, but he did disagree with him in some key respects. His main objection stemmed from the fact that, in his eyes, the French minister approached economics backward: surely, in focusing on trade and industry, he had misunderstood the ancient basic precept that agriculture was the source of all national wealth. Smith believed that Colbert had fallen prey to the "sophistry of merchants," that he had written too many repressive trade regulations, and that, "unfortunately," he had "embraced all the prejudices of the mercantile system." Commerce alone, Smith felt, would not create wealth, because it ignored the force of nature and the virtues of farming while allowing merchants—whom Smith detested—to dictate policy and create monopolies. The job of government was to help agriculture dominate industry so that trade could operate freely, according to the laws of nature.[8]

Rather than being opposed to one another, Colbert and Smith represent different, though related, historical strains of free market thought. Over time, however, Smith's critiques of Colbert became magnified in the minds of laissez-faire economists and historians, solidifying the myth of Colbert and his school of state-led industrial market-building as necessary antagonists of the free market. Smith's concept of the mercantile system evolved—completely out of context—into the modern concept of *mercantilism*: a simplistic, blanket economic term used to characterize early modern economic thinkers as proponents of an interventionist, taxing, subsidizing, and warring state whose goal was to simply hoard gold. In 1931, the Swedish economic historian Eli Heckscher, in his monumental study *Mercantilism*, juxtaposed Colbert's "mercantile" economics with a pure, laissez-faire system, which he felt Smith embodied, that allowed for individual and commercial freedoms without state intervention. A powerful and simplistic binary continued thereafter, one that informs our own vision of the free market today. We can see it still in Friedman's work.[9]

Yet, for most of the very long history of market philosophy, foundational economic thinkers saw the state as an essential element in creating the conditions under which free and fair exchange could take place. Smith's school crystallized a current of free market thought, dating back to Cicero and the traditions of feudalism, that saw agricultural production as the source of all wealth, its closeness to nature imbuing it with inherent moral superiority. To maintain what was perceived as nature's equilibrium of constant production, landowners had to dominate government, in order to make sure farming was untaxed and unregulated. This did not mean no government. It simply meant that the government had to aggressively liberalize the agricultural sector in the hope that farming would dominate society and drive the economy.

But the other tradition in free market thought, today mistakenly called mercantilism, focused its energies instead on innovation, trade, and industry. From the Florentine philosopher Niccolò Machiavelli to Jean-Baptiste Colbert and Alexander Hamilton, its advocates espoused an unapologetically strong government presence to foster the kind of innovation and industrial development they thought would create healthy interior markets while also allowing a nation to compete internationally. Economic freedom was essential to wealth production, according to these pro-industrial thinkers, but it was no more self-sustaining than it was necessarily based in agriculture; to the contrary, it required a pro-industry government to help design and foster it.

The give-and-take between free market models changed in the nineteenth century, when the United Kingdom became the undisputed economic master of the world, with British free-market thinkers finally embracing the potential of industry along with the theory of general equilibrium. Surely, if markets were free, liberal economists thought, then the hardworking, frugal Christians of the British Empire would continually produce innovation, wealth, and peace between nations. Then, in the twentieth century, as some economists became increasingly convinced of the market's capacity to regulate itself, they sought to define free markets as the absence of anything but the most minimal role for government. They insisted that, by simply allowing supply and demand to operate without interference, market systems—as well as societies—would magically sustain themselves. Alas, we now know that they will not.

To HELP US understand how ancient beliefs in nature and farming slowly evolved into a modern theory of free industrial markets, I move beyond the study of economic treatises themselves in this book to engage with a range of sources, from state archives to private letters, as well as books dealing with morals, the natural sciences, religion, literature, and politics. Some of the material will be familiar to readers of economic history and philosophy. Some of it, though, is likely to be new, and even seemingly out of place. But all of these disparate elements—from the classical ethics of Cicero, to the manuals and balance sheets of Florentine merchants, to the state papers and internal memos of French government ministers, to the courtly letters of dukes and archbishops—are absolutely essential to understanding why the field of economics so constantly eludes clarity or consensus.

The goal is to show that, in order to understand economics, it is not enough to formulate theories based on equations and data sets. One must also excavate the historical assumptions and ancient belief systems that are so embedded in our modern habits of thought that they go unexamined. Today, as markets and societies have continued to prove too complex to be explained through general equilibrium theory, orthodox free-market thought has found itself on the defense. But as I show in this book, the great pioneers of free market thought always knew that systems of exchange could not be considered in isolation from the real, flawed, fallen human beings who maintain them and function in them.

In the end, free markets cannot liberate humanity from itself. To flourish, they require as much labor, as much attention, and as much careful moral reasoning as any other human endeavor. What is remarkable is that, in spite of so many failures, economists, philosophers, politicians, and others still cling to the dream that the economy can be completely self-regulating, and express shock when they find that it is not. But then it is hard to relinquish an idea that is not only so attractive, but also so ancient, one that grew from the philosophy of Marcus Tullius Cicero (106–43 BC), the most influential thinker of the Roman tradition, whose work would serve as the linchpin of economic thought for almost two thousand years.

CHAPTER 1

THE DREAM OF CICERO

For Nature is so much more stable and steadfast, that
for Fortune to come into conflict with Nature seems
like a combat between a mortal and goddess.

—CICERO, *On Duties*, 44 BC

To UNDERSTAND THE origins of free market thought, it is first
necessary to understand Cicero's philosophy, which provided the
idea that through aristocratic farming and moral behavior and
politics, humans could tap into nature as an infinite and self-
perpetuating source of wealth. Cicero's work gave the impression
that the Roman Republic had achieved a state of equilibrium that
brought peace and prosperity for centuries. His ideal of Rome
would be a source of inspiration for free market thinkers well into
the nineteenth century.

In fact, Cicero lived in a time when the Roman Republic was
collapsing. As an aristocratic Roman senator of the first century
BC, he was defending the old order. He was appalled by the greed
of merchants hungry for profit and by the ambitions of would-be
tyrants, such as Julius Caesar, who became dictator in 49 BC.

Cicero believed that ideal market exchange, as a lever for wealth production, transpired between noblemen who lived peacefully by farming and who followed the laws of the republic. Over the course of his political and writing career, he developed a theory that by following Stoic morals and providing disinterested service to the state, the leaders of the republic could emulate the stable laws of nature and maintain a self-perpetuating system of wealth.

Cicero's economic vision was far from "natural," however. It reflected the values of the nearly five-hundred-year-old Roman Republic, whose ancient elite had lived off the great wealth of their estates since the era of Romulus, who, as legend has it, founded Rome in 753 BC. Cicero's writings show that economics are never divorced from the specific historical, cultural, and material conditions that produce them. He was convinced that trade should support Rome's ruling class—a philosophy, and indeed, an agenda, that, while pertaining to different elites, would echo all the way into the age of the steam engine. Even today, it is discernable in modern free-market thought.

HISTORIANS HAVE NOT seen Cicero as a key to understanding the origins of modern economic thought. Yet Cicero was the first to claim that morals and feelings sparked the market to work autonomously to create an economic equilibrium. As he saw it, friendship between educated, landowning equals created not only trust, but also the philosophical basis for ideal market conditions. Born eighty miles southeast of Rome in Arpinum, in the Lazio, Cicero hailed from an agricultural background, as his less-than-illustrious name—Cicero means "chickpea"—vividly illustrates. His family belonged to the *equites*, the equestrian order, a group of lower nobles that grew in prominence in the second century BC. Their status, below that of the senatorial class, was marked by their symbolic donation of a horse in place of serving in the cavalry. Though they often worked in public finance, tax collection, or moneylending, the equestrians were first and foremost landowners and farmers. As an upwardly mobile *novus homo*—a "new man," someone who had only just gained aristocratic status—he had powerful connections through his family that helped him rise in politics. Cicero carried a certain social stigma even after he became a member of the Senate, however, and even after he attained the very highest republican office, that of consul. It was paradoxical—or perhaps not—that the man whose work would define aristocratic ethics in the European tradition was himself never fully a true aristocrat. Yet he had reached the summit of the Roman system, and he now sought to preserve it.

In the first century BC, the empire had a population of more than forty million, and Rome itself had more than a million inhabitants. Only five million inhabitants of the empire were privileged as full citizens, receiving free bread and enjoying legal and civic rights. Slaves made up 10 percent of the population, with the rest of the Roman noncitizens consisting of the lower classes. At the very top was the ruling class, which comprised only seven hundred or so senatorial families and thirty thousand equestrians. Roman elites were thus tightly knit and knew each other's family histories. Sharing easily identifiable forms of dress and education, they organized themselves around kinship and clientele networks. They exchanged goods, made loans, and bought property from one another. Theirs was a closed market that, by Cicero's time, had worked for centuries, lending it the appearance of an immutable natural order.[1]

Growing up in the orbit of Roman senatorial power, Cicero was steeped in practical politics, law, and philosophy from a very young age. His family consorted not only with Rome's great figures of learning, but also with powerful politicians. The prestigious Scaevola and Crassus families, conservative intellectual defenders of the senatorial order and culture, served as Cicero's tutors. They defended the *mos maiorum*: the customs and codes of Roman agricultural life, and the natural laws and social hierarchy they believed it represented. As such, they loathed any change and defended the ancient Roman constitution. The republic ideally functioned through popular assemblies, including commoners elected to the Plebian Council, which was supposed to work closely with the Senate, and the consuls, who ran the executive branch. In reality, though, the republic had long since ossified into an oligarchy, with the Senate ruling, and more and more, with unscrupulous dictators looking to rule over the Senate itself. Still, Cicero was imbued with a strong sense that defending the senatorial class, the republic, and a virtuous market society was to defend Roman concepts of the natural order.[2]

At the center of this identity was an understanding of nature and agriculture, and Cicero drew diligently from a long line of agrarian thinkers. Essential to his vision was the archconservative soldier, historian, and defender of Roman patriarchy Cato the Elder, whose book *On Farming* (160 BC) explained that noble wealth depended on good agricultural management. Nature's bounty was every bit as stable as the republic if one knew how to farm correctly. For innovation and trade, Cato simply expressed disdain. Only large-scale landownership was truly "good" and capable of producing virtuous citizens and soldiers.[3]

The majority of the population in Cicero's Rome toiled, and that was it. Not much thought was given to the toil itself. There were merchant and service classes in Roman society, but the greater part of the population did manual labor, some as slaves, others as freedmen for meager wages. Cicero was not interested in any of them.

In the scheme of nature, toil was fate. The peasant was meant to remain a peasant and the slave a slave. All "must be required to work," he insisted, and they must be given "their dues," and no more. The nobleman alone was above this toil. He did not earn this natural position as a property owner; elite status was part of the state of nature. For this reason, Cicero and his class abhorred land taxes. They owned all the land and the labor on it. To tax nature's bounty, then, was surely a mark of tyranny. The job of the landowner was only to squeeze work out of slaves and laborers to meet basic production yields and create wealth for those entitled to it.[4]

By virtue of their closeness to nature, members of the landowning class saw themselves as duty-bound to study what they believed were nature's divine laws in order to perpetuate their aristocratic society. When the "best men" rule in "moderation," said Cicero in his *On the Republic* (54–51 BC), the "citizens enjoy greatest happiness" through peace and prosperity. Wealthy aristocrats, burdened by "no cares or worries," could focus on government operating solely on virtue itself. Cicero's belief in the "best men" was based on the idea that nature did not create people equally. And if nature drew distinctions, then it was only right for men themselves to follow suit. True political and economic freedom was only for the landowning few.[5]

Nobles, in Cicero's worldview, were "indifferent to riches." They naturally despised professional moneylenders and the hawkers of the marketplace. Claiming to loathe greed and money for money's sake, he viewed commercial values as necessarily debased morally, and used the Latin term *mercator*, or merchant, as an insult. Cicero believed that the ideal market led men to use common possessions for the common interest while, at the same time, preserving private property. According to the Stoics, he explained, "everything that the earth produces is created for man's use." This notion led to the concept of free and self-perpetuating exchange. Similarly, moral and philosophical reasoning would guide men to contribute to the general good through debate and acts of kindness, in order "to cement human society more closely together, man to man." If the exchange of privately held goods began with the exchange of ideas, Cicero felt, then once they were expressed, ideas belonged to all, to be shared in the common pursuit of truth and noble service to the state. Intellectual exchange should follow a Greek proverb: "Amongst friends, all things in common." Virtuous philosophical trade served the "common interest" of the Roman Republic and its leaders.[6]

Duty was essential to Cicero's system. It meant a "good man's" service to the state in what was a civic religion. Yet while one had duty to "fellow-citizens, and all human beings," Cicero warned that one could not help the "infinite" number of the needy. One had to reserve the lion's share of one's personal resources for family and friends. Such a closed, elite market, based on the "common bonds" of "friendship" and "kindness," Cicero believed, "preserved justice" and maintained wealth and society. He went on to describe true, intimate friendship as adding a "brighter radiance to prosperity," for it "lessens the burden of adversity by dividing and sharing it." Lasting wealth did not come from greed, or from profiting from another, but from the common bond of "goodwill." It was this honest sentiment that "holds up houses and allows fields to be tilled."[7]

Thus, 1,800 years before Smith's idea of the free market, Cicero designed a morally sound system of free commercial exchanges between members of the like-minded ruling class. Such bonds of decent exchange protected society in critical ways from unnatural, if otherwise likely, alternative scenarios: "For a man to take something from his neighbor and to profit by his neighbor's loss is more contrary to Nature than is death or poverty," said Cicero. Exchange

had to be self-supporting or it led to "despoliation." High morals—
"courtesy, justice, and generosity" in the act of exchange—were the
principles that led to a harmonious and rich society.[8]

So it was that through their contributions to the state, Roman
aristocrats donated bread to citizens through a vast distribution system of wheat—the *annona civica*—that was the backbone of the
economic system. Imperial fleets distributed wheat across the Mediterranean, or, as the Romans called it, *mare nostrum*, "our sea." The
Mediterranean was like an organ to the Roman body—in his *Natural History*, the naturalist and military leader Pliny the Elder called
it the *mare intestinum*, "intestine sea," as it facilitated the free flow of
the Roman economy. Wealth, therefore—beginning with the landed
class's wheat harvests—appeared to move naturally across the empire according to the self-regulating laws of nature. Rome produced
goods and fed itself through the invisible hand of the seasons—and
with help from the seemingly eternal state and its senatorial class.
The state subsidized both markets and shipping lanes between Italy
and North Africa and beyond, to Iberia, Greece, Anatolia, and the
Black Sea. Goods flowed freely in the giant Roman trade zone.[9]

IF CICERO'S ASCENT to power in Rome was stunning, his demise
was all the more dramatic, and it came directly from his defense
of the Roman constitution, the aforementioned rules of virtuous
exchange, and the fundamentals of private property and free trade
in which he believed. In 63 BC, at the age of just forty-two, Cicero
became one of the two consuls of Rome, the highest office of government. His year as a head of state was marked by violent rebel-
lion, and he soon came into conflict with the senator Catiline, who
was running for consul on a reformist platform of debt forgiveness and land distribution for the poor. Cicero scorned all popular
reformers who worked outside the aristocratic ethos. Promises of

land to the poor, he felt, undermined not only market rules, but the existing order itself. And so in the Senate, with Catiline present, Cicero began his famous orations. For days, he condemned Catiline's lawlessness and the indebtedness of his friends and questioned his motives for poor relief. Finally, Cicero successfully pleaded for the execution of several of Catiline's coconspirators. When Cicero exclaimed, "O tempora, o mores!" (Oh the times, Oh the customs!), he was referring to Catiline's complete disregard for the laws, as well as his financial corruption and greed. He was also defending what he saw as the natural, moral economic order.[10]

Cicero's dramatic defense of the status quo gives us insight into how he saw honor as essential to the market. To bribe or use fraud was not only "unjust" but "hypocritical." Cicero passed a law, for instance, against the trading of votes for favors, the *Lex Tullia de ambitu*, in 63 BC. It must be noted that many, including Julius Caesar himself, believed Cicero to be corrupt, however, and many more believed that he was simply a self-promoter—a point impossible to deny. Yet unlike Caesar, Cicero defended strict senatorial legality, and never attempted to overthrow the constitution.[11]

Julius Caesar began to assert permanent dictatorial powers over the republic in 49 BC. Then, on March 15, 44 BC—the famous day of the Ides of March—a group of pro-republican senators, led by Marcus Junius Brutus, assassinated him. While not himself involved, Cicero nonetheless hoped now to guide the Senate back to republican government. It is a testament to Cicero's brilliance that in the midst of the violent turmoil that characterized the fall of the Roman Republic and the rise of the empire, when his own fortunes were at their lowest, he wrote his most enduring work, *On Duties* (44 BC). Ostensibly directed to his son, this book of philosophical advice became one of the most influential books in the Western tradition and a blueprint for free market thought.[12]

Cicero's economic vision in *On Duties* was that friendship and the quest for knowledge brought harmony and peace, protected property, and produced a just society based on political service, affection, kindness, and liberality. Good morals, in other words, drove a healthy market, allowing ethical people to make exchanges in confidence. Trust was a mechanism that freed trade. Central to perpetuating this trading process were Cicero's ideals of decorum and Stoic self-control. One can see how these ideas would later appeal to Christians and, later yet, to eighteenth-century Enlightenment philosophers, who were for a moral model for trade.[13]

The sophistication and gentle decency of *On Duties* was partly a response to the rampant violence that Cicero witnessed in Roman society and often described in his letters. In the book, he also denounced not only the broad target of Caesar's illegal, dictatorial ambitions, but a more widespread tendency toward greed. This was where Cicero drew a moral line in the sand, condemning the bestial force of the lion as "unworthy of man," and the "fraud" of foxes as even "more contemptible." Such animal pursuit of power and wealth must not be permitted, as it was "insatiable," he told his readers. The elite could not give in to the vices of dictatorship, but had to remain self-disciplined and in harmony with the laws of the constitution.[14]

In economic affairs, duty had to outweigh not only greed, but also pleasure. Cicero could not accept that self-interest or desire drove economic interaction, or, as Greek Epicurean philosophers proposed, that all of life centered around a quest for pleasure. He attacked the schema that life was a quest to avoid pain and find pleasure as hopelessly simplistic, noting that what might be construed as pain could, after all, lead to pleasure, just as to forgo pleasure might serve to avoid pain. Duty, learning, and friendship were surely superior goals and, moreover, contributed to the foundation of trust that was essential for free exchange.[15]

In his *Academica* (45 BC), Cicero defined the "chief good" as human learning to understand nature. Rather than pleasure, it was the search for truth through skeptical philosophy that "supplied the courage to face death" and provided "peace of mind, for it removes all ignorance of the mysteries of nature." The virtue of learning created the kind of discipline and trust that allowed humans to move beyond base self-interest. Studying Greek theories of physics, for instance, Cicero looked to understand the self-regulating system of the universe, which he discussed in the last chapter of his work *On the Republic*, in the famous passage entitled "The Dream of Scipio." Looking for a "first cause" that creates the "eternal motion," he arrived at love, not greed, as the most fundamental market principle. Virtuous exchange was part of these divine mechanisms and, allowed to play out, would produce reliable wealth.[16]

Yet Cicero's dream of a natural, self-regulating, noble world of learning, affection, and free exchange struck a dissonant note with the actual world around him. In the fight for supreme imperial power, leading citizens dropped all pretense of senatorial precedent. Constant civil wars wracked Rome in the first century BC, ending in Cicero's moment of glory but also in his gruesome demise, for he now stood between the powerful general Marc Antony and Octavian (the future emperor Augustus) in their battle for power.

It was in the fray of this tragic war that Cicero delivered his famous orations against Marc Antony, *The Philippics*—an attack on, among other things, immoral exchange. On the floor of the Senate, he sarcastically berated Antony for breaking the laws of the republic, mocking his sloppy lawlessness, corruption, and false account books. "How was it," he asked Antony, "that before the first of April you ceased to owe the forty million sesterces that you owed on the fifteenth of March?"[17]

It is remarkable that Cicero thought he might survive making such a public attack on all the corrupt parties of the disintegrating republic. Perhaps he was emboldened by the belief that he had the support of Octavian. The future emperor's primary goal, however, was to protect his own claim on imperial power. As he and Antony negotiated over which of their foes to kill, exchanging names in a deadly political barter, Octavian eventually betrayed Cicero, giving in to Antony's insistence that he be executed. This was hardly the sort of exchange that Cicero had envisioned. But with no more powerful friends left, he was alone in defending a republic that had already died.

Upon hearing of the sentence, Cicero fled to a country house where he could honorably prepare to die. Then, when the soldiers came, he asked them to make a clean cut of his head. It took three strokes. Along with the ill-fated philosopher's head, a soldier also cut off a hand. Living up to the brutal vulgarity of which Cicero had so eloquently accused him, Marc Antony now ordered Cicero's head and hand nailed onto the *rostra*, the primary speakers' tribune that faced the Senate in the Forum. Here was what was left of Rome's greatest orator and the defender of the republic, a symbol that would resonate for millennia. Predating Jesus of Nazareth, Cicero, whose secular, republican martyrdom lent an almost Christian poignancy to his vision of political and economic virtue, became a leading figure in Western history. He had realized his own ideals, battling tyranny and the vices of corrupt exchange. He tried to preserve the natural order and economic morals, revealing a virtuous path to wealth.

In this way Cicero anticipated a central tenet of Adam Smith's later market thought: if elite, educated men focused on agriculture and exchanged goods righteously and ethically, then the market would work on its own and produce wealth, and the republic would prosper. And as Christianity began to dominate Western Europe, this model of equilibrium would become one of the most lasting conceptual frameworks of economic philosophy. Christians would replace civic earthly politics with heavenly salvation as the ultimate goal of society, and God would enter into the system of exchange.

CHAPTER 2

THE DIVINE ECONOMY

Give bread and seize paradise.
—Saint John Chrysostom, "Homily 3:
Concerning Almsgiving and the Ten Virgins,"
circa AD 386

A little more than two hundred years after Cicero's death, not only had the Roman Republic given way to the empire, but Rome began its long fusion with Christianity. The Roman Empire, as such, still existed. But its new Christian leaders sought to amend Cicero's economic vision. Early Christianity mostly eschewed the idea that civic morality was a virtue. Instead, the Christian thinkers of the third and fourth centuries AD created a new ideal of life, and with it, a new vision of market exchanges. Cicero's tenet that commerce should be based on a moral code remained. But in the early Christian economic system, good moral choices had to come from a sincere desire to trade worldly goods for a place in heaven. Morality became centered on the afterlife rather than on some earthly "chief good" deduced from nature's laws. This was a market centered around a desire for individual salvation and a quest for a spiritual reward.

Christianity thus transformed the idea of commercial exchange by grounding it not just in duty and virtue, as in Cicero's system, but also in human desire. This was not the desire of the Epicureans, who sought earthly pleasure. Rather, Christians believed that if humans chose to live piously and reject wealth, then the "invisible hand of God"—Saint Augustine meant the term literally—would bring them the treasure of heaven. The Christian concept of salvation would provide a conceptual model for later free-market thought. Individual choice could lead to a paradise of endless heavenly wealth. Early Christianity bequeathed a major legacy to modern economic culture: the idea that constant aspiration is necessary to reach a perfect, though still nonexistent, state of market conditions.

EVEN AS CHRISTIANITY spread in the empire, paganism remained a powerful force. Although the emperor Constantine the Great converted to Christianity in around AD 312, until the end of the fourth century Cicero remained prominent in school curricula. The Fathers of the Church, in the centuries following the birth of Christ, hailed primarily from the Roman nobility, which means they had grown up in a pagan imperial culture. They had to know Roman law, and they counted on the emperor to ensure stability. Church Fathers such as the Bishop of Milan, Saint Ambrose, and the writer who would become the most influential theologian of Western Christianity, Saint Augustine, wrestled with the thought of Cicero, looking to supplant it with a new Christian version of morality. Ultimately their approach to wealth was more individualistic and democratic than that envisioned by Cicero.

Cicero wrote that desire was inherently negative. Christians, however, believed that desire was moral if it was for salvation—if, for example, one were to satisfy that desire by giving money to the poor and renouncing earthly pleasures in return for heavenly rewards. With a basis in the Gospels of Saints Matthew and Luke, this desire for the treasure of heaven was seen as not only good, but holy. Drawing from the Gospels and from other scriptures, Christian salvation was formulated in an economic language of interest, choice, will, exchange, and reward. In fact, the basis of Christ's crucifixion was itself a transaction: "Without shedding of blood," there is no forgiveness of sins, the author of the Book of Hebrews wrote. In other words, Christ paid the collective debt of humanity.[1]

While the Christian Church depended on the Roman Empire for protection and even financial support, the Judeo-Christian tradition expressly rejected Cicero's belief that the finest thing one could do was to study philosophy and serve one's country. Messianic Christianity brought with it instead eschatology: a rejection of the secular world and its imperfections and an aspiration for the end of days prophesied in the Book of Revelation, with God's wrath coming down upon those who clung to earthly wealth as he bestowed a heavenly, eternal afterlife upon true believers.

Saint Luke the Evangelist insisted that Christians rid themselves of earthly possessions by giving to the poor so that they could attain the treasures of heaven. In his gospel, Jesus says, "Sell that ye have, and give alms; provide yourselves bags which wax not old, a treasure in the heavens that faileth not, where no thief approacheth, neither moth corrupteth." Saint Matthew, a tax collector before Jesus called him as a disciple, echoed this message. He followed both Mark and Luke in quoting Jesus in the New Testament using an old Jewish saying—that a rich man had a slimmer chance of going to heaven than a camel did of fitting through the eye of a needle. He also quoted Jesus on the fleeting nature of earthly treasures, saying he described them as "where moths and rust destroy, and where thieves break in and steal." He called on believers instead to find eternal treasure in their hearts. And in Matthew's telling, like Luke's, Jesus portrays salvation as in fact predicated on poverty, a process of exchange wherein one must give to the poor in order to receive it: "Jesus said unto him, If thou wilt be perfect, go and sell that thou hast, and give to the poor, and thou shalt have treasure in heaven: and come and follow me."[2]

Yet Matthew gave conflicting messages about wealth. He claimed Jesus said that those who did not invest their money for a good return were sinners. In Jesus's "Parable of the Talents" in his gospel, a master calls his servant who has failed to invest his money "slothful" and "wicked." Jesus warns, "For whosoever hath, to him shall be given, and he shall have more abundance: but whosoever hath not, from him shall be taken away even that he hath."[3]

The offer of treasure in heaven was not metaphorical. Because of the hopeless poverty of so many within the Roman Empire, the offer of actual treasure in the afterlife resonated powerfully, and Christian preachers used the promise to win converts. There is little doubt that the general squalor of living conditions in Palestine, and across the Roman Empire, was at the basis of the Christian obsession with poverty. The idea that the poor had to be protected had arisen earlier in Jewish thought and theology, which preached almsgiving and even social equity: "He that hath pity upon the poor lendeth unto the Lord; and that which he hath given will he pay him again" is one of the proverbs of Solomon. Saint Matthew echoed this concept when he described Jesus equating charity to the poor and communion with God.[4]

The most important material commodities in Rome's economy during the earliest days of Christianity were gold and silver. But the Gospels dealt as well with other worldly interests, including sex, the body, and the pursuit of pleasure. Saint Matthew's Jesus regards sexual abstinence and even self-castration as a gift to God.

"For there are some eunuchs," he observes, "which were so born from their mother's womb: and there are some eunuchs, which were made eunuchs of men: and there be eunuchs, which have made themselves eunuchs for the kingdom of heaven's sake. He that is able to receive it, let him receive it." Pleasure, along with wealth and self-interest, was cast in terms of the system of market exchange for personal salvation.[5]

Nowhere was this more clearly demonstrated than in the lifestyle of the early Fathers of the Church, which contrasted with the Roman tradition of noble opulence. Christian leaders practiced extreme forms of self-denial inherited from a long tradition of asceticism. In *The Rich Man's Salvation*, Clement of Alexandria, while recognizing that earthly wealth had to exist, explained that there were rules about how to use that wealth, not least by giving it away according to a pious plan of "providing." The rich man who gave away all his wealth to the poor and to the Church and, in so doing, focused his passion on Jesus, would find salvation.[6]

The basic tenets of asceticism had spread throughout the Roman Empire in the first century BC via a work by Sextus, a pagan Greek moralist, who helped create the concept of a self-regulating market of spiritual exchange, and whose maxims were interchangeable with the new Christian mores. *The Sentences of Sextus* describes a monetary process in one's relationship to God and the afterlife. Only those who "relinquish the things of the flesh are free to acquire the things of the soul," Sextus wrote, adding bluntly that "it is difficult for a rich person to be saved." He expressed the Platonic idea that one could become a "sage" close to God through spiritual study and self-denial. By "conquer[ing] the body," the sage can "give everything possible to the poor." Earthly attachment—even attachment to one's children—was to be scorned. Sextus exclaimed, "A faithful man bears the loss of his children gratefully." The sin of

27

earthly pleasure, he warned, would be "called to account by an evil demon until the last penny is paid up."[7]

Sextus's maxims soon spread throughout Greek Christian communities. Leading theologians—including the Alexandrian Christian scholar Origen, who, in the third century, marveled at the "multitudes" who read Sextus's book—embraced them. A series of Christian works followed echoing the idea that the worldly market had to be replaced with a heavenly one. Original Sin meant that humans could not truly enjoy the earth. This idea was central to *The Shepherd of Hermas*, for example, which appeared sometime between AD 90 and 150. It contained the basic principles, first laid out by Saint Matthew, that rich men were poor "in the things of the Lord," and added that only through poverty and humility could man enjoy God's bounty. The text lauded fasting and an ascetic life, themes that pervaded the religious literature of late antiquity. In the Book of Revelation (AD 95), John of Patmos recounts Jesus reproaching seven Anatolian cities for their sins. These cities—Ephesus, Smyrna, Pergamum, Thyatira, Sardis, Philadelphia, and Laodicea—were considered metaphorical references to the world itself, representing a biblical distrust of the flesh and commercial urban life. With equal drama, in around AD 208, the theologian Tertullian railed against Rome as a modern Babylon drenched in the blood of martyrs. He, too, called for the repression of sexual urges, and even discouraged remarriage after the death of a spouse. He lauded the sanctity of devotion only to God through widowhood and virginity. Virgins, he insisted, should be veiled, so they could gaze all the better upon Christ. Thus protected from sin, they were "worthy of paradise."[8]

Such extreme voluntary sexual self-denial in exchange for salvation made Christianity fundamentally more transactional than Judaism. Money, lust, pleasure, and even eating, talking, and smiling—these were all bad things, products of Original Sin, in the Christian view, and had to be forsaken in return for the reward of heaven. In the first decades of the third century, Origen wrote a fundamental work about life after death in which he argued that this prize was achieved only through self-denial. Origen took this view of chastity as an exchange of pleasure for salvation to extreme lengths when he castrated himself. Edward Gibbon, the great Enlightenment author of *The Decline and Fall of the Roman Empire*, famously commented that Origen's literalist reading of the scriptures was an "unfortunate" mistake.[9]

The holy market and its aspirational model, emphasizing choice, discipline, payment, and reward, became central to Christian life. Origen was only one of many people in late antiquity to engage in dramatic forms of self-sacrifice in the hope of a holy exchange. Male chastity became a valued form of self-discipline in the quest for the treasures of the city of God, and it would become the basis of the tradition of priestly and monastic celibacy. The Desert Fathers set the tone of this new monasticism and economy of asceticism. Generations of cenobitic monks took to the deserts of Egypt and accepted only the most meager of donations as they lived solely to commune with God. Most famous perhaps is Simeon the Stylite (ca. 390–459), who lived on a small platform on top of a pole near Aleppo for thirty-seven years.[10]

Simeon was a shepherd's son, but many of the Christian leaders who rejected wealth and society came from rich noble families. In the vein of the Roman ideal of civic service, some of these noblemen became bishops and leading theologians. Notable examples include the Church leaders Saint Basil (ca. 329–379) and his brother Gregory of Nyssa (ca. 335–ca. 395), Saint John Chrysostom (ca. 347–407), and Saint Ambrose (ca. 340–397). Virtue, for them, was "prayer" and a rejection of the flesh. Friendship should be based on

Christian fellowship alone. Rejecting the pagan Ciceronian worship of the natural world, Gregory would write the words of what later became a Christian mantra: "Nature is weak and not eternal." It was God, who made nature, who was eternal, and all natural systems originated in the deity.[11]

PART OF THE evangelical mission of the Fathers was to win over the Roman nobility to the Christian faith, which seems a rather impressive ambition, given the contrast between hedonistic noble lifestyles and the Christian insistence on poverty and abstinence. The Fathers as well needed to make the case for heavenly salvation over the earthly pleasures of Rome. Ironically, evangelism did not come cheap. With limited funds for the legions of needy souls, to say nothing of its buildings, priests, and missions, the Church asked its wealthy followers to give money so that the bishops could feed the hungry with both food and the spiritual ingredients of salvation.

From Antioch to Carthage to the new imperial capital of Constantinople, bishops had to contend with populations of Greeks, Syrians, Druze, and Jews, among others, who were still steeped in the ancient religions of the empire. The archbishop of Constantinople and a leading Greek evangelical, Saint John Chrysostom, not only had to keep his Christian flock in line but also aspired to convert Constantinople's masses. The son of a pagan military officer, he himself had converted in around 370. Chrysostom knew the sins of the great capital were present every day, as even Christians attended games and erotic performances. He needed an approach that instilled fear in the hearts of his parishioners and also offered them a tangible sense of salvation in return for conversion and pious behavior.

Using fear and the theatrics of fanaticism to inspire local populations, Chrysostom preached passionately against Jews and homosexuality, and warned of damnation to those Christians who enjoyed the salacious shows of Constantinople. In the city of Ephesus, he called on the mobs to tear down the great Temple of Artemis, one of the Seven Wonders of the Ancient World. He made appeals to the economic sensibilities of those who listened to him preach in Antioch: his "Homily 3: Concerning Almsgiving and the Ten Virgins" (ca. AD 386–387) is a succinct and forceful plea to put all pleasure and economic activity into a logic of holy exchange.

Rather than engaging with a world of civic-minded aristocrats making transactions to maintain the status quo of Rome, Chrysostom insisted that Christians should operate solely in the spiritual marketplace. He questioned why people go into debt and impoverish themselves when they might forgo money altogether, casting away both debt and poverty to "gain the profit" of an easy "ascent into heaven." It began, he said, with a simple pledge of repentance. Once one made the personal decision to "profit" from salvation alone, one then needed to perform concrete acts of exchange. Chrysostom maintained that almsgiving was the social act of paying "the debt demanded by sin." His language was strikingly economic. A woman who pays alms to the poor, he claimed, "has her own bill of sale that she holds in her hands." She could exchange it for the treasures of heaven.[12]

Chrysostom made clear to his listeners that they literally had to leave the market of earthly goods. Poverty alone did not get one into heaven: "The sky is cheap," he said. To "buy the sky" was to enter into a covenant with God of total material self-denial and giving. It meant that, in the right circumstances, even giving away a glass of water would set in motion the self-perpetuating chain of salvation. Nor was this lesson simply an allegory. In an extraordinary passage, Chrysostom explained that "heaven is a business [or an undertaking of trade] and an enterprise.... Give bread and seize paradise." He lamented that people were willing to buy as many cheap products as they could, but unwilling to invest in their souls.[13]

Chrysostom's Homily 3 provided a model of divine exchange for Constantinople and the Eastern Roman Empire. It would also create a template for Saint Ambrose, arguably the most influential Latin Christian leader of his time. He, too, used the idea of an economy of spiritual exchange, but in his case as the basis of a project to Christianize the Latin West. Saint Ambrose was born into an ancient noble Roman family in what is today modern Belgium. He trained for high service in the Roman state and was brought up and educated in an imperial system, studying rhetoric, law, and philosophy. Like the pagans of the East, he was versed in the learning of ancient Greece and Rome. But he bridged the civic and religious worlds. He was a cousin of Quintus Aurelius Symmachus, one of the richest nobles of his day and consul of Rome. Indeed, Ambrose himself would go on to become governor of the Northern Italian province of Aemilia-Liguria, with Milan as its capital.

Ambrose, a Christian, governed as a Roman-Christian governor. In 371 he stepped down to become the bishop of Milan but still served in the court of the Christian emperor of the Western Roman Empire, Valentinian I. Looming over Ambrose was the ever-present Cicero, martyr of Roman civic virtue and model of public service. Training for an imperial leadership role, Ambrose must have struggled with Cicero's legacy. This was, after all, Ambrose's vocation as a Roman praetor, and later as a bishop. Ambrose had the most contradictory of jobs. He had to serve Caesar while preaching the rejection of the earthly world.

As an imperial Roman, a civil servant, and a Christian leader of the Western Empire, Saint Ambrose was thus a remarkable transitional figure. His challenge, as he recognized, was to Christianize the very heart of the empire. Central to his mission was the status of money. As an administrator, he worried not only about finding converts, but also about finding resources to sustain the Church. In true Christian form, he had given up his own immense private estates to the Church and attacked trade as unchristian. He was unequivocal on personal wealth: Money was "the root of all evil." Leading men should have "no desire for filthy lucre in common with Syrian traders and Gilead merchants, nor to place all their hope of good in money, or to count up their daily gains and to calculate their savings like a hireling." Ambrose invoked metaphors of free movement and aspiration for something greater to be gained through a freely chosen exchange. No one should hoard treasure, Ambrose believed, because if it stood still, money would "rot" with "worms." Movement, on the other hand, made money "sweet" and "useful," like "water," which could put out fires. The way to spur the market into circulation was to bestow "silver" on the poor. Only then would God give the return gift of "friendship of the saints and eternal habitations."[14]

Mixing imperial administrative duties with firm Christian belief made Ambrose an evangelical realist. He believed he had to directly confront Cicero to transform the very notion of duty. It should not be surprising, then, that one of Ambrose's most important works, *On the Duties of the Clergy* (ca. AD 391), was an attack on Cicero's work. He denounced his rhetorical theories, insisting that elegance and beauty were not to be found in the art of words, but rather in God. Real knowledge could only come from divine revelation, not from earthly science. Ambrose also directly attacked private property: "We state nothing to be useful but what will help us to the blessing of eternal life." Surely, it was impossible for humans to own things, because God bestows more on humans than humans can possibly bestow on God, making humans inevitably "debtors in regard to their salvation."[15]

Ambrose was in such conflict with Cicero that he tried to bend Ciceronian moral language to fit the terms of the Christian spiritual market. Giving to the poor and to the Church, he observed, was the great "duty," for it gave grace, where a true love of God was superior to earthly friendship. Beyond simply focusing on the afterlife, however, Ambrose exhorted the clergy to build the body of the earthly Church through fellowship and "the bond of baptism."[16]

Most importantly, Ambrose described Jesus's self-sacrifice as a commercial, divine exchange. Jesus had given his blood on the cross, after all, out of "divine liberality" in exchange for human "redemption." Rather than living and dying for empty republican ideals, humans thus had to live for salvation. With the empire now on the edge of collapse, the proposition appealed to many converts.[17]

OF ALL THE Church Fathers, Saint Augustine (354–430) would have the greatest lasting power and the strongest influence on economic thought. Augustine believed that God created a self-regulating order in the Christian universe through predestination. This meant that it was not by one's own choice or will that one might be saved, but only by God's decision of grace—a decision already made before one could act. Predestination meant that God not only chose which souls were to be saved in heaven, but also which of his flock would be rich on earth. This did not absolve good rich Christians of the responsibility to freely give their money to the Church. In making such a claim, however, Augustine opened the door to a new idea about wealth that transformed Christianity.

Augustine was born into a Latinized North African family of the Roman upper classes. His mother, Monica, was a devout Christian, and his father was a pagan. Augustine himself initially embraced a truly pagan life, studying Platonic philosophy and Ciceronian rhetoric in Rome. Practically living in brothels, he worshipped wine and had a child out of wedlock. In 386, however, two years after becoming chief rhetoric teacher for the imperial city of Milan, he had an epiphany when he heard a child speaking in God's voice calling on him to read the scriptures. After reading Saint Paul's critique of debauchery in his Letter to the Romans, Augustine converted to Christianity, fervently rejecting paganism, Ciceronian skepticism, and his erstwhile taste for carnal pleasures. Due to personal needs and the powerful pull of Christian evangelism, he decided to replace all earthly pleasure and knowledge with faith. For Augustine, the fall of man through Original Sin and redemption through devotion to God was a personal story. Saint Ambrose publicly baptized Augustine in 387, and in 395 the new Christian rose to become bishop of Hippo (present-day Annaba in Algeria).[18]

Before leaving Italy, Augustine began writing *On Free Choice of the Will* in a quest to understand good, evil, and predestination. This work is key to understanding the logic of the moral market of grace and salvation. In it, Augustine explained that in order to receive grace and to be freed from Original Sin, a person must first be chosen by God. In other words, humans had to be divinely intended to choose rightly. While God had total foresight, he left open the door for radical human freedom and error. Augustine revealed the influence of Cicero's Stoicism when he declared that, in the marketplace, one could either use disciplined virtue or be a "slave of desire."

Augustine's idea of free will had vast ramifications for economic thought. If God helped people do good, and if by their own free will they then were pious and nonmaterialistic, their possession of money and goods could be positive, especially if they decided to give that money to the Church. Augustine had now used his authority and powers of persuasion to suggest that some earthly wealth was in fact God-given and therefore good. This notion was contrary to the asceticism of earlier Christian writers. It meant that rich Christians could be virtuous while making money. This pious rationale for earthly wealth was a paradox. But Augustine recognized that people could not be self-denying ascetics all the time. Some would have money and power, but they would have to mix this earthly wealth with an attitude of charity, goodwill, and the truly "voluntary" quest for grace. Earthly wealth flowed according to a mix of God's will and free choice. This was a dramatic change in Christian thought. The Church no longer had to condemn all wealth.[19]

Like Cicero's economic beliefs, which reflected his allegiance to the Roman agricultural elite, Augustine's theology was strongly influenced by his experiences as bishop of Hippo. North Africa was not Italy, and although Hippo was a relatively prosperous city, with around thirty thousand people, Augustine had to build the Church there from the ground up. He did this by encouraging donations. The task was not easy. Unlike Ambrose, Augustine was not fabulously wealthy; he depended on the Church for a living. For him, the Church was a portal necessary to reach heaven, but it was still a very earthly tool. Out of necessity, Augustine was more concerned than Ambrose with the mundane details of survival. He acknowledged that he had to struggle to find money to maintain Church buildings, clothe and buy food for the priests, and protect them in the hostile environment of North Africa. And he felt no shame in grubbing for money. If his flock did not give, there would be no Church.

Surrounded by a poor countryside filled with heretics, who were often violent, along with rich, aggressive pagans and an often unruly flock, Augustine was under physical siege in a way that the other Fathers of the Church were not. Ever a threat was the Donatist heresy, which had taken root in Carthage (near modern-day

Tunis), three hundred miles away. The Donatists were founded by a Berber bishop, Donatus Magnus, who preached that the clergy had to be completely free of sin—"free of stain or wrinkle," to quote Ephesians 5:27—to effectively preach and administer the sacraments. This orthodox rigorism called for a "church of saints" in which all who took part were completely pure. That meant Donatus rejected anyone who had ever negotiated with or capitulated to the Roman government in times of Christian repression. Augustine believed that no one was free of sin, and that such inflexible views only served to undermine the Church. It was heresy to suggest that a small group of believers had a singular grasp on God's inscrutable plans, a monopoly on virtue that could not be challenged. Donatists, however, would physically attack other priests who did not accept their beliefs.[20]

For Augustine, limiting the Church to a small, chosen few not only was wrong, but also posed a danger to its survival and expansion. His fight against the Donatists was an earthly and spiritual battle that made money all the more necessary. Evangelism did not come cheap. The Church needed access to money and markets in order to fight its foes and rebuild a Christian Rome. It would have to take part of the place of Cicero's republic, with priests the servants of a semi-theocratic state. This is clear in one of Augustine's sermons, where he calls for alms to be made directly to the Church rather than distributed "indiscriminately" to the poor. It was not ideal for individuals to give charity to others without spiritual expertise. The Church alone could administer alms and the sacraments to bring salvation. The path, then, was not simply about renouncing the world; it was about earthly exchanges that benefited the Church and allowed it to grow.[21]

As with all earthly things, this new Christian Rome was not to last. Alaric, king of the Visigoths, sacked Rome in 410 and the city fell. Some Roman elites fled the invading Germanic hordes all the way to Augustine's Hippo, where, justifiably, there was panic. Hippo did not have the military resources to defend itself. However, for Augustine the earthly challenges of the Church presented an opportunity to develop his thoughts on individualism in the economy of salvation. Cicero had shown the power of literature in facing the great adversity of the collapse of the Roman Republic. Now, the literal fall of Rome inspired Augustine to write his monumental *City of God*, in which he explained the necessity of earthly wealth and its place in the divine economy.[22]

Not all money could be renounced or given to the poor, he said. Rather, the Church needed its followers to create a Christian market economy based on free will. Those who were moral, Augustine insisted, were simply more likely to live better and to keep their wealth. "God," he explained, "shows more clearly his manner of working in the distribution of good and bad fortune." After all, he claimed, the moral and pious had suffered less at the hands of the Visigoths: "Those who obeyed their Lord's advice about where and how they ought to amass treasure, did not lose even their worldly riches in the barbarian invasions." The chosen were not just destined for heaven; God could bestow on them earthly treasures and protection.[23]

Augustine's message could hardly have been more radical or more influential. The spiritual market directly influenced the earthly market. Augustine said that God had created the world with his invisible hand: "God's 'hand' is his power, and God achieves even visible results by invisible means." This was not yet Adam Smith's invisible economic hand, but it made clear that a higher power could regulate wealth. Once one freely entered into God's system and fulfilled the necessary exchange, there was nothing to worry about. God's grace would take over. As with Cicero's system of nature, Augustine saw salvation as "a stream" that conjoined and "caused" all things, and that could deliver one to God in heaven.[24]

In one of his last expositions on the Psalms, written near the end of his life, Augustine was explicit in connecting piety to an invisible system of wealth. "Is not this then happiness, to have sons safe, daughters beautiful, garners [storehouses] full, cattle abundant, no downfall, I say not a wall, but not even of a hedge, no tumult and clamor in the streets, but quiet, peace, abundance, plenty of all things in their houses and their cities?" God, he said, would make sure "the righteous" would have all this. "Did not Abraham's house abound with gold, silver, children, servants, cattle?" he asked.[25]

If one believed Augustine's view of earthly riches and in God's role in the balance between free will and predestination, then it was possible to go one step further than Augustine, such that God might stretch the eye of the needle for a chosen few to pass through. Augustine and the Fathers of the Church who followed him erected a model of economic hope. For even as Rome itself collapsed, their theology promised that chastity, giving to the poor, and helping the Church would all lead to wealth in this life as well as treasure in the afterlife. It was the original win-win. One simply had to have faith in the system.

But the Christian market of salvation did not bring quick riches on earth. It would be hundreds of years after the death of Augustine before Europe found its way to earthly wealth—divinely sanctioned or not. When it did, the model of the divine economy would once again provide the philosophical concepts and language for the earthly economy, in this case, for early capitalism and free market theories. But after Augustine, with earthly riches came a new Christian embrace of secular, Ciceronian values.

CHAPTER 3

GOD IN THE MEDIEVAL MARKET MECHANISM

It is the fact of rarity, or the difficulty in finding something, that makes things more necessary.... According
to these criteria, wheat is worth more in periods of
shortage... than when it is abundant for everyone.
—PETER JOHN OLIVI, *TREATISE ON CONTRACTS*, 1293

WHEN THE ROMAN Empire collapsed in the early 400s, with it
went the economic system and market that supported the pagan
philosophers, the senatorial lords, and the powerful new Fathers
of the Christian Church. So, too, shrank the state and the coffers
of the Church itself. With the fall of the empire went the idea of
an overarching, natural economic system. When effective human
government collapsed, nature suddenly seemed less harmonious
and nurturing, and the idea that the economy was self-regulating
and generous no longer made sense. Untamed nature now seemed
a threat. With the Germanic invasions, the Church began to turn
toward the earthly economy to survive. It would have to organize

itself as a state, and it would have to help create and sustain economic growth. The market was not coming back on its own.

For medieval thinkers, wealth-generating exchange was not latent in nature, awaiting the steadying hand of the virtuous legislator to keep it on course, as Cicero had imagined. Nor was it a predestined divine order that individual free will could set in motion by trading worldly for spiritual goods, as Augustine had preached. Instead, human management and oversight, including the building of strong government structures and the development of innovative technologies—the ninth-century heavy plow, for instance, which yielded greater returns, and late thirteenth- and early fourteenth-century double-entry accounting, which allowed for effective financial management—were all necessary to developing the modern market and its mechanisms. Scholastic philosophers of the Church, meaning those who worked via deductive reasoning to resolve the contradictions of theology, dominated universities in the 1100s. (Their most famous debate was about proving the existence of God through arguments for and against.) In their quest to understand human freedom, these medieval philosophers pioneered ideas of individual rights and agency. They believed that the state—ecclesiastical and secular—would have to play a large role in rebuilding European societies and economies. Between 1200 and 1400, a later generation of Christian thinkers began to theorize about how to create earthly wealth, and also how to reject it. They did not believe in one overarching free market; rather, they studied self-regulating market mechanisms on a limited scale and sought ways to work them into their own Christian moralities.

WHEN THERE IS political stability and a developed economic system, it can seem as if markets just emerge on their own and sustain themselves. The fall of Rome, however, showed that when society collapses, strong and sustained state intervention may be necessary to build back the market. Imperial shipping routes, guaranteeing the stability of the Mediterranean for private trade, had given the impression that the free movement of goods was part of the natural order of things. In fact, it was a great achievement of the Roman state. Trade in olive oil, pottery, and other goods followed the flour fleet. This state-made free flow created wealth. But when the flour fleet disappeared, and when the Vandal invaders took North Africa, not only did security collapse in the *mare nostrum*; so, too, did the entire Roman commercial system. Money became scarce as ore mines in Spain, Gaul, and Austria closed. Slowly, trade dried up, and the Western Roman Empire became impoverished.[1]

The Western cities and provinces lost contact with the empire's trade and communication systems that had connected them to the Eastern Greek Empire and North Africa. Somewhere between 10 and 30 percent of the population of the Roman Empire lived in cities, with one million living in Rome itself. There were dozens of cities with populations of more than one thousand. With the decline of international commerce and cities between AD 400 and 700 came the decline of the wealth of urban elites. Poverty supplanted relative prosperity as a more precarious rural economy took hold. Meanwhile, a declining temperature, of perhaps 1.5°C (2.7°F), led to lower crop yields and colder winters, adding to the economic crisis.[2]

Along with this pervasive poverty came illness, plague, and demographic decline. As civic management and the state food system ground to a halt, an array of diseases struck the weakened population. Viral pandemics were common. Unmanaged marshlands bred malaria. Leprosy, or Hansen's disease, once rare in the Roman world, now spread throughout Europe due to poor hygiene. Worst of all, in 541 the bubonic plague made its first appearance in the empire. The Greek Byzantine historian Procopius described Justinian's plague of 541–542 as a mysterious disease that came from Egypt: "The whole human race came near being annihilated," he reported. Killing as many as fifty million people in the Eastern and Western parts of the Roman Empire, the plague decimated working populations and what industry remained on the Mediterranean rim. By 600, there was a sense of total collapse in the former Western Empire. Merchants and artisans could not fill in the gap because they were simply gone. There was no longer a market, and no longer any way to circulate goods. In northern Gaul and the Rhineland, agricultural land gave way to forests, and small family farms, clustered in villages, replaced the larger and more organized Roman villa system. With poorer soils and smaller tilling animals came hardier grains in northern Europe, such as rye and oats.[3]

Ironically, the collapse of the Roman Empire brought the Church closer to the earthly civic spirit of Cicero. Without the powerful state, and faced with chaos, poverty, and plague, the Church stepped into the role of leadership in the new Germanic kingdoms and became a worldly force. It did so not just to protect its own interests, but also because there was no other civil organization remaining. Church leaders looked to harness their own institutions and governing power to develop the larger European economy.

In Western Europe, monasteries became great holders of authority and wealth, as both the Roman emperors and the German kings—in need of its organizational prowess—supported Church expansion with gifts of land and the freedom of self-rule. The founder of the Christian monastic movement, Saint Benedict of Nursia, saw that monasteries would have to help rebuild and organize the economy. The Roman system of villa-based farms bequeathed to the early Middle Ages an agrarian slave labor system.

Monasteries now became centers for the stewardship of wealth. Monks prayed and worked, and they also oversaw the slaves who worked their increasingly rich lands. Benedict's monastic Rule (516) was essentially a set of instructions on how to manage a large monastic community. These wealthy institutions used their vast estates to produce valuable agricultural products, such as spun wool, milled wheat, cheese, sausage, wine, and beer. The abbot of the monastery became the "dispenser" of the wealth of God on earth.[4]

For these holy "custodians," or "cellarers," wealth creation was not a product of nature, or even of farming in the classical sense, but rather of the good management of scarce goods. There was no concept that a market or a single individual spontaneously produced this new wealth. It came from collective discipline, powerful institutions, and large slave farms. In other words, the government of the Church developed and built much of the early medieval economy.[5]

Clerics had to manage goods according to both scarcity and codes of morality. The Church had to make sure that its members got enough food and clothing. Pope Gregory I (reigned 590–604) equated good administration with the redistribution of "wealth" (*largine*) for "charity" (*caritas*). Later, major religious institutions, such as the wealthy Durham Cathedral Priory in northeastern England, became centers of financial management. They kept extensive account ledgers to manage stocks and stores, households, personnel, rents, and tolls.[6]

By 1050, with the advent of heavy plows, harrows, hoes, and new harnessing equipment, crop yields had multiplied, not only improving living standards but leading to a population boom. With demographic growth came the rise of cities and the expansion of commerce. Where before there had been only the Church, kings, noble warlords, slaves, serfs, and intermittent trade, now the

Western European rural economy gave way to burgeoning urban centers filled with merchants and skilled artisans, who enjoyed freedoms that set them apart from the great mass of rural subjugation.[7]

Medieval cities pose a challenge to understanding free trade because, at first, commercial freedoms came in the form of clearly determined monopolies: the Church and the state both granted and limited free trading privileges to cities and their guilds. This combination led to economic development and market expansion. In 1127, in Saint-Omer in the County of Flanders, in northern France, the count, William Clito, granted the burghers—Saint-Omer's urban citizens—the privilege to be judged for all crimes by courts within their own city. Moreover, he exempted them from military service and from paying tolls and numerous taxes within Flanders. Free from feudal constraints at large, these burghers paid neither the German *hansa* tax, nor safe-passage money required by the Holy Roman emperor, nor French royal tolls. They were also free to maintain local monopolies, with the count guaranteeing that all contracts within the city be honored. In a customs document, the count listed all the foreign rulers with whom he had agreements to protect the burghers' tax exemptions. Furthermore, the count guaranteed the town military protection.[8]

By no means did city dwellers enjoy the freedoms of kings, churchmen, or lords. However, they had now secured individual liberties that gave them freedom of passage; protected them from feudal agricultural labor, duties, taxes, and arbitrary imprisonment; and granted them the right to vote for city governments. In exchange for privileges of free trade and local monopolies, burghers made money, brought wealth to Flanders, and paid taxes to the count. It was from this mix of urban freedoms, monopolies, and professional regulation that European markets first arose and, with them, early capitalism.[9]

Though Adam Smith would see guilds as purely repressive—the antithesis of free market culture—they were essential to market development. Guild laws emerged at the very moment when urban wealth began to expand. Much like monasteries, guilds had strict rules. Those who ate in the guild house paid a discounted rate, and outsiders had to pay more. Anyone who tried to sneak a cup of wine out of the guild house would be fined. There were also fines on fighting and striking other guild members with "loaves of bread or a stone, since no other weapons are available." As it was for monks, clothing, food, and prayer were regulated (for example, no one could wear wooden clogs in the guild house without paying a penalty). One of the benefits of the guild was privileged treatment for members within a given town. Guild members received discounted products, while nonmembers paid higher prices. Most importantly, though—and this is what Smith missed—is that guilds in cities such as Florence and Siena were centers of expertise, innovation, and wealth.[10]

Theologians were often wary of merchants. Because they toiled for profit and did not work the land, they were considered spiritually poorer than even the poor themselves. In the tenth century, Rathier of Verona categorized merchants as "wanderers and paupers." But by the eleventh century, ideas about business had evolved. Some leading thinkers, from the Italian bishop and legal theorist Gratian to the theologian Bernard of Clairvaux, saw the pious merchant in a positive light. The Benedictine monk and ecclesiastic reformer Peter Damian said that a good bishop should manage his diocese like a good merchant. Certainly merchants were good if they gave their fortunes to charity. In this way, the Church could make clear who was and wasn't part of the natural economy: "infidels" and "Jews," for example, who were considered guilty of usurping legitimate Christian wealth, were "bad" merchants and could not trade with any moral authority. But for the most part, the Church did not want to fight merchant wealth; it just wanted its share. And so it sought to use its undeniable influence to regulate the growing economy while at the same time adhering to Christian morals in the marketplace.[11]

The Church did not have the authority to control commercial life, but it did provide guidance to the guilds in setting moral prices, which were to reflect both market value and the principles of just and equal exchange, which included limitations on profit. Having defined their own community of moral commerce and new market rules, Christians could trade freely if they traded in a Christian way. Here were echoes of Cicero: as the priest Robert of Flamborough wrote in his *Penitential* (ca. 1208–1213), exchange based on the "civil friendship" of Christian relations was a virtue.[12]

IN MANY WAYS, the story of medieval economic thought begins with the life of the founder of the Franciscan Order, Saint Francis of Assisi. He was born Giovanni di Pietro di Bernardone in 1181 in Umbria, Italy, his father a silk merchant and his mother a noblewoman from Provence. The family was part of a new class of wealthy merchants who inhabited the Latin Mediterranean from Italy and southern France to Barcelona. It was a socioeconomic stratum that Francis would reject. In 1205, he had a mystical vision that led him to forsake earthly wealth. He renounced his inheritance and, in a stunning display of his dedication to total poverty in the name of Christ, stripped his clothes off in public, driving his horrified father to disown him. From then on, he wore only coarse peasant garb, walking and dwelling among the poor as a mendicant monk and living only from donations. The first true ecologist in the European tradition, he saw animals as spiritual beings and preached to them. He believed that his church had no walls and was nature itself, and spurned the very essence of wealthy monastic life. His followers, the Franciscans, and their vow of total poverty posed a real threat to the religious institution that had become the center of wealth throughout Western Europe.

The renunciation of riches brought with it a profound philosophical examination not only of what wealth was, but of how prices were created both morally and through market forces. Franciscan Scholastic theologians—trained to use dialectic and deductive reasoning to resolve philosophical questions—centered at the University of Paris, drew upon Plato, Aristotle, and Cicero to understand how markets could function according to Christian morality. They mixed an Aristotelian interest in balance with a reliance on Roman natural law as described in Gratian's *Decretals* (1140), the great legal textbook of the Middle Ages. The founding medieval compendium and textbook of Roman Church law, *The Decretals* declared that every unfair loss—a deal that was not deemed of equal value for both parties, or a fraud—had to be "restituted" with something exactly symmetrical in its worth. This idea came from Aristotle's *Nicomachean Ethics* and the principle of giving "equal for equal." *The Decretals* also described how exchange was based on private property, contracts, and consent. This was the basis of just price theory, by which no price should reflect anything more than the fair balance of the trade, and those involved in the trade should profit equally.[13]

The challenge for Scholastic thinkers was to establish what was the fair and moral price for a product or service, and how to calculate the equal values. Public authorities and producers set prices. Churchmen believed that to determine fair value, traders could make moral commercial decisions by using a logic of neutral individual choice. This did not really mean individual autonomy in the modern sense, only that merchants could make professional

decisions about prices. They simply had to mix moral considerations with the market values of the time to create prices and profit
margins that were just and fair, according to Christian thinking.

In his *Summa Theologica* (1265–1274), the Dominican friar and
Italian Scholastic thinker Saint Thomas Aquinas agreed with the
Franciscans that merchants had to be moral and use "just" prices.
Yet Aquinas did not agree with Francis's vow of absolute poverty.
He argued that poverty should not be a requirement or rule, but a
personal choice or aspiration. Indeed, he believed that total poverty
was not possible, because man always owned things, and felt the
Franciscans risked mortal sin and damnation, for breaking a vow
one has made to God was a serious matter. It was perhaps a con-
venient piece of argument, for the Dominican order was wealthy,
with huge feudal landholdings, and Aquinas did not have any
qualms about what he considered morally acquired wealth: he felt
that the Church needed to be rich. This belief influenced his sense
of the natural workings of the market.[14]

Honest business and profits, Aquinas said, were not a sin. In
a contract, prices could be clearly agreed upon to the advantage
of both parties. If one party in a sale or exchange tried to have an
unfair advantage over the other, the public authorities (secular or
religious) would have to intervene and seek restitution. Aquinas
cited Cicero when he argued that it was the duty of all traders to
declare in advance any defect in their product. Aquinas followed
Cicero's belief that good morals formed the basis of commerce and
politics. In this highly restricted moral way, one could be pious and
earn a profit.[15]

The challenge facing Franciscans was enormous. If they acciden-
tally owned wealth or used it beyond their bare necessities—for example, if they owned any piece of clothing that was beyond what
was necessary for utilitarian purposes—they would be damned for

breaking their sacred vow. The Franciscan Order began to study pricing and valuation mechanisms to be sure their members remained in "total poverty." The rules of the order denied its members the right to live in monasteries, which were too rich. Nor could they own any sort of property. They were not even supposed to touch money. Friars could help the poor, the sick, and the pious, laboring faithfully and devoutly, but they could never work directly for money.[16]

The strictness of Francis's own Rule caused consternation among members of the Church. It seemed impossible to have a monastic order without a hierarchy, property, and funds for housing, sustenance, and charitable works. Aquinas believed that the Franciscans were too radical and would lead to a rejection of all institutional and social hierarchy, as well as private property. The Church was the greatest feudal property owner of the time and collected taxes across Europe. The vow of poverty threatened the temporal Church and its vast wealth. Peasants and even kings chafed at this great power, thus it had to be forcefully preserved. Even more, figures such as Aquinas worried that the Franciscan vow implied that members of the Church who did not live in poverty—or lived in great luxury—were impious sinners.

Franciscan poverty posed a real threat to the Church. While most Franciscans preached peace, other groups of radical mendicant friars, such as the Northern Italian Dolcinian sect of the early 1300s, periodically led powerful and violent movements to overthrow the social order and destroy the Church as an institution of private property. The Church sent armies against them, and in 1307, the leader of the movement, Fra Dulcino, was captured and burned at the stake.[17]

The Scottish Franciscan monk and Scholastic philosopher John Duns Scotus took a more nuanced view of pricing than Aquinas, proposing that prices came neither from balanced exchange nor from moral rules. Rather, he believed they came from a freely working secular market process. Private property was not the purview of the Church, which was ill equipped to understand all the market activities that went into creating value. As Duns Scotus saw it, prices came from quantity and from the value of labor and expertise. To understand a price, one had to take into account "diligence, prudence, care, as well as the risk one accepts in doing such business." Therefore, it was very difficult for churchmen to calculate market prices. And because this was the case, it was equally difficult for Franciscans to be sure that they were truly obeying their vow of poverty. To keep their vows, they needed to consult with merchants and those expert in secular market prices.[18]

As it happened, Franciscans often came from well-educated, commercial backgrounds, which meant that some had a particular awareness of the workings of commerce and pricing. Franciscan leaders and sympathizers came to believe that the way to manage the vow of poverty was to more carefully codify it. The Franciscan theologian Saint Bonaventure's *Constitutions of Narbonne* (1260) was a detailed analysis of wealth and poverty meant to create strict rules to hold Franciscans to their vows. One of the most important topics was clothing, a prominent sign of wealth in Italy, where cloth production was at the center of its flourishing economy. Saint Francis himself considered clothing a material impediment to poverty and a sign of riches. The rules of the *Constitutions* thus decreed that each brother own only one tunic, even going so far as to specify what a friar should do if a tunic fell apart, for instance, or if one had to use pieces of other cloth to repair it.[19]

In 1286, the Franciscan Order began to examine how books—vellum manuscripts, which were very expensive—could be viewed not as valuables, but purely as tools of learning. The Franciscans calculated that an expensive book, if it was used for strictly utilitarian spiritual purposes, was not an object of wealth within the strict economy of the order. Thus, a layman could give books as gifts to individual monks or monasteries, but the institutional leader or custodian would have to decide who could actually use them. In 1297, one Brother Bartholomeus of Bologna received two books from another friar. He then bequeathed them to a certain Brother Hugolinus. To be sure, they were following rules of spiritual utility. Friars were careful to record such goods and describe exactly how they used them so that the order could calculate the value of the goods in worldly and spiritual terms.[20]

Pope Nicholas III (reigned 1277–1280) defended the Franciscan vow, which he believed had been proved valid by the pious examples of many of the order's members. In his *Exiit qui seminat* (*Confirmation of the Rules of the Friars Minor*) of 1279, he came up with a revolutionary approach to realizing the vow of poverty. Franciscans could not break their vow, Pope Nicholas maintained, because the pope was the actual owner of all Franciscan property, meaning that the Franciscans themselves never actually "owned" anything. But Nicholas went further, using market valuation to explain that, even if the Franciscans had goods and property at their disposal, the value of these assets was not inherent, but dependent on where, why, and how friars used them. Each thing's value changed according to its practical and spiritual utility. The abdication of property, Nicholas insisted, did "not seem to lead to a renunciation of the use of things in every case." The value of objects, he explained, comes from "places and seasons," and related to specific duties. "Science requires study," he noted, and this exercise was impossible without "the use of books." Nicholas thought that religious authorities could oversee the valuation process, not only to make sure that Franciscans owned things only out of necessity, but also to assuage their fears of breaking their vows. With his papal decree, Pope Nicholas had embraced a belief in market mechanisms in order to solve a conflict within the Church.[21]

That same year, a French Franciscan, Peter John Olivi, wrote *De usu paupere* (Treatise on poor use)—a work on the restricted use of goods within the vow of poverty—in which he specifically addressed the question of how to keep the vow while owning worldly things. Olivi created some of the earliest, most innovative concepts of specific self-regulating market mechanisms. He was originally from Montpellier, and spent time in both Florence, Italy, and Narbonne, a city of thirty thousand people in Provence. This placed him in the center of the Mediterranean world of commerce where Franciscans often worked as confessors to merchants. Having served in Nicholas III's papal administration, Olivi sought to defend the Franciscan vow and, to this end, created the first theory of the law of diminishing marginal utility, by which a good loses value as access to it, and consumption of it, increase. Olivi said that if people used things "generally" or "conventionally" it would affect their value. The more available something is, the less it is worth. Commodities such as oil and vegetables, produced in great quantity for a great number of people and obtained "with ease," are worth less than rarer products.[22]

Utility and value were based on the number of those who benefited from a product. If hundreds of people had access to something, it was not of great worth. Olivi claimed that if something was so rare that only one person owned it—a rare manuscript, or a jewel—then its scarcity made it precious. He noted that "durability," too, affected price. With foodstuffs, for example, freshness was a key factor, as recently harvested food was more valuable than older, "corrupted" products, which rapidly lost value. Longevity mattered, too. Storable goods, such as grain, were also worth more. The value of clothing, or houses, which were more lasting, had to be calculated according to their durability. What this meant was that no single authority could assign or fix a fair price to something. Olivi insisted that fair prices could be based on moral precepts, but even more, they were subject to a self-regulating and constantly changing system of quantity, utility, accessibility, and durability.[23]

Olivi's contention that utility and not morality created value was a challenge to the Church and even to secular authorities, who had long seen it as their role to judge such things. Added to this, Olivi had also critiqued Saint Augustine's idea that human cognition relied on divine illumination, insisting instead that judgment in the human mind came from free will. This idea took agency away from God and the Church and centered it more on the individual. This was too much for the leaders of the Church, and especially for the powerful doctors of the University of Paris. They declared Olivi's thought heretical. Authorities brought him before a tribunal of seven Franciscan judges in Paris, who condemned him, ruining his chances of teaching there.[24]

Olivi eventually cleared his name, managing to win a teaching position in Narbonne, and in 1293 wrote what is arguably one of the most visionary works of economic theory of the Middle Ages, his *Treatise on Contracts*. In it, he insisted that churchmen could not understand pricing, and thus needed to rely on secular merchant "experts" to illuminate the workings of the market. One of his main concerns was that if people did not understand contracts, they could not understand their sins. This was also true for Franciscans, who, in their administrative duties, inevitably had to sign contracts while keeping their vow of total poverty. Olivi was worried that his brethren could be damned if they could not effectively describe their failings to keep their vow in confession—without economic expertise they could not confess to sin. Thus, it was essential to understand contracts not only in order to manage the vow, but also to confess to having broken it.

Olivi believed that only the "judgments" of the merchant "community" could fairly establish prices, for only they understood the relationships between "goods and services" and knew the demands of "the common good." Olivi believed that honest and accurate business decisions were the causal spark of market mechanisms. Of course, merchants were not always honest, and Olivi never explained if fraud could also drive market mechanisms. Still, he did have the insight to understand that businessmen knew the value of labor in a specific market, and could add this value to the price of a given product. One could estimate the price of products by a knowledge of their "utility," which "the buyer" set according to need. For example, during periods of sickness, certain rare medicinal herbs became more expensive, particularly when they were perceived to be necessary for survival.[25]

Olivi observed how merchant labor and expertise often added extra value to products. He reminded his readers that traveling for business was dangerous, and required significant background knowledge. Merchants had to know their trade routes, not to mention the customs and currencies of the foreign countries. Long-distance commerce entailed serious capital investment and risk. Nearly nine hundred years before Karl Marx, Olivi was the first thinker to discuss the market concept of capital. Money lacked intrinsic value, he observed, "because money alone, by itself, is not lucrative." Value came, rather, "through the activity of merchants in their business dealings." He saw money as capital for future investment; its value could grow, but this value was uncertain and subject to the skill of merchants and their decision-making, along with the more diffuse dynamics of the market.[26]

While Olivi saw naturally occurring mechanisms that set prices, he nevertheless believed they needed to be tempered by morality, warning that scarcity was not a moral excuse to raise prices unjustly. Merchants had to resist the temptation to overcharge for scarce goods. Even more, he believed that simple resellers were immoral. Those who did not produce, or use skill to add value to capital, but simply brought something to market to sell it at a higher price with no extra labor involved, were so immoral that the community should "expel" them. Assessing which merchants were truly and morally productive was an enormous responsibility. Therefore, Olivi suggested that the Church would have to learn about the labor, skill, and the risk-taking that went into a product to assess whether merchants' prices reflected just values.[27]

Franciscan thought would take a revolutionary turn in the work of the brilliant Scholastic philosopher and English Franciscan William of Ockham, whose ideas moved toward a modern concept of individual and subjective choice in the marketplace. In the 1320s, Ockham, like Olivi, defended the idea of perfect and absolute poverty, but he had a new approach to defending the vow. Ockham believed that no law could force someone to own something against their will, preaching instead the necessity of "permissive" laws, such as the right to refuse private property. Personal choice meant that Franciscans could refuse property just as easily as they could own it.[28]

A temporal prince with rich domains and considerable military forces, Pope John XXII, the second Avignon pope (reigned 1316–1334), believed that the Franciscan vow of poverty did, in fact, undermine private property. In his 1322 papal bull *Quia nonnunquam* (Because sometimes), John attacked the vow and excommunicated a group of extreme Fraticelli, or Spiritual Franciscans, who fanatically believed that the example of Christ taught the total renunciation of private property. Pope John maintained that private property was divinely instituted. Overturning Nicholas III's *Exiit qui seminat*, he insisted that the apostles had owned possessions, just as the Franciscans, and not the pope, owned their own property and goods. In this way, Pope John sought to dismantle Nicholas's defense of the Franciscan vow.[29]

William of Ockham rebutted Pope John with the long-established view that private property was a secular institution, founded after the Fall from the Garden of Eden. He boldly claimed that the pope had no right to make general decisions about property. Like Duns Scotus, Ockham believed that God had rendered worldly possessions unto Caesar, or secular princes and lords, and it was they who had the ultimate authority over earthly questions of property. Secular laws allowed humans to exercise "evangelical liberty" in economic questions, following their personal free will rather than religious authority. Ockham further insisted that no one could deprive free individuals of "possessions, rights, and liberties." Thus merchants and Franciscans had the freedom to choose, and the Church could neither police nor repress them. The pope and the Dominicans could elect to make money, but it was equally within the Franciscans' power to refuse all possessions.[30]

In a series of theological acrobatics, Ockham argued that in heaven, as in the Garden of Eden, all things were held in common. But with the Fall, Adam and Eve's Original Sin created the permanent stain of human imperfection. Humans lived in a flawed world and they had to navigate it and seek salvation through their own moral decisions. In other words, the Church could not "bid" someone to follow a moral precept. The "papal principate," Ockham insisted, could not force moral decisions such as charitable giving, virginity, or sexual continence. Secular princes, on the other hand, could make and enforce laws, so long as their authority was "founded on love, not fear, and by popular election." It was a remarkable vision of individual liberty, as well as an early defense of a free market of economic choice.[31]

Today, Ockham's views of religious, political, and economic freedoms appear almost modern. But they had an echo in the constitutional, republican city-states of Northern Italy, where citizens enjoyed relatively high levels of personal and economic liberty. Ockham's theory of property also happened to serve the secular interests of Edward I of England, who was even then trying to force the clergy to pay taxes. By no means did Ockham's belief in secular power usher in an age of individual rights, however. In most parts of Europe, feudalism still ruled. And feudalism was not based on individual natural rights, but on feudal customs and privileges. It was only via contracts that princes and lords granted merchants urban freedom. Ruling over their long-suffering serfs, they extracted not only labor, but wealth itself, often through violence and their own personal judicial systems.[32]

However, urban dwellers enjoyed far greater freedom. For completely opposing reasons, merchants, too, began to study how the market worked. They believed that a more secular ethos was needed to match their flourishing markets' astounding new wealth. Florentines, in particular, came up with a new idea central to free market thought: that it was in fact virtuous for hardworking merchants to earn wealth and even to celebrate it.

CHAPTER 4

FLORENTINE WEALTH AND THE MACHIAVELLIAN MARKETPLACE

Well-ordered republics have to keep the public rich,
but the citizens poor.
—MACHIAVELLI, *DISCOURSES ON LIVY*, 1517

AT THE VERY time William of Ockham was writing to justify individual freedom in defense of Franciscan poverty, Florentine merchants were seeking a philosophy to justify individual freedom in the pursuit of wealth. By the 1300s, merchant republics with constitutions, civic freedoms, complex markets, and remarkable material riches—such as Siena, Florence, Genoa, and Venice—stood apart from the feudal realms of kings and lords. Their wealth came not from traditional farming and feudalism, but from industry, trade, and finance. The merchant elite who ruled these medieval cities knew their situation was unusual. Indeed, there were no important texts in Christendom that wholly praised mercantile wealth. Now wielding real authority, some sought to change this by describing and celebrating how markets worked.

Unlike Ockham and the Scholastic philosophers, Italian merchants did not view the desire for money in a negative light. Embracing Cicero's ideals of service to the state, wealthy Italian traders and Renaissance humanists saw individual self-interest and profit-seeking as essential to creating a virtuous commercial republic and a healthy market. This was a profound cultural shift between 1250 and 1450, as it meant that commerce, not agriculture, was key to maintaining such virtues, and that earthly desires and aspirations for riches could be good.[1]

By the 1200s, the Tuscan city-state of Siena had already become a leader in European banking as a result of the financial expertise of its citizens and international confidence in the republic's institutions. Siena's government officials were conscious that for borrowers and investors to work and bank in the city, they had to believe that the market would function according to expectations. From 1287 to 1355, the Nine Governors and Defenders of the Commune and the People of Siena focused on maintaining the rule of law and a reputation for good financial administration. The government oversaw not only a highly organized taxation system, but also stable credit networks.[2]

The values of good government and commercial virtues permeated society. In Siena's famous medieval public administration building, the Palazzo Pubblico, a series of three frescoes by the painter Ambrogio Lorenzetti, *The Allegory of Good and Bad Government* (1338–1339), suggests that law-abiding merchants uphold good government. In a clear reference to Cicero and the Roman philosopher Seneca (AD 4–65), the frescoes depict good government surrounded by the Stoic virtues of justice, wisdom, peace, fortitude, prudence, magnanimity, and temperance. Lorenzetti equated Stoicism with good business practices. He renders Siena as a city filled with rich citizens, full shops, merchants, and artisans. The moral and economic message is clear: good, elite republican government, supported by the rule of law, could create the conditions necessary for wealth-creating trade. Healthy markets, in turn, would support the republic. Another frame repeats an old Ciceronian message: that political tyranny led directly to corruption, undermining not only trust and peace, but the marketplace itself and the wealth that would otherwise spring from it.[3]

The celebration of virtuous Stoic government and urban wealth soon became commonplace among the merchant writers of Florence. By the late 1300s, Florence had eclipsed Siena as the center of Tuscany's economic life. The Tuscan classical humanist scholar and writer Francesco Petrarch undertook to resurrect Ciceronian thought to support the idea that secular civic service was a virtue. Both a poet and a papal official, Petrarch led a movement to find and restore the texts of the ancient Romans. The Black Death of 1347 and ensuing wars had led him to reject the notion that God was punishing Italy; rather, he believed that humanity had brought the cataclysm on itself by forsaking civic virtue. Italy thus needed to renew itself by emulating Rome to build better government.[4]

Petrarch looked for a philosophy to attract elites to civic service. He found it in Cicero's idea of *paideia*, or moral, civic education, which he hoped would lead to a Florentine renaissance of Roman virtue. Petrarch explained that the Tuscan elite would have to work to achieve Cicero's civic *summum bonum*, or "the highest good," by studying ancient ethics, rhetoric, and law to learn how to govern well. In his treatise *How a Ruler Ought to Govern His State* (1373), he used the works of Cicero to describe his ideal rulers as morally just. They worked for the love of the republic and for the common good of "the multitude." Rather than arms, Petrarch saw wealth and a good citizenry as the foundation of a successful state.

Following Cicero, he noted that leaders should be honest and efficient managers.[5]

Petrarch's discourse on *paideia* appealed to the old families of the Italian republican elite and to the new men who entered their ranks after the plague. With the rise of trade, Florentine merchants saw themselves as legitimate leaders of a new elite based not on feudal or divine power, but on commerce and secular law. Long portrayed as moral paupers by the Church, merchants were now some of the richest men in Europe. Understandably, they sought to portray their wealth and political service as virtuous.[6]

Florentine merchants wrote about these new ideals in letters, account books, and formal business and family memoirs called *ricordi*, or books of the merchant arts. Taking these writings to be little more than practical paperwork, economic historians have, for the most part, failed to integrate them into the formal history of economic ideas. And yet, on examination, they reveal radical new beliefs about commerce and its virtues. In his *Ricordi* (1393–1411), the Florentine merchant Giovanni di Pagolo Morelli lauded the market itself, boasting about the "abundance" of the "markets of Tuscany" that had made not only Florence but his family rich. He was proud of his ancestors' acquired wealth and, even more, proud that they had "died rich"—something he considered a particular honor. However, the quest to accumulate personal riches independent of civic virtue, and independent of one's duty to the republic, was suspect. In 1428, the Florentine humanist and historian Matteo Palmieri was explicit in saying that the quest for profits had to directly serve the interests of the state. Quoting Cicero, Palmieri insisted that merchants needed to mix "eloquence" and "virtue," and they had to avoid petty greed and focus on channeling the desire for wealth toward "the useful merchant arts," which had "great utility" for those who took part in "public government."[7]

The most extensive and brilliant of all these writings was Benedetto Cotrugli's *The Book of the Art of Trade* (written in 1458, though only printed a century later, in 1573). A merchant from the Venetian trading city of Ragusa, modern-day Dubrovnik, Cotrugli (Kotrulj in modern Croatian) admired and emulated Florentine values. More than any other figure of his time, he developed the idea that good Ciceronian ethics and decorous behavior created the trust and political stability necessary for the market to function. This is a central point. Greed and necessity are everywhere, Cotrugli observed, and even the poorest places have markets, but not all markets create wealth or magnificent cities. He made it clear that for commerce and investment to flourish, a market ultimately needs institutional support, confidence, and cooperation, without which trade could not properly function.[8]

Well acquainted with every element of this complex market system, the Cotrugli family saw Florence as its stabilizing core. Dyers who dealt in wool, grain, and bills of exchange, they had strong connections well beyond Ragusa, in Venice, Florence, and Naples. Cotrugli was inspired by what he considered to be the superior business practices he discovered in all of these places while working with the Florentine Neroni company, which traded with Ragusa in silver and wool.[9]

Essential for modern free-market thought was Cotrugli's idea that the merchant's hunger for wealth was a form of self-interest that created a greater good, an idea that admittedly required some twisting of Cicero's philosophy. In his eyes, Cicero's *On Duties* was a guide to making money. Wealth, or "honest gain," may be seen as the basis for the "dignity of a merchant," for through wealth, he explained, the merchant "contributes to the advancement of public welfare with the splendor and opulence of his own house." This meant that owning magnificent residences, furnishings, and clothes as well as forging profitable matrimonial alliances for one's children were all good acts. They supported urban wealth, the state, and, in the end, the common good.[10]

Like earlier merchant writers, Cotrugli changed Cicero's noble equation to put merchants in the leading role, replacing agriculture with commerce and industry. Erroneously claiming that Cicero said "merchants are the resources of the state," Cotrugli wrote as if Cicero agreed that a class of well-educated merchants who followed commercial laws were the natural leaders of society. He thus transformed the Roman senator into a hardworking Tuscan trader. Cotrugli proceeded to follow Cicero's model in arguing that the "gushing spring" of the mercantile "ingenuity" of "nature" spurred markets. Merchants, he said, worked "in the hope of gain." In doing so, they facilitated the "maintenance of the human race." Trade supported "households and families, republics and principalities, kingdoms and empires," and produced an endless source of earthly wealth.[11]

Before the Anglo-Dutch philosopher Bernard Mandeville's famous eighteenth-century idea that the private vice of greed led to the public virtues of wealth and cooperation, Cotrugli argued that the honest gains of merchants were the drivers of commercial states: "Profit for the good of all coincides with honest gain, as Cicero has it." Cotrugli was well enough versed in ancient philosophy to know perfectly well that he was bending old virtues to make new ones. Indeed, he twisted not only Cicero, but also Christian rules of trade, agreeing with the Church's traditional attitudes about moneylending while paying lip service to just-price theories. Certainly almsgiving was a moral necessity for merchants. Yet Cotrugli would have been horrified by the idea of giving away one's fortune entirely. Money was needed for investment capital, earthly dignities, and to support the secular state.[12]

COTRUGLI'S WORK REPRESENTED an ideal defended by powerful merchants in the trading centers of Europe. However, by the end of the 1400s, Italian merchant republics had gone into decline with the rise of the great European monarchies in Spain and France with their vast coffers and huge armies. These new great powers were dominated by kings and landed aristocrats who still held ancient agrarian ideals. When both Spain and France began invading Italy in the late 1400s, Italian merchants either bought their way into the landed nobility or lost rank and status. In 1492, in the name of the Spanish monarchy, Christopher Columbus reached the so-called New World, opening up trade routes that brought a sense that wealth was bound only by the limits of the globe. Great merchant families, such as the Florentine Medici, could no longer exercise the kind of political and economic influence they had in the early 1400s without becoming rulers themselves and tapping the wealth of the state.

The Florentine Cosimo de' Medici won fame with his skill in banking and his support of learning and the arts. Yet he rejected all Ciceronian notions of virtue when he weakened his city's republican constitution to become the de facto ruler of much of Tuscany in the mid-1400s. The second half of the century saw a slow collapse of the Florentine constitutional republic. In 1494, hoping to claim the throne of Naples, King Charles VIII of France invaded Italy with more than twenty-five thousand troops. Ironically, the French feudal king drove the Medici tyrants out of Florence, allowing for a brief return of the old Florentine republic. Vigilant to the dangers of oligarchy and tyranny, the leaders of the restored republic sought to bring back the constitution and the rule of law. Foremost among them was Niccolò Machiavelli, who created a philosophy to defend republican laws and a well-balanced marketplace.[13]

During the eighteen years of the new republic, Machiavelli worked in many positions, becoming second chancellor in 1498.

But for all his acumen, the founder of modern political science bungled the defense of the city against the cardinal Giovanni de' Medici, who forced the city into submission by unleashing Spanish troops against the nearby city of Prato, so that his family marched into Florence almost unopposed in 1512. The Medici then dissolved the republic and installed themselves back to power. Suspecting Machiavelli of plotting against the new regime, although his part in the foiled plot was never proven, the Medici had him tortured "with the rope" and then, upon the election of the same cardinal Giovanni as Pope Leo X, he was freed in a general amnesty and self-exiled to his country house. Embittered, he began working on his two great books: *The Prince* and *The Discourses*.

The intellectual historian Albert Hirschman claims that Machiavelli was "the source" of the modern concept of society as a battlefield of self-interest where "passions" collide and drive market forces. Machiavelli was especially interested in how to master passion to realize self-interest. He agreed that the pursuit of individual wealth was important. He feared the tendency of private wealth to tip into corruption and oligarchy. Machiavelli insisted that the state had to be strong enough to manage and oversee these private passions and interests, so that no one person could dominate the city.[14]

Machiavelli's belief in the primacy of the state was a counterpoint to the tyranny of the Medici and other oligarchs and princes throughout Italy. When the Medici took over, they favored family and friends, using the lawless state for private power and gain while emptying its coffers. Such self-interested tyranny ruined Florence and decimated its free trade. Machiavelli had no faith, then, in the virtue of patricians. To survive in Machiavelli's Italy, as in Cicero's Rome, one had to either live in a powerful republic that respected the rule of law, or else protect oneself by any means possible. In other words, Machiavelli believed in the rule of law, if one could get it.

As a politician and as a historian, Machiavelli was eminently practical, and his writings, like merchant manuals, were meant to be applied to life and, literally, as he said, to managing one's "fortune." To this end, while he agreed with Cicero's civic republicanism, Machiavelli rejected the noble optimism that rulers could be morally generous and good, and even make friends with their subjects, as Petrarch had suggested. Machiavelli had seen that economic inequality and bad government brought violence and strife. In response, he promoted the idea of a republic of laws that would guarantee peaceful and stable government and functioning markets. There was something profoundly Augustinian in Machiavelli's pessimistic vision of humanity.[15]

Written in 1513 in a bid to gain employment with the new Medici regime, Machiavelli's *The Prince* remains an enigma. Some still see it as an invitation to immoral behavior, hence the modern term "Machiavellian," meaning deviously self-interested. Others see the book as a critique and an exposé of the evils that tyrants commit. Most likely, it was both. Machiavelli, after all, hated oligarchy and tyranny, just as he loved politics and dutiful service to the republic. Even after the Medici had taken over, he wanted to both serve and criticize.

Machiavelli did not believe in Cicero's rejection of all immorality; he saw human faults as facts of life. But he agreed with Cicero that the best antidote to corruption was republican government. Tyrants and ambitious men act like beasts, Machiavelli warned. As such, there needed to be some sort of legal oversight if one wanted to avoid the kind of violence Italy had known in the mid-1400s. Machiavelli explained that the state had to protect individuals from the destruction of the unchecked self-interest of capricious and perverse monarchs, and gave practical examples from the Roman Republic and Empire in the hope of providing tools to fight corruption and tyranny. In his *Discourses* (1518), Machiavelli famously exclaimed that "well-ordered republics have to keep the public rich, but the citizens poor."[16]

This did not literally mean that citizens had to be poor. Machiavelli governed in a merchant republic and supported commercial wealth. What he feared was the concentration of money in the hands of an oligarchy, threatening the stability of the republic and its markets. He had watched the rise of the Medici as they corrupted the state and undermined its representative and legal systems with their riches. Machiavelli understood that the republic's finances had been used to the advantage of the patricians and to the weakening of the republic. In opposition to the oligarchic Cicero, he lauded the Roman agrarian laws that redistributed land to the poor and checked the powers of the nobles. He believed that limiting vast wealth inequality had enabled Rome to maintain peace and order. If the rich gained too much power, as they had in the Roman Civil Wars and during the imperial ascent of Julius Caesar (a stand-in for the Medici), it would lead to "the destruction of the republic."[17]

Machiavelli saw the Revolt of the Ciompi (1378–1382), an uprising of Florence's laboring class, as a lesson about economic freedom. In his *Florentine Histories* (1525), which he dedicated to the second Medici pope, Clement VII, he argued that oligarchic monopolies were dangerous and hindered stable trade and wealth. Oligarchy and economic inequality, he said, had brought the civil war to Florence. The republic and its markets could not function without a degree of economic fairness. Using Cicero's terms, he critiqued merchants who gained their fortunes "by fraud or force," which he called "ugly acquisition." Machiavelli disapproved of the

Florentine patricians who had limited the representation of the journeymen Ciompi workers in the guilds, believing it had led to bloodshed, instability, and radical politics. It was only at the point when the republic fails, *The Prince* suggests, that the laws of animals take over. Only a stable state could ward off the bestial and dangerous actions of "foxes" and "lions" to uphold virtue and defend good trade and markets.[18]

Machiavelli had the same misgivings about professional guilds. For them to work, they had to represent the interests of both the patricians and the workers. Two centuries later, the idea that guild oligarchy was antithetical to free, functioning markets would be a fundament of Adam Smith's economic thought. Smith believed that professional guilds were repressive cartels that depressed wages. As a citizen of Renaissance Florence, however, Machiavelli took a more nuanced view. He believed that guilds were necessary to build and maintain trade, quality, and trust. As Florentine merchants proclaimed again and again, these professional associations had made Florence rich. Most medieval and Renaissance merchants knew that the rules of their guilds provided some of the original framework of the constitution and government of their commercial republics. This is why the coats of arms of each guild adorn the Palazzo Vecchio, the famous towered seat of Florentine government. However, Machiavelli insisted that guilds had to make sure that wealth went to all citizens, and that newcomers could join. He saw the *catasto*—the Florentine land tax—as essential to the republic, because it "placed a partial restraint on the tyranny of the powerful" and kept the market functioning fairly.[19]

The great founder of modern cynicism, Machiavelli believed that unchecked self-interest could destroy the market. For stability, one needed the secular state to be richer and more powerful than individuals. Thus, Machiavelli outlined an economic argument that remains relevant even today: he believed that a strong state had to oversee a balance between patrician and plebian classes to guarantee political and economic stability and to avoid oligarchy and tyranny. It was perhaps his greatest lesson, and it would serve generations of future market-builders who looked to curtail the power of landed oligarchies in order to develop free commercial societies.

CHAPTER 5

ENGLAND'S FREE TRADE BY MEANS OF THE STATE

For when Trade flourisheth, the King's revenue is augmented, Land and Rents improved, Navigation encreased, the poore employed. But if Trade decay, all these decline with it.

—EDWARD MISSELDEN, *FREE TRADE, OR, THE MEANES TO MAKE TRADE FLOURISH*, 1622

THE BEGINNING OF the sixteenth century brought rapid change in Europe. In 1517, the very year in which Machiavelli wrote his *Discourses*, the German founder of Protestantism, Martin Luther, nailed his Ninety-five Theses to the door of Wittenberg Cathedral, setting in motion a process that would splinter Christianity. The first Protestants shared Machiavelli's deep pessimism about humanity's base nature and believed that humans were fallen and acted on bestial tendencies. But they also shared Machiavelli's belief in the power of individual choice and self-interest. Through the proper exercise of personal choice, humans could shape their own destinies.[1]

During the same period, the Spanish explorer Juan Ponce de Léon discovered and explored Florida. The Americas gave Europeans the impression of a natural wealth that was more expansive than they had ever imagined. Philosophers increasingly saw science and discovery as keys to unlocking these riches. However, this new global quest brought with it the realization that the state had to take a leading role in underwriting and protecting long-range seaborne trade and empire, which were too expensive and complex for individuals and companies to pursue alone. Sixteenth- and seventeenth-century economic thinkers consistently stressed that wealth production required a mix of state investment and individual enterprise.

Europe was on the cusp of a scientific revolution that would usher in the discovery of natural laws governing everything from planetary motion to the circulation of the blood, so it is not surprising that sixteenth-century economic thought witnessed a profusion of innovative new theories about how natural market mechanisms worked. Coming to the fore were such free market concepts as the quantity of money theory, the law of diminishing returns, and notions about barriers to entry, inflation, labor productivity, and entrepreneurialism—all of which pioneering economic thinkers saw as dependent on certain forms of state involvement.

BY THE 1530s, Europe was flooded with gold from German and Bohemian mines as well as from the Portuguese and Spanish Empires. The Spanish fleet brought mounds of precious metals from the New World that landed on the shores of the Guadalquivir in Seville or in the Flemish port of Antwerp. While more gold brought riches, it also caused inflation and even monetary shortages, destabilizing economies from Bohemia to Madrid, Paris, and London.[2]

In response to this sudden instability, philosophers began to examine money and what imbued it with value. They began to appreciate that market forces played a central role. Just as early Scholastics had understood that individual behavior created the market mechanics of pricing and value, late Scholastics, especially in Spain, believed that royal fiat and states could not fully control monetary value. A school of legal thought now arose at the Universities of Salamanca, in Spain, and Évora, in Portugal, focused on understanding market mechanisms. In the 1550s, the Spanish-Basque theologian Martín de Azpilcueta developed a quantity of money theory, showing that money's value came from both how much currency was circulating (more coinage depressed currency value, and such inflation, in turn, caused currency shortages) and what people thought money could buy.[3]

The insight that market forces set currency values led to new thinking about moneylending. Christian and Scholastic thinkers had long believed money to be evil. According to one argument, money, they said, following Aristotle in *Politics*, was "sterile" and could not produce wealth without the exchange of goods. Thus, it should not "breed," so earning interest was unnatural, and even a kind of theft. In another argument, money was made of nothingness, and nothingness was evil. It had no utility in itself. Only things had value, and money merely reflected the value of those things. Because money was nothingness, earning interest—creating wealth—was a form of black magic. Usury was also associated with the Jews, who were presumed to be evil. However, if quantity and utility set the value of money, it implied that earning interest was not evil or theft, after all, but a critical part of a market mechanism. In view of this, Protestant economic thinkers soon took the giant step of ending the ancient ban on usury.

The German Protestant Calvinist reformer Martin Bucer most forcefully defended lending at interest, challenging not only the

Catholic ban on usury but also the underlying idea that money was inherently sterile.[4] Part of a growing number of theologians who saw commerce as positive, if done in a purely Christian context, Bucer helped dismantle this prejudice against money (although not against the Jews, whom Bucer wished to expel from civic and commercial life). Due to religious strife, in 1547 Bucer sought refuge in Protestant England, where King Henry VIII received him at court. In 1549, he became Regius Professor at Cambridge, where he wrote *On the Kingdom of Christ*, outlining his vision of lending as economically beneficial if it is mutually agreed upon without "abusive" interest rates. Bucer used quotes from Cicero and Saint Ambrose to justify profit for the good of the Christian community, "in order to purchase peace for the people of God." His focus on supporting civic life through commerce represented a move within Christian thought toward the secular world. "Money is also God's gift, and God demands that we use it rightly," he stated in his *Treatise on Usury*. If money helped Christians live well and supported Cicero's old chief good of civic stability, then it no longer had to be sterile.[5]

Calvinist Protestantism had great influence in France, then the most populous country in Western Europe, and potentially the richest. Yet the French Wars of Religion, which began in 1562 and spanned more than thirty-five years, threatened to destroy the country as Catholic extremists attacked Protestants and even Catholic moderates. Cities and rich industries collapsed. Seeking a theory to stop religious strife and rebuild, some French thinkers embraced Machiavelli, whose ideas they saw as essential for stabilizing the state and society as well as for creating favorable market conditions.

One such thinker was the French jurist, historian, and natural philosopher Jean Bodin. At the height of the Wars of Religion, he wrote political theories defending absolute monarchy as an institution that could not only maintain political peace, but also develop the French economy. His theories were a reaction to the Saint Bartholomew's Day Massacre (1572), in which Catholic fanatics killed hundreds of high-ranking Protestant nobles in Paris, as well as thousands of others across the country. The unprecedented violence traumatized France and left it unstable, as mobs destroyed cities and commercial wealth. Absolutism was Bodin's response to religious faction and civil strife. If the economy was to work by natural processes, Bodin believed, the state had to stabilize society and rebuild markets. Adopting Machiavelli's ideas in defense of the stability and power of the state, Bodin was more explicit yet in his belief that the state fostered wealth and allowed the market to work as a natural system. Of course, Bodin was in a very different position from Machiavelli—he could afford to be explicit, as he was an internationally respected scholar, lawyer, and counselor to kings.

Bodin's *Six Books of the Republic* (1576) explained that absolutist monarchy was the only response to the "passions" that consumed the body politic. Bodin did not agree with Machiavelli's defense of immorality, but he did believe that Machiavelli was right in focusing on political stability above all. Hatred and fanatical religious belief unbalanced the harmony of the body politic and destroyed commerce and wealth. Like many market theorists before him, Bodin also drew on Cicero, proposing that a moral, law-giving prince would practice Stoic moderation and bring nature's balance back to the economy.[6]

Bodin followed Machiavelli's precept that in order for the state to be stable, it had to be rich. He, too, believed that having a fabulously wealthy oligarchic class was a threat that destabilized market mechanisms. "Excessive wealth for a few" and "extreme poverty for the majority" inevitably caused civil strife. Only a strong state could manage the "plagues" of extreme wealth and poverty. But, like Cicero, Bodin saw attempts to create "equality" as another dangerous mirage. He believed that the economy needed to grow, and that a healthy state created ideal market conditions by inspiring confidence and trust, which meant taxing fairly and forgiving debts. Following the model of Rome, the state also had to raise funds by expanding colonial growth. For Bodin, good government meant good public financial management. He thought the state should try to understand public net worth by "counting people," so that they could be valued for labor productivity and possible urban industries. This early form of economic demography would prove essential to understanding markets.[7]

In Bodin we see the complexity of sixteenth-century economic thought: while a staunch defender of the role of the state in stabilizing the economy and guaranteeing market conditions, he also was the premier monetary theorist of his time, providing groundbreaking observational analyses of market mechanisms. Early in his career, in 1568, Bodin had faced Europe's inflation problem by writing his *Response to the Paradoxes of Monsieur de Malestroit*, a full-throated defense of the quantity of money theory, in which he stated that the amount of coinage in circulation affected currency value.[8]

Malestroit was a royal counselor and accountant who, in 1566, wrote that the value of money was intrinsic, and that devaluations, coin purity, and coin clipping (literally clipping the edges off of gold and silver coins) were at the basis of the inflation crisis. Malestroit believed that prices had not changed in three hundred years, and that inflation came from the quality of the coinage itself. Bodin knew that coins had only limited intrinsic value, and that the better part of what they were worth came instead from market forces. As a historian, he had studied archival data on coin values over time. He understood that the influx of gold and silver from German and

Spanish mines, as well as from the New World, had caused a rare metals glut. It was the quantity of coin, not the quality, that was causing inflation. Changing the official value of money and fighting coin clipping would not stop it. If the increased quantity of bullion weakened currency value, and states could not control the inflow of metals, then the state had to intervene to help the economy grow. Generating more trade was the only way to fight inflation, put money into circulation, and stabilize currency values.[9]

Bodin's *Response* represents one of the first data-driven, practical studies of monetary and market functions. Following the Scholastics, he saw quantity as a causal force in determining value and prices. For example, the more coinage there was in circulation, the less it was worth. The same was true for grain. (Bodin also provided fully historical, documented reasoning as to how one could paradoxically have more gold and more poverty at the same time.) Historical prices worked like the movement of planets, he observed; in drawing on the Polish astronomer Nicolaus Copernicus's theories of causality in planetary movement, Bodin explained how abundance could lower prices. Size and speed were natural forces of movement that regulated how planets revolved around the sun. Copernicus believed that planets and money followed the same laws, and Bodin echoed this powerful analogy.[10]

Bodin used Cicero's famous death at the hands of Marc Antony to show that human affairs, like nature, were not always harmonious. It was up to the state to ensure that these conflicts did not deteriorate into mass upheavals like the fall of the Roman Republic, or the religious wars of his own time, and the attendant risk of currency collapse. Bodin was certain that with God's providence and Stoic human prudence, moderate Catholic monarchs would win out against extremist factions and bring balance, peace, and prosperity back to France.[11]

Machiavelli, the Scholastics, and Bodin all inspired the economic and political thought of the Savoyard Jesuit priest, philosopher, and diplomat Giovanni Botero. One of Botero's most important ideas was that cities fostered industry and spurred markets. As opposed to farmland, they were centers of discovery, innovation, and manufacturing, with large accumulations of assets that created a dynamic process of constant wealth production. This meant that states had to focus on cities, managing and investing in them. Sharing Machiavelli's idea that a state had to make hard decisions for its own survival and prosperity, Botero was the first to call this idea "reason of state." Economic historians associate what would later be called *raison d'état* in French with the modern concept of mercantilism, by which a prince or leader must do everything within his or her power to strengthen the state economically, whether it meant hoarding gold or subsidizing industry and commerce. However, Botero did not think that the state alone could manage economies; rather, the state needed to work in partnership with merchants themselves to create the right conditions for maximizing production.[12]

While advancing the Ciceronian argument that all energies had to be focused on stabilizing the state for the civic good, Botero nonetheless moved away from Cicero's agrarian ideals, as well as those of contemporary aristocrats who continued to believe that trade and industry were dishonorable. Botero replaced the notion of infinite agricultural and mineral wealth with what he saw as the boundless possibilities of human industry. He described how cities across Europe had become rich by focusing on urban wealth over agriculture; they were the sites of universities, law courts, and local industry, all of which fostered skills, which in turn created more industry.[13]

Central to realizing such possibilities, Botero noted, was human cunning and the use of expedient devices in creating wealth.

Artifice could mean the Machiavellian dissimulation of emotions in politics. But it could also refer quite literally to the "skilled human hands" of the artisans themselves and the seemingly boundless array of innovative "devices" and "artifices" they worked to produce, expanding society's wealth. Botero had seen firsthand how the "industriousness" of artisans "far outstripped" the wealth that "nature," agriculture, or even mining could produce. In his eyes, nature was as limited a driver of wealth as it was inefficient. He pointed to the powerful economic hubs of Venice and the Dutch Republic as examples of urban centers that had become incomparably rich through creativity. The further away an urban economy moved from agricultural raw materials by adding value to them via manufacturing and global trade, he wrote, the more efficient and expansive was their wealth creation.[14]

The Neapolitan philosopher Antonio Serra also used market analysis to defend industry over agriculture. His 1613 *Short Treatise on the Wealth and Poverty of Nations* spelled out in detail how agricultural products brought diminishing returns, which pushed up production costs and, at best, produced a limited surplus. Agriculture simply did not create enough wealth for large-scale investment. Only manufacturing, with its "multiplication of products, and therefore of earnings," could produce lasting goods that did not quickly depreciate in value. As the volume of production increased, Serra explained, costs would fall, making it possible to increase wages and lower prices at the same time. This was the mechanism of increasing returns. Competing industrial markets, then, had great potential—at least until the increasing returns described by Serra created what later came to be called "barriers to entry": a mechanism creating oligopolies and monopolies.[15]

Like most Italian urban dwellers, Serra believed that for this manufacturing strategy to work, the state had to support industry through regulations and standards. For this reason, modern economists consider Serra a "mercantilist" rather than a free market thinker. Yet Serra certainly didn't see it this way. More aware of market mechanisms than anyone else of his time, with a keen understanding of how depreciation, marginal costs, and building capital for commercial investment worked, he simply sought to explain what he saw: that in Northern Italy, stable, commercial states, such as Venice, Genoa, and Milan, helped make manufacturing and trade far more productive than agriculture.

Italy was one of many centers of sixteenth-century commercial development. England, too, was on the rise, again through a balance of state intervention and free market policies. Unlike France, where civil war had weakened great trading cities spread thinly over the tissue of vast agricultural feudal domains, England saw more and more towns become manufacturing and trading centers. Between 1550 and 1570, for example, the number of shops in Southampton doubled. By the 1570s, the town had three hundred shops that offered more than a thousand different products, with more than a hundred types of cloth, more than a thousand different types of fishhooks, as well as a seemingly endless supply of iron and coal. As England's population increased, almost 30 percent in the last half of the sixteenth century, the density of its cities grew, with urban expansion taking hold even deep in what had only recently been countryside.[16]

England's economic development was accompanied by a national rise in legal commercial contracts and credit fundamental to market growth. When a greater demand for money led to currency shortages, the English turned to credit, and debt now rose in all parts of English society. Far from simply illustrating a fall from economic virtue, this pervasive indebtedness was a sign of market development. Soon, a vast network of loans, bonds, and contracts was at work to create liquidity, spurring further commercial growth. Between 1560 and 1640, economic activity based on credit grew, with more loans and with a new regularity of contracts signed in the presence of witnesses. Economic trust grew continually, and even modest English merchants might boast that they could access a large loan on short notice. Along with contracts, British numeracy also grew, the general knowledge of accounting spreading along with a sense of trust in the system of investment. Nicholas Grimalde's popular 1558 English translation of Cicero's *On Duties* quoted words popular at the time: "Faithfulnesse is the foundation of justice: which is in worde, and covenaunt, a trouth, and stedfastnesse."[17]

The flourishing of trade, trust, and credit accompanied a wave of important English economic writings. Attributed to the parliamentarian, Cambridge scholar, and pioneering market thinker Sir Thomas Smith, *A Discourse on the Common Weal of This Realm of England* (ca. 1549) claimed that the government needed to free the agricultural market while at the same time highly regulating industry to spur urban manufacturing. Parliamentary intervention in creating enclosures out of ancient common agricultural lands, Smith claimed, undermined crop production, which in turn undermined the wealth of cities. Subscribing to the idea of an international market system of industrial supply and demand, Smith also had a vision of how the state could help entrepreneurial artisans. While he trusted in the inherent power of a rich market to expand itself, he quoted Cicero in claiming that the state must help and even "force" urban industry to develop with "rewardes" and with the "paine" of regulation. And whereas agriculture needed freedom, Smith felt, industry needed state oversight, along with support in the development of international markets. Expanding industry created a flow of national enrichment by which "townes and Cities would be replenished with all kind of artificers; not only clothiars, which as yet weare oure natural occupation, but with cappers, glovers, paper makers, glasiers, pointers, gold-smithes, blacke smithes of all sortes, coverlet makers, nedle makers, [and] pinners." All these trades and businesses supported each other, creating a market system of economic growth.[18]

The English government now supported not only English industries, but also the expansion of English markets into the colonial world. Queen Elizabeth I helped fund Francis Drake's project to circumnavigate the globe in 1579. She also chartered Walter Raleigh to lead his 1595 expedition down the Orinoco River, in what is now Venezuela, where Christopher Columbus thought he had found a path to heaven. Some one hundred years after Columbus, Raleigh described his trip in a self-promotional book called *The Discovery of the Large, Rich, and Beautiful Empire of Guiana, with a Relation of the Great and Golden City of Manoa Which the Spaniards Call El Dorado* (1596), in which he, too, claimed he would find endless wealth, "the mother of gold."[19]

While many in England believed that states had to take part in building empires, they also sought to understand what they saw as the natural laws that made the market constantly productive. The Anglo-Flemish merchant and commissioner of trade in Flanders, Gerard de Malynes, in his *Lex Mercatoria*, or *Law of Merchants* (1622), took a remarkably sophisticated view of the role of regulations and freedoms in building commerce. He cited biblical, Spartan, Cretan, Carthaginian, and Ciceronian law, as well as the works of Jean Bodin, to insist that the state had to strategically support trade.[20]

Also like Bodin, Malynes confounded the modern free-market/mercantilist dichotomy with an economic theory relying in equal parts on state intervention and self-regulating free-market mechanisms.

Natural law dictated that if the elements of nature behaved in a certain way, or moved according to certain fixed principles, then human behavior and trade should mirror such principles. But such "mirroring" was not a spontaneous process; it required human oversight and maintenance if the system was not to steer off course. Describing trade as an alchemical process, Malynes drew from those who believed that through science they could transform basic stones and elements into gold and elixirs. It was, in part, the proto-science of alchemy that led to the belief that money could be created out of money. It also led Malynes and other thinkers to believe that gold and wealth creation were part of natural processes that could not only be understood by philosophers, but harnessed by scientists.[21]

Malynes agreed with elements of Bodin's quantity of money theory, but he went further. For him, a host of natural and human elements—such as the passage of time, depreciation, quantity, and the authority of the crown in minting and regulating quality coins—all affected currency value. Malynes's *The Maintenance of Free Trade* (1622) warned that if a country lost too much coin to another via a trade imbalance it would undermine its industry. If the English bought too much Dutch cloth, then English gold would go to Holland and there would not be enough coinage for trade. As a bullionist, Malynes believed that the quantity of coin and precious metal in a country equaled national wealth, and he defended this belief as the basis of industrial development and free trade. Malynes was talking about current affairs. England was experiencing a monetary shortage, so that merchants did not have enough coins for trade, or to pay taxes. He believed that the shortage undermined investment to expand England's cloth industry.[22]

At the same time, Malynes felt that the government had to protect wool merchants from potentially destructive foreign competition. Only by government tariffs could the "English Merchant" be assured of a fair price, and thus support "free trade" with foreign nations. What seems like a contradiction from the perspective of modern free-market thought was simply a reaction to England's coinage shortage. Early seventeenth-century English economic thinkers were not economic primitives, who did not understand laissez-faire wealth creation; rather, they were trying to channel precious metals back home to restore trade and industrial development. Malynes and other merchants saw the state as the only force capable of carrying out this feat, and, therefore, as the necessary guarantor of economic freedom and stability. Tariffs would bring back enough money to allow internal commerce to grow, so that England could freely and favorably compete in international markets.[23]

Malynes was not alone in his beliefs. Most English economic leaders subscribed to the idea that the state could be instrumental in creating the conditions of free trade. Foremost among these influential voices were the director of the East India Company, Thomas Mun, and the merchant Edward Misselden. For Mun and Misselden, there was no contradiction in the idea that protectionism by the state would spur freedom of trade. And so, while economic historians have long considered them mercantilist theorists for insisting that the crown protect English shipping and manufacturing through duties, we also need to see them as pioneering free-market thinkers.

For Mun, the surest path to free trade was to allow the market to set prices while the government protected and fostered the growth of English industry. As director of the East India Company in the 1620s, a time of economic depression, Mun adopted a mix of liberal policies and protectionism in order to help the crown reverse its trade imbalance. Under attack by the public for trading away precious silver for luxury goods, Mun defended his oversight of the company by saying that this trade enriched England. Only an "orderly flow of goods," propelled by the "movement of purchasing and paying," would strengthen the value of English currency, meaning that less currency could buy more, thus stemming the flow of money out of the kingdom. While Mun thought free trade would help regulate the currency crisis, he did not feel that this was enough. He believed that market solutions along with state intervention were needed to reinforce England's capacity to trade freely. He supported a host of tariffs on foreign goods that competed with national industries, and he maintained that English shipping should be done only on English vessels, such as those of his company. This might not look like free trade today, but to Mun and other business leaders freedom of trade entailed creating optimal conditions to face the Dutch, who operated at a considerable advantage.[24]

In his *Free Trade, or the Meanes to Make Trade Florish*, Edward Misselden expressed similar ideas. He opposed monopolies and believed that trade worked as a naturally perpetuating and growing system of buying and selling. He believed that markets set monetary value in relation to the "wares" that coin could purchase. Yet, like Mun's, Misselden's idea of free trade was nuanced by the realities of the rough international market and the fact that England was not yet the dominant economic power. England's industries were fragile, he believed, and had to be protected. And while he thought that monopolies were unhealthy, he nevertheless felt that the state should oversee trade: "Those that Trade without *Order* and *Government*," he wrote, "are like unto men, that make *Holes* in the bottome of that *Ship*, wherein themselves are *Passengers*." Without government oversight, "unskillfull and disorderly persons" would destroy trade and undermine trust and value, not least with counterfeit products and mislabeled commodities.[25]

While religious wars between Catholic and Protestant powers ravaged France and the German states, helping to divert trade to England in the 1620s and 1630s, England's own civil war (1642–1651), which pitted the Stuart king Charles I against the Puritan Parliament and the military leader Oliver Cromwell, soon threatened to undermine its industry. Its luxury trades depressed and its international shipping blockaded, the country now found itself losing hard-earned commercial advantages to the Dutch Republic. Finally, with the Puritan ascent to power in 1651, Parliament passed the Navigation Act, the culmination of a long campaign by English merchants and traders to protect their market against foreign competition and to create a legislative front against the Dutch commercial juggernaut.[26]

The act protected national industries and limited all shipping into the country to English ships. It also brought fiercer competition with Holland. No sooner had the English Civil War ended than the first Anglo-Dutch War began in 1652, and the ensuing two years of struggle did not bring a decisive English victory, either. Although the English were victorious at the Battle of Scheveningen in 1653, they failed to knock out the Dutch fleet or to blockade its coast. With Holland retaining its position as the dominant commercial country, policy makers followed Mun and Misselden's recommendation that the English government create tariff systems to help foster national industries. They also sought state aid to challenge the Dutch domination of global trade from India and Africa to North America, and the slave trade in particular.

And so it was through a mix of expanding commercial capital and government legislation, spurred by the strong influence of merchants on government, that England began its commercial ascent. This state and commercial partnership worked well, and by the mid-seventeenth century England had become an advanced commercial nation with an influential business class that worked hand in hand with the state to refine its tariff laws. The people who built England's formidable seventeenth-century economy did so with state aid. It was not paradoxical to them that free trade meant limiting foreign competition to protect their young industries in the battle for competitive advantage and infinite treasure. England had begun its slow but steady rise as the premier commercial country in the world. But first, it had to overcome the competition of Holland and France.[27]

CHAPTER 6

FREEDOM AND WEALTH IN THE DUTCH REPUBLIC

God created man αὐτεξούσιον, "free and *sui iuris*," so that the actions of each individual and the use of his possessions were made subject not to another's will but to his own....Hence the saying: "every man is the governor and arbiter of affairs relative to his own property."

—HUGO GROTIUS, *DE IURE PRAEDAE COMMENTARIUS*, 1603

IN 1576, AS the Dutch revolted against their hereditary Spanish ruler, King Philip II of Spain, his troops sacked the great trading city of Antwerp. Almost half of its population fled north to Amsterdam, which now took its place as the center of global trade. In 1581 seven of the northern Dutch provinces broke from the Spanish Netherlands to form the Dutch Republic. A decentralized state of city provinces dominated by Calvinism, the Dutch Republic was characterized by relative religious tolerance and governmental rule by its merchant class. As leaders of the new republic, these merchants naturally promoted their vision of a country based on innovative ideas of free markets and an aggressively pro-business state.

Even as England methodically built its commercial strength, Holland continued to dominate the European economy. The so-called Dutch Golden Age fostered complex ideas about economics, and free markets in particular. However precocious this free market thought may appear in hindsight, it, too, like English and French economic thought, operated on the assumption of a heavy dose of government involvement in the economy. The realities of politics and imperial economics did not always fit neatly into the ideals of freedom espoused by Dutch republican thinkers. As during many other periods of history, free market ideals coexisted with the more complex reality of state intervention.

ONE OF HOLLAND's leading humanists, Simon Stevin, moved from Bruges to Leiden when the Dutch Republic came into being. Hailing from a family of modest merchants, he nonetheless befriended Maurice of Orange, Count of Nassau, later Prince of Orange, while at university in Leiden. When Maurice, the son of William I the Silent, became the stadtholder, or steward, of the Dutch Republic in 1585, he chose Stevin to become his principal adviser and tutor. Maurice remained stadtholder until his death in 1625. During his years in office, he named Stevin to direct the all-important waterworks—the canals, levees, dikes, and sluices that keep out the sea—made him quartermaster of the army, and helped him found Leiden's engineering school. A polymath, Stevin wrote an influential accounting manual, *Accounting for Princes* (1604), arguing that governments had to be run by those fluent in the art of commerce.[1]

Stevin explained how essential double-entry bookkeeping was for commercial firms and stressed the necessity of state and municipal administrations building trust in the Dutch internal market. A healthy commercial republic was one in which all members were financially literate, he said. Once everyone could read a balance sheet, they could do business, make confident financial audits, and regulate themselves and others. Merchants, he assured the prince, would make better treasurers than the bureaucrats and taxmen in the prince's employ, just as a prince versed in accounting could read treasury books himself rather than having simply to take the treasurer's word.[2]

Stevin and other Dutch leaders believed that tolerance played a key role in inspiring market confidence and in attracting foreigners to the Dutch Republic. Calvinist textile manufacturers fled the Spanish invasion of the Netherlands during the Eighty Years' War, or Dutch War of Independence (1568–1648), seeking refuge in the cities of the northern republic. By 1609, Amsterdam had an equal number of Calvinists and Catholics, along with many Jews and Lutherans. All of them had the right to invest and create companies. Tolerance and confidence, along with financial literacy, transparency, and efficiency, would spur an already rich and growing market culture.[3]

Not surprisingly, the Dutch market expanded. The country harnessed huge amounts of combustible peat along with an endless supply of water and wind as natural energy sources for manufacturing. In 1592, the Dutch started building a massive network of windmills for industrial purposes, such as cutting timber. Windmills were the product of Dutch traditions of communal investment dating from privately funded medieval public works. Up to seventy investors, for example, could hold stock in a single windmill. This meant citizen investors worked together to create public infrastructure. This long tradition of private-public partnership laid many of the commercial foundations of the republic.[4]

By the middle of the seventeenth century, the Dutch economy had become the most sophisticated in the world. Understanding that economic growth was based not on agriculture, but rather on industry, Dutch farmers focused on growing crops for manufacturing and began to import wheat for food. They saw that farming purely for agriculture was not as productive as farming with more complex industrial ends. They grew madder, a perennial whose roots produced a red pigment long used for leather and textiles. They also developed an advanced tobacco industry, growing the crop in the countryside and then processing and packaging it in Amsterdam.[5]

Via powerful municipal administrations, the state took a leading role in developing the economy, ever aggressively writing self-beneficial trade treaties. Constantly outsmarted by Dutch diplomats, the infuriated French and English would respond with tariffs. But with its own incomparable market, not to mention control of access to the North and Baltic Seas and Hanseatic League cities, and widespread demand for its manufacturing, the Dutch Republic remained economically dominant for the entire seventeenth century.[6]

Like Florence before it, Holland relied on its guilds to develop industry and quality controls. Artists, bakers, bankers, tailors, and tanners all had their guilds. Cities such as Deventer provided privileges and monopolies to lure foreign textile manufacturers to develop their crafts locally. They even offered cash subsidies and used tariffs to protect infant industries. This produced local specialization. The city of Gouda, for example, had twenty thousand inhabitants, of which four thousand worked making long clay pipes for tobacco—as, indeed, one manufacturer in the city continues to do today.[7]

With a fleet that was now bigger than Venice's had ever been, and bigger than those of France and England combined, the Dutch were the most skilled, literate, and efficient merchant sailors in Europe. Their two-hundred-ton flute ships needed a crew of just nine or ten sailors, whereas a similar English ship required thirty. With the end of the Spanish trade embargo in the 1590s, the Dutch were sailing down the coasts of Africa. By 1634, they had expanded to the West Indies, capturing Aruba, Bonaire, and Curaçao, which they used as beachheads for the slave trade.[8]

Setting up trading posts in the Spanish and Portuguese Empires to siphon off trade, Dutch merchants succeeded in making more money than anyone else in Europe. In 1599, Jacob Cornelius van Neck's spice expedition to the East Indies made a profit of 399 percent. New companies proliferated across the Dutch provinces, eliciting concern that too much competition among the Dutch themselves might actually undermine trade. The land's advocate, or prime minister, Johan van Oldenbarnevelt, one of the country's most important leaders, insisted that all the companies of the seven provinces of Holland unite as a single federated corporation for foreign trade. Thus, in 1602 he helped found the United Dutch East India Company (in Dutch, the Vereenigde Oost Indische Compagnie, or VOC). The charter of the company illustrated the mixture of private capital and state interests that Oldenbarnevelt felt would best serve the republic. The company was charged not simply with developing a trade monopoly, but with upholding national interests. Much like the English East India Company, it was a private business built by the state and then given monopolistic prerogatives, such as the right to build its own navy and army. Internal company documents show that the legislature oversaw and regulated the VOC and other companies and played a major role in forming commercial slave-trading policy in the 1620s. The Dutch state took part in decision-making and shared its archives and intelligence with the company to help form strategy. Thus, in Holland,

as in England and France, the enterprise of empire and the formation of the first large-scale global companies emerged from state
and private-sector collaboration.[9]

Soon after founding the VOC, in 1602, the state, along with
company shareholders, undertook a massive project in market-
building. With help from the company, Oldenbarnevelt and the
Dutch authorities founded the first true stock exchange in Amsterdam to facilitate the trading of VOC shares. The VOC was the first
publicly traded company, and its shares were sold across Europe.
This pioneering and sophisticated market did not simply spring up
on its own. In 1609, Amsterdam's leaders founded the Exchange
Bank, or Bank of Amsterdam, in the city hall, and oversaw its op-
erations in order to create confidence, guaranteeing the value of
precious metal currency and deposits for the purpose of making
payments to the VOC.[10]

The VOC's charter stipulated that any Dutch citizen could buy
shares in the company and that "there shall be a distribution of dividends as soon as 5% of the proceeds from the return of the cargo
have been cashed." The company was directed by seventeen principal stockholders, the *Heren Seventien*, and the next sixty or so largest unlimited-liability investors, the *Bewindhebbers*. Dutch citizens
could freely invest in and divest of the company simply by buying
and selling shares, rather than by removing their capital investment
from a partnership in the company. The Dutch stock market was a
victory of commercial creativity as well as a victory for trust in the
market. For the first time in history, investors had confidence in
publicly sold paper shares to represent parts of ownership.[11]

The public invested in the new company at an unprecedented
level. The VOC's capitalization of 6,424,588 guilders was ten times
that of the English East India Company. This meant that the vast
imperial ambitions of the charter could be realized. Investors' funds

were effectively used to build ships (the English leased theirs) and to send military forces to fight against Spanish and Portuguese interests in Mozambique, Goa, the Moluccas, and Ambon.[12]

The VOC represented a potent mixture of entrepreneurialism, careful state stewardship, and use of market principles balanced with government regulations. Dutch leaders achieved this through trust-building exercises. In the Dutch spirit of open government, the VOC's charter claimed that accounts and audits would be made public every six years in a full public hearing, or audit. As a private company, it answered to its shareholders, who could appeal to the state. In 1620 the company paid no dividends and faced accusations of insider trading. Profits made by sweetheart deals within the company, and a failure to include share capital on balance sheets, made assets appear larger than they were. VOC rates of return dropped from their average of 18 percent to 6.4 percent. Public opinion began to turn against the VOC, whose stocks were now being sold not on financial data, but on rumors in the marketplace. Secrecy and accounting fraud, it seemed, were undermining the first public stock-offered capitalist venture.[13]

In 1622, a shareholder revolt finally convinced Prince Maurice to audit the company. It was becoming clear that "natural" market mechanisms only functioned reliably if investors had trust in the stability and probity of state regulation. And so the head of state did a private audit, put an end to corruption by the managers, and began to rebuild public trust in the company. The VOC would go on to make vast profits and high returns for another century.[14]

AFTER SUCCESSFULLY DECLARING independence from Hapsburg Spain in 1581, the Dutch Republic sought entry into Spanish and Portuguese markets and trading posts that had been closed to them. The VOC's plan was to dominate Asian trade. Piracy played a large role in how the Dutch harassed and stole the treasure and business of the Iberians. In February 1603, the Dutch captain Jacob van Heemskerck attacked and captured the Portuguese ship *Santa Catarina* east of the coast of Singapore. The Admiralty had given van Heemskerck direct orders not to take part in warlike actions. However, the value of the treasure from the ship was a good deal more compelling than Dutch law. Carrying 1,200 bales of rare Chinese silk and hundreds of ounces of musk, on its return to Amsterdam the *Santa Catarina* had a bounty worth well over 3 million guilders—300,000 pounds sterling. Van Heemskerck had, of course, no legal authority to take the ship. And while the Dutch Admiralty Court would ultimately decide that the capture was a legitimate prize, such outright theft was considered immoral by some shareholders, posing a challenge for the VOC, which was moving aggressively into new imperial markets.[15]

The Dutch Republic's desire to enter into Iberian imperial trade would produce some of the most influential free-market philosophy of the period. As the scandal of the *Santa Catarina* raged, the VOC called on van Heemskerck's young cousin, the famous humanist legal prodigy Hugo Grotius, just over twenty years old, to write a treatise to defend its interests. They wanted him to argue that the company had a moral right to use piracy to battle its way into the markets of the Spanish and Portuguese Empires. The son of a noted scholar and politician, Grotius had matriculated at the renowned University of Leiden at age eleven. There he steeped himself in the classics, with a particular fondness for the works of Cicero. Grotius's life would prove as colorful as that of the great Roman jurist himself. Grotius would escape from prison in Loevenstein Castle and go to Paris in what was supposed to be a box of books (the box is still on display in Loevenstein) and survive a shipwreck before going on to become a statesman. He would use his humanist erudition to become the most important legal theorist of his time as well as a Calvinist theologian.

Grotius's *Commentary on the Law of Prize and Booty* (1604), a powerful and influential text on free market thought, inaugurated Grotius's career as the founding legal author of modern natural rights theory. The *Commentary* used the logic of universal natural law to defend the Dutch attacks and even incursions into Portuguese imperial territory. The manuscript was long and technical and probably not the piece of propaganda the company had expected. However, it set the framework for Grotius's future writing. Grotius borrowed from Cicero the idea that moral, natural laws are universal, and that any individual, using reason, can figure out what these laws are. By trying to control the seas of the world, the "perfidious and cruel" Portuguese had caused moral harm. Further, by refusing to allow the Dutch to trade with the indigenous peoples of their empire, the Portuguese had taken away Dutch natural rights, and this, according to Grotius, was a crime. Therefore, the Dutch capture of the Portuguese ship was justified spoils, taken in "good faith." Since sovereignty was a natural right and not exclusively Christian, the indigenous peoples of the Spanish Empire had the right and freedom to choose the Dutch as their trade allies. Given the size of Dutch cannon and fortresses, this indigenous free choice against Iberia could be made quite compelling.[16]

Grotius took chapter 12 of the book, *The Free Sea*, and published it anonymously in 1609, not only for the VOC, but also as his public debut as a legal scholar. It was a remarkable coup of both philosophy and propaganda. Grotius made arguments about the fundaments of nature, the sea, and individual freedoms that would lay the foundations of the thought of Samuel von Pufendorf and John Locke later in the seventeenth century and other European natural and human rights thinkers who followed.

Grotius's argument was that liberty came from nature, and God created nature for all beings. While Cicero believed that humans created the very concept of property with communal agreements, Grotius objected that there existed some things too large for human or even national ownership. Quoting Cicero's *On Duties*, he observed that earthly things "were brought forth by nature for common use." The sea, for example, covering the whole world, is "infinite" and cannot be possessed; nor can its infinite fish be claimed by any one country. There were no "foreigners" to fishing, in other words, and the English and the Portuguese bans on Dutch fishermen off their waters were thus a violation of their natural rights of free trade on the seas.[17]

Again quoting Cicero, Grotius asserted that any nation interfering with this freedom would be inviting a just war. This argument would be central to Grotius's towering work of international law, *The Rights of War and Peace* (1625). In laying out the laws by which nations should interact, Grotius insisted that individuals had the natural right to choose their own actions. The "law of nations," as separate from natural law, made it clear that individuals had the positive freedom to do what they chose, so long as it did not harm another. This is still the basic argument for private property possession. Expansive parts of nature that "cannot be exhausted" cannot be possessed by any one country; only finite things, located firmly within borders, such as "Lakes, Ponds, and Rivers," can be owned by individuals or nations.[18]

Key to Grotius's arguments in *The Rights of War and Peace*, as well as his arguments in support of the VOC, was his defense of slavery. Like the French jurist Jean Bodin, Grotius believed that the enslavement of those captured in a just war was legal. He claimed that slavery was far better than death, as "Life is far preferable to Liberty." God gave those captured in war a "free" choice:

they could elect death or else accept their new status as "captives." In a grim moral and economic calculation of market mechanisms, it was the prisoner's choice, or natural right, to choose death or captivity. Clearly, captives meant indigenous peoples.[19]

Grotius was obviously aware that the VOC made its money in the slave trade, just as he knew that those captives were not really war prisoners. And it is impossible to imagine him defending slavery as a response to capture in a European war, though this idea was enshrined in Roman law and had been in practice in Europe until around the year 1000, when agrarian feudalism replaced agrarian slavery. Feudalism, though far less cruel than chattel slavery, nevertheless retained many of the latter's coercive elements. Predicated on the idea of a freely entered contract by which laborers chose servility in exchange for protection by their lords, feudalism was related to the logic that Grotius used in his Roman formulation of overseas and wartime slavery. Thus, slavery was enshrined in Grotius's vision of natural law and rights. It was a perverse reading of freedom of choice within the logic of war and peace, but it served the lucrative interests of the VOC, which depended on slave labor.[20]

Defense of the slave trade aside, Grotius's work was threatening not only to the Spanish crown, but also to the Netherlands' more friendly trading neighbors. The Scotsman William Welwod saw it as an attempt to pilfer Scottish fishing stocks held around all the islands and "narrow seas" of Scotland. However, many English thinkers saw the usefulness of Grotius's argument in opening the imperial world to the English themselves, who had begun their own East India Company in 1599. In 1609, the colonial promoter Richard Hakluyt translated and published an English version of Grotius's text with the possible intention of using the same arguments for British colonial expansion, and a number of related works soon appeared on the same topic.[21]

While theories of free seas, free trade, and the economic and po-litical rights of the individual were clearly stated in Grotius's text, the reality was much murkier. The Dutch East India Company re-lied on the state and its own brutal military power in pursuit of its free trade while also ignoring Grotius's concepts of human rights and freedoms when it came to slavery. In the end, the sea was free for exploitation by whichever powers were strongest. England and France would eventually supplant Holland as the premier powers in the Indian Ocean, working together as a cartel to maintain their colonial might.

The realities of overseas economic power did not much concern Dutch economic thinkers, however. The most important work of Dutch economic theory of the mid-seventeenth century—at the apex of Dutch commercial supremacy—was by the Protestant cloth manufacturer, economist, and free market and republican theorist Pieter de la Court, who wrote *The True Interest and Political Max-ims of the Republic of Holland* (1662). In what was one of the most sophisticated pieces of free market theory of the time, de la Court claimed that political liberty and free trade trumped monarchi-cal might. Written with the support of the grand pensionary, the de facto prime minister Johan De Witt, it was a virulent attack against monarchy and a detailed outline of how political and reli-gious freedom, free trade and competition, and manufacturing and shipping were all part of a self-regulating economic system. De la Court made direct references to the Anglo-Dutch merchant writer Gerard de Malynes and his *Lex Mercatoria*, or *Law of Merchants* (1622), in asserting the ascendance of merchants over princes.[22] De la Court argued quite simply that monarchies were bad for economic growth, and that the inhabitants of Holland could "re-ceive no greater mischief in their polity, than to be governed by a monarch or supreme lord." "Earls" destabilized politics through their attempts to gain power, and "Sycophantical Courtiers" undermined what made countries rich: "Navigation, Manufacture, and Commerce."[23]

"Fish and Traffick," de la Court argued, were not enough to maintain the country's economy. Wealth came not from agriculture and natural bounty but from "manufactures." Only industry, by taking commodities, turning them into goods, and selling them on the international market, created true wealth. Nature, then, was to be harnessed to commercial ends. Key to Holland's successful manufacturing and shipping was its "frugality and good Husbandry" in the efficient use of water power. It was not enough to collect the goods of nature; they had to be processed through manufacturing and a complex market system of distribution.[24]

De la Court claimed that the Dutch economic system worked only because of the "state of Freedom" of its inhabitants. Personal, religious, and economic liberty were "the true Interests" that created the wealth of manufacturing. The Dutch Republic had prospered, he believed, because religious institutions did not control significant wealth. Dutch citizens should be free not only from guilds but even from the monopoly of the Dutch East India Company itself, argued de la Court. He also saw the republic as successful because it welcomed and integrated foreigners with tolerance, granting them the freedom to create and join manufactures. It was through freedom of trade, as well as personal and religious freedom, that Amsterdam had become the center of the world commodities market.[25]

With the riches of empire stocked in Dutch "warehouses," its skilled merchants could manufacture raw materials and get them quickly on ships, which they could then circulate at unmatched speeds. The Dutch Republic managed this even with high taxes. During the wars with Spain, it handily dominated its English rival. Its civic freedoms attracted talent from across Europe. De la Court was aware that almost all countries were pitted against Holland and furious at its trade policy; still, he claimed that Holland's "interests" were for the "common good" and "mutually beneficial" to all of Holland's allies. De la Court's arrogant tone did not convince Holland's trading partners that its commercial policies were fair. Sparked by political, colonial, and trade interests, the Anglo-Dutch Wars broke out from 1665 to 1667 and from 1672 to 1674. France invaded Holland from 1672 to 1678.[26]

The Dutch Republic experienced unparalleled economic success until its infamous *Rampjaar*, or Disaster Year, in 1672, when De Witt tried to suppress the most powerful Dutch nobleman, Prince William III of Orange, in his attempt to control the republic. That year, even as France's bellicose King Louis XIV invaded the republic, William tried to assert his own authority over Holland. William claimed the title of captain-general of the armies for life, encouraging rumors that France intended to make him king. With the republic on its knees, William became stadtholder on July 9, and now openly threatened De Witt's and de la Court's influence. On July 23, Orangists in Dordrecht captured and tortured De Witt's brother, Cornelis, accusing him of plotting against William. William ordered Johan De Witt to pay a heavy fine to free his brother. When Johan arrived in Dordrecht, he thought he could calm the angry Orangist crowds, only to be attacked and stabbed. The crowd murdered both brothers, beheaded them, strung up their bodies, and ate their body parts—violence that William did not disavow.[27]

With the rise to power of the Prince of Orange, so began the decline of the Dutch Republic and its freedoms. William took out massive loans and built up the army to cement his power. But he had bigger plans. He began secret negotiations to become the Protestant king of England, eventually overthrowing the Catholic

James II. On February 23, 1688, William and his wife, James's sister Mary, became the constitutional monarchs of a new Britain. But if England's Glorious Revolution marked the beginning of an age of constitutional liberty and economic expansion, it sounded the death knell for Dutch republicanism and, along with it, Dutch dominance of global trade.[28]

France and England now took the Dutch Republic's place as the commercial leaders of Europe, inaugurating a fierce competition that would last until the nineteenth century. Sliding into monarchy, Holland was unable to truly compete with French and English commerce, science, imperial might, and industry. In the end, Dutch freedom had not fulfilled de la Court's confident predictions; nor had it produced a decisive laissez-faire movement. The most powerful and lasting articulations of free market thought would emerge, instead, from the enduring conflict between the great powers of France and England.

CHAPTER 7

JEAN-BAPTISTE COLBERT AND THE STATE-MADE MARKET

To re-establish commerce, there are two things necessary: certainty and liberty.

—JEAN-BAPTISTE COLBERT, "MÉMOIRE CONCERNING COMMERCE WITH ENGLAND," 1651

EVEN AS HOLLAND and England vied for commercial dominance in the mid-seventeenth century, the sleeping giant of France began to wake. It was a behemoth, with a population in 1660 of around 23 million, dwarfing England's 5 million and Holland's 1.8 million. In spite of its size, civil war had left France weak. On top of the Wars of Religion, there was the Fronde (1648–1653), another series of wars, during which powerful nobles rose up against royal central authority. The crown won the battle in the end, but when King Louis XIV took power in 1661, the monarchy was all but bankrupt and France's commerce stagnant. France, a European leader in wool production at the beginning of the seventeenth century, saw its output drop precipitously by the 1640s. Its merchant marine and navy, its colonies, and its trade networks and manufacturing base lagged far behind Holland's and England's. France's great commercial cities of Lyon, Bordeaux, Marseille, and Rouen, after so much religious and civil unrest, had been emptied of quality artisans, leaving France as a whole at a distinct competitive disadvantage.[1]

A young, ambitious, and relatively poor king, Louis XIV needed new sources of income. With the rich landowning nobles and the high clergy exempt from taxes, the state depended on funds brought in by taxing rural peasants and such French commerce as was able to lumber on in these slow decades. It was not enough to bankroll the Sun King. As the Neapolitan economist Antonio Serra had warned, harvests were not dependable, yielding, at best, limited surpluses and uneven tax revenues. A modern kingdom needed industry, innovation, and economic expansion.

In 1661, Louis XIV chose as his de facto prime minister Jean-Baptiste Colbert, whose discreet and surgical administrative skill, ruthlessness and loyalty, and intimate knowledge of industry and trade Louis appreciated. Colbert came from a world connected to the old Florentine mercantile tradition. His home city, Reims, was the capital of the Champagne region, and part of the Lyon-Florence cloth trade axis that grew from the great Burgundian wealth of the Middle Ages and the fairs of Flanders. Much like those of earlier Florentine merchants, Colbert's family's fortunes rose through the wool trade, finance, and service to the state. A trained accountant, Colbert worried that France had neither the commercial skill nor the discipline to compete with the Dutch and English. He was also frustrated that the crown relied on agriculture rather than on industry for its income. Great powers such as "ancient Rome, the kingdoms of Asia, France and Spain," Colbert wrote, did not "apply themselves to commerce," and thus undermined their own capacity for glory. He blamed France's economic focus on agriculture for "undermining industry," believing that France needed what one would call today a new "brand" as a nation of industry, innovation, and luxury. Thus, Colbert sought to mix the technical expertise and cultural influence of Italy with the imperial might of Spain and the commercial prowess of Holland and England in order to create a France that could take its rightful place on the global stage.[2]

From the beginning of his career, Colbert saw his work to industrialize France through what is today called development economics. The state would have to help commerce and industry to become more competitive. Certainly, Colbert did not expect France to surpass Holland's commercial prowess in his lifetime. He knew that the Dutch and English states had enormous advantages, having worked for decades to build companies and manufacturing, not to mention, in the case of England, drafting the protectionist Navigation Laws that had allowed its commerce to grow. Now it was the turn of the French state, and it had to act faster and on a larger scale. And this it could do: Colbert recognized state power and centralization as a tool for development that France had and England lacked. While the Stuart kings had pushed for absolute rule, they clashed with Parliament and ultimately failed in their quest, resulting in the overthrow of James II by William III. In England, kings and their ministers could not legislate large-scale economic policy by fiat. In France, however, they could. Adopting a proto-authoritarian approach to pull France into the early-industrial age, Colbert would develop a model of market-building that still has resonance today in the dynamic authoritarian economies of Asia.

ONE OF COLBERT'S central ideas was that before France could participate in an international free market, it first needed stable market conditions within its own borders. Since these did not yet exist, the state would have to build them. In 1651, Colbert had complained that civil unrest had caused France to "lose the skills and the advantages of commerce." Merchants had lost the "liberty" and "confidence" to "transport their goods." France was large, agrarian, and feudal, with medieval internal tariffs; local systems of privileges, courts, and tolls; and closed provincial markets—all of which, Colbert complained, undermined trade. In his eyes, business could not function without confidence and the means to freely circulate. Colbert looked to free France's internal market while building up infrastructure and, with it, commercial confidence.[3]

Also a challenge to growth was the overly litigious legal system and the shady municipal debt market of bond trading, which he felt "inhibited" commerce and undermined trust. Added to that was the mischief wrought by French merchants and guilds, which, Colbert believed, set low standards while tolerating piracy. Colbert sought to bypass local constraints and create national industrial standards as well as uniformity in sizes, names, and the quality of products, in particular cloth. These new regulations would be enforced with a repressive system of state inspections. By the 1670s, he was insisting that all mayors and guild masters "constantly keep in hand the rules and instructions that I have sent for the factories and dying-houses, so that they are systematically executed." Colbert was convinced that uniform standards created confidence and, supported by better infrastructure, freed trade between cities and regions.[4]

Colbert also created a massive, and still disputed, plan to develop France's weak industrial base. His approach to fostering business looked a lot like that of Italian merchants, and even like Dutch cities, which had a long history of enticing foreign workers with grants. Colbert established new state-subsidized industries, such as the Gobelins tapestry works and the Saint-Gobain glassworks. He attracted Dutch manufacturers to Rouen to build the cloth trade, and Dutch engineers to help build canals. Much as in modern tax-free development zones, Colbert offered these newcomers state pay, funding, and even monopolies to help them start their industries and develop new technology.[5]

Colbert took a great interest in successfully building the wool and silk industries in particular, looking to bring in new weaving techniques and revive the textile industry in cities such as Amiens. He built ports, and with them, the shipping industry that was to serve France's colonial enterprises. He expanded existing companies in India, North America, Africa, and the French West Indies. France would now compete with Spain, Portugal, Holland, and England in the race for a world commercial empire of expanded territories and lucrative slave and sugar plantations.

Innovation was not Colbert's only focus. In the name of strengthening the state, he used spies, brutal internal police, and rough prison sentences for counterfeiters and anyone who published pamphlets against the king. In modern eyes, this makes Colbert a confusing figure: at once a visionary market-builder and a pioneer of early authoritarian government. For him, though, the two were not mutually exclusive.

Colbert's success has long been debated. However, statistics show that his reforms expanded manufacturing and set the basis for long-term growth. As he upgraded textile weaving methods, for example, the number of textile apprentices doubled in cloth-producing cities such as Rouen and Amiens. As he subsidized Amiens's *sayetterie* fabrics (combinations of wool or goat's hair and silk), more expert artisans appeared on the rolls of the city, expanding quality and capacity. In the 1680s, more than eight hundred new textile-related professions appeared in manufacturing centers such as Lille. Even if the progress of this development was moderate, it was nonetheless real. It was during this period that the French developed successful woolen, silk, and cotton twill industries. Colbert's industrial exports competed with those in Flanders, Holland, and England, and the techniques he introduced would play a crucial role in French economic expansion in the eighteenth century. Rouennais cotton production grew at an annual rate of 3.2 percent, reaching eight hundred thousand pieces by the 1780s.[6]

Colbert's economic projects were not all explosively successful, and English growth was far superior. Still, if England led in coal, metal, cotton, and ship production, France led in the powerful industries Colbert developed, from the all-important wool industry to canvas, lace, and Lyonnais silks. In the eighteenth century, fear of these French industries would lead Britain to reject calls for laissez-faire and enact protectionist policies. While it is estimated that the English were 20 percent more productive per person, France's volume of trade remained more or less equal to England's throughout the eighteenth century. This was no small feat for a country that, by 1650, had lost its commercial competitiveness.[7]

Then as now, the world of international commerce was rough and dangerous, often entailing outright war. Colbert certainly believed that France needed a powerful navy to compete with the warring maritime powers of Holland, England, Spain, and Portugal. In spite of Colbert's reputation as a militarist, however, all evidence in his correspondence and in internal government documents points to his believing that war was bad for economic growth. Opposing Louis XIV's wars with Holland until they became inevitable, he far preferred deterrence and trade treaties, firmly believing that they would succeed in puncturing Dutch and English dominance. Colbert wrote that France needed to find "security and liberty" by fighting the Dutch and English through diplomacy. This would bring "liberty of commerce" back to France.[8]

The Dutch were Colbert's biggest concern, because in spite of all of Pieter de la Court's high-minded language about free markets, the reality was that they had an aggressive, nationalist trade policy and a dominant navy. The "bad state of French commerce," Colbert constantly railed, as well as France's negative trade balance of 4 million pounds, was the direct result of Dutch treaties that freed their trade at the expense of their competitors. Dutch incursions into France, and in particular their hijacking of various French exports—they controlled the trade of French wine and spirits in the rich market of the Baltics, for instance—infringed upon France's natural rights, Colbert felt. Additionally, the Dutch barred entry to French merchants and artisans who might truly compete in their national market. France was not yet in a position to compete; Colbert knew it was still too weak. And if he closed the borders to Dutch trade, it would only undermine French development. What he sought, therefore, were not trade barriers, but well-designed trade treaties that brought at least reciprocity between countries. For this, Colbert believed the government needed to recruit experienced merchants in administration as well as in writing commercial treaties and laws.[9]

Colbert based part of his strategy for building French industry on his understanding of the English Navigation Act of 1651, which he (and later Adam Smith) believed to be the key to England's developmental advantage. Colbert also claimed that the Dutch had created tariffs to suffocate French trade and manufactures. In 1670, after long negotiations with the Dutch, he still complained that they were excluding all French goods from their markets while targeting the city of Lille to suffocate its industry. The Dutch were also bent on controlling trade in the French West Indies, forcing the French islands to buy Dutch goods.[10]

Colbert believed that French protectionist tariffs were justified, as the Dutch excluded French traders in some French border cities and even in the French colonies. Therefore, what he sought was to bolster free trade for the French within France's territories. He suggested that the population of the Antilles arm themselves to defend against Dutch interference, so they could do business in "complete liberty." In a letter to Jean-Charles de Baas, the brutal governor of the slave colonies of the French Antilles, Colbert said that "liberty of commerce" was not just for the monopoly of the French West Indies Company. This liberty had to extend to all French traders for what Colbert called the "general good." His was still a medieval concept of economic freedoms as a state-granted privilege. Liberty did not extend to serfs, indentured servants, criminals, or slaves. It was restricted to nobles and to those French traders and free settlers who carried the king's passport. Rather than a universal natural right, the privilege of economic liberty was the state's to give. Still, no matter how limited, it constituted a vision of free trade.[11]

COLBERT'S EFFORTS ON numerous fronts succeeded in turning France into a great, lumbering commercial powerhouse across the globe. To be sure, France was not as successful as England, but by the early 1700s it had surpassed Holland as England's main trading partner and competitor. And if Colbert's attempts to dominate Asian trade largely failed, the old French Caribbean slave and sugar colonies continued to expand production, competing favorably with England and Holland. France also succeeded in dominating Levantine trade in the Mediterranean. One can judge Colbert's economic success by the fact that the English emulated and admired many of his practices. This was precisely what he wanted. The very desire by others to copy France, he believed, was key to making its markets work. Colbert was convinced that if other countries had confidence in and admired France and its products, they would buy French goods and in turn spur the economy within. Thus Colbert in no small part helped create something that has withstood the test of time: a brand of luxury and expertise that remains potent today.[12]

Market-building was not just about economic development and reform, however. It was also about trust and confidence. Free markets are based in great part on perception and choice. People buy things as a result of an odd and often self-contradictory set of sentiments and situations: need, availability, pricing, desire, obsession, faith, and confidence. Some commercial sentiments are rational and objective, and some are not. Colbert came up with a plan to create trust and confidence in France, both merited and imagined, convinced that his mix of branding and policing would give France a powerful commercial image.

To this end, he issued sets of commercial laws and standards with stiff penalties for anyone who broke them. Colbert's brilliant and ruthless chief of police, Gabriel-Nicolas de La Reynie, oversaw Parisian markets and streets—butcher shops, tailors, prostitutes, street lighting, and the printing trade—and regulated the trade guilds to make sure members followed rules. He cracked down on the illegal circulation of foreign printed cloth, which flooded the country as contraband and undermined French industry. The Italians, Dutch, and English had long taken advantage of lax commercial oversight in France. In response, Colbert instituted a system of stamps to signify quality inspections of French cloth, which gave confidence to foreign markets. When the English found ways to counterfeit the French royal stamps, La Reynie seized thousands of reams of foreign cloth. He helped ensure that the French woolen industry would pose a serious commercial threat to that of England.[13]

For Colbert, creating confidence in France's reputation was as important as regulation and protectionism in building commerce and foreign colonial trade. Thus propaganda (or what one would today call advertising) was key to his project of building French commercial markets. He regularly drafted respected scholars to serve as the spokesmen for his projects to boost France's reputation as a center of knowledge, culture, and technological innovation. In 1663, as he was establishing the French East India Company, Colbert asked the academician and scholar François Charpentier to compose a discourse on the history and usefulness of East Indian trade. It was a work intended not only to spur French commerce, but also to advertise it to foreign competitors. Following Colbert's line, Charpentier claimed that "dangerous laziness" had taken over France, thus undermining prosperity in the kingdom owing to the damage done by war and upheaval. Commerce was "like the liberal arts"—it could be "cultivated" by focus and concentration. And so Charpentier challenged his audience to navigate new seas and find new "wealth" from discoveries. "Inventors," he said, create riches.[14]

Colbert also hired the Jesuit scholar Pierre-Daniel Huet, bishop of Avranches and an erudite member of the Académie Française, to write commercial histories comparing Louis XIV's France to the glories of the Roman Empire. In the preface to his *History of Commerce and of the Navigation of the Ancients* (1763), Huet explained how Colbert had used the "advantages" of the state to show how important commerce could be for a country. The French would have to turn to navigation and to empire-building if they were to compete commercially. The Roman Empire succeeded because of trade and empire, he explained; now France would follow the model to become a new commercial Rome.[15]

Colbert saw the path to "reestablishing" confidence and certainty as based, as well, in the quality of state financial management and accounting. He hoped to sweep away talentless, "corrupt" state officials who could not keep good books to measure liabilities or depreciation. During his first ten years as minister, he managed to bring France's public finances into the black for at least one brief historic moment in the early 1670s. Adam Smith would later laud Colbert's management of public accounts as key to creating a market society.[16]

Colbert's 1663 "Memoirs on France's Financial Affairs to Serve History" followed Machiavelli, Bodin, and Botero in the proposition that a state can only survive if "its means are well administered." In other words, ministers had to run the state with financial competency, effectively collect taxes, and manage income, expenditures, assets, and liabilities. This good stewardship would create confidence, grease the wheels of trade, and, according to the formula he oft repeated, create "liberty of commerce." Colbert was using every economic model and tool available—from Machiavelli's vision of the state, to Holland's focus on accounting, to England's developmental protectionism—to bring confidence to markets.[17]

Reaching out to the reading public itself, Colbert sponsored a series of books he thought would instill French citizens with mercantile knowledge and confidence. He commissioned the mathematician and accounting master François Barrême, for example, to produce both double-entry accounting manuals and works on money-exchanging. Accounting schools came to use his handbook on practical mathematics, *The Arithmetic of Sir Barrême* (1672). In the preface, Barrême noted the shortage of financially literate people in France, even at the highest levels of the state: "Monsieur Colbert had always hoped to keep double-entry books for all the business of the King, but he could not find enough people familiar with the practice so that the old affairs of the Chamber of Accounts could be brought up to date." Barrême's work was so successful that it became the *Barrême Universel*, an accounting manual published well into the nineteenth century.[18]

In 1673 Colbert published his famous *Commercial Code*, written with the merchant and trade expert Jacques Savary. It is for these famous laws that Colbert's relief portrait is one of twenty-three of the great lawgivers that adorn the gallery of the US House of Representatives, along with Moses, Lycurgus, Justinian, and Thomas Jefferson. Surprising in its simplicity, the *Commercial Code* comprises 122 articles under 12 titles to offer not just a legal framework and a standardization of best practices for trade, but also a description of how double-entry accounts should be kept, paperwork completed, fairs organized, and, very importantly in Colbert's eyes, how bankruptcies and litigations should be handled. The code even contains the formulas and uses for bills of exchange and promissory notes.[19]

Savary expanded Colbert's project, publishing a far more detailed business manual and reference book, *The Perfect Merchant* (1675)—a modern version of the Renaissance merchant Benedetto Cotrugli's *Book of the Art of Trade*. Savary claimed it would bring "confidence to business" because it published commercial laws, rules, and best practices. A unique compendium of commercial information, Savary's book was also a staggeringly successful piece of French propaganda. Colbert was showing that France was a world center of business standards and expertise, something unthinkable twenty years before. Facts mattered in all manner of trades, Colbert knew, but so did illusions. Even after his death in 1683, his program of codification (and advertising the codification) continued to great effect. In 1685, the French government published the infamous slavery laws, the *Code noir*. Adam Smith would later applaud how the horrific *Code* made French slavery less brutal and more effective than British slavery—as if such a thing were possible.[20]

Colbert is known, of course, for building Versailles and founding Louis XIV's academies of learning, which exist to this day. Historians have seen culture as part of Louis XIV's quest for "glory" and a tool to fashion his image as the Sun King. Certainly Colbert's building of Versailles and the founding of the famed royal academies boosted Louis's image, but this is a somewhat superficial view. What Colbert hoped these institutions would truly promote was commercial confidence in France itself. If France had the best scientists, the most beautiful art and buildings, and the most desirable fashions, it could build an international trade for French products. Colbert understood very well the central relationship of image to market confidence.[21]

Colbert saw that he could take scientific expertise and verification and commercialize it. In his "Mémoires," he stated that the "great men" of science, arts, and letters would bring "reputation" to the kingdom and attract foreign consumers and trade. For this reason, Colbert wrote directly to famous scientists and historians throughout Europe, such as the Dutchmen Nicolas Heinsius in Stockholm and Isaac Vossius, who was then at Windsor, explaining that Louis XIV wanted to show his appreciation of their "merit," and was sending them a large cash "gratification." If they chose to dedicate important works to the Sun King, it went without saying, his appreciation would continue to their mutual benefit.[22]

In 1663, the famous academician and architect who designed the east façade of the Louvre, Claude Perrault, began working with Colbert on a plan to create the Royal Academy of Sciences. More than simply a place to celebrate Louis XIV's glory, it was also a place, Perrault wrote to Colbert, to advertise the credibility of French science, "to publish its findings, to make them known," and give France "éclat in the world." The first notes on the plan reveal that the fields of study—chemistry, anatomy, geometry, astronomy, and algebra—were practical and could be of use in French commercial and financial ventures. The goal was to make the academy a center of experiment and of public teaching that would place scientific authority in the hands of the crown, and then advertise it to the world.[23]

In 1666, with the help of the Dutch mathematician, physicist, astronomer, and inventor Christian Huygens, Colbert founded the new royal library and Academy of Sciences in the palace once belonging to Louis XIII's prime minister, Cardinal Mazarin. Huygens wrote in 1666 that the academy would measure and establish the meridian line and longitude, and that these measurements would be put to use to "Measure the size of the earth...[and] Advise on the means of making geographical charts with greater exactitude than hitherto." These new authoritative maps would not only improve navigation but also facilitate France's ability to make colonial territorial claims. The long list of Huygens's astronomical and practical scientific experiments included what would become one of Colbert's great achievements: to "establish once and for all the universal measure of sizes by means of pendulums." Huygens outlined his plan to create a practical pendulum clock that could be used as a "maritime clock" to calculate longitude on board ships sailing on colonial missions.[24]

Huygens convinced Colbert that one of the most important activities of the academy would be to publish natural histories that explained scientific experiments in a "common" and easy-to-understand language that made the works accessible to the public. In 1665, Colbert began sponsoring Denis de Sallo's project of creating a state-controlled scientific journal, the *Journal des sçavans* (Journal of the learned), which would make France the trusted source of scientific authority. It claimed to tell "what was new in the Republic of Letters," or the international world of learning. The publisher noted that it would focus on that which was "useful," and would be the place to find the "principal things that take place each year." Even later, when Louis was at the height of his wars and political and religious repression, scholars across Europe saw the journal as a major authority on science, philosophy, mathematics, mechanics, philosophy, and, importantly, "arts and crafts," or engineering. It brought France international credit even in a time of war.[25]

Colbert directed the Royal Academy of Sciences to begin work on a huge illustrated encyclopedia of mechanics and industry. In it, Colbert gave practical, commercial knowledge equal footing with formal learning, therefore giving the former prestige. Huygens and Perrault, among others, submitted plans for inventions. Colbert's encyclopedic projects, which would have monumental influence in the eighteenth century, would guide future developments in the arts, sciences, and technology and were therefore essential to France's economic expansion.[26]

These scientific publications gave France a reputation—even an exaggerated one—as an industrial and commercial leader. The strategy was successful and, in the 1670s, the English began to see France as a greater commercial power than Holland—something unimaginable in 1661. In 1668, Colbert sent his brother Charles Colbert, marquis de Croissy, as ambassador to London, where he made a great impression and managed to convince the English king, Charles II, to secretly support France's economic moves against Holland in exchange for annual personal payments of £230,000. In a few short years, Jean-Baptiste Colbert had managed to make the country a true commercial competitor, and even—in appearance at least—a leader.[27]

The famous English diarist and secretary to the admiralty Samuel Pepys was impressed by Colbert de Croissy, whom he and others knew was, on his brother's orders, spying on English industries and naval programs. This made Jean-Baptiste Colbert seem all the more formidable. Pepys was also an avid reader of Colbert's commercial propaganda. On January 30, 1669, Pepys wrote in his diary that he "fell to read a French discourse" on navigation, which, he worried, gave the impression that France's navy and capacity for trade would soon surpass that of England. This was none other than François Charpentier's book of propaganda on the founding of the East India Company, and it had clearly worked, lending Pepys the impression that France had already transformed itself into a successful trading nation and England's most important competitor. France's technical expertise was also a source of admiration. In his Naval Minutes from the 1690s, Pepys noted that France had the finest shipbuilding techniques, boats, ports, and sailors, referencing Colbert's 1671 rules on shipbuilding and 1673 rules for galleys. Pepys believed that these books showed the French navy to be far more advanced than the English navy, lamenting, "Is there any one good rule in our Navy that has not been long established in France?" Colbert's policies and propaganda had hit home.[28]

By THE TIME he died in 1683, Jean-Baptiste Colbert had succeeded in opening the English market to France. France even managed to gain a trade surplus with England. This was a crisis for English merchants, who felt France was gaining the upper hand and now needed to be stopped. The advancement of free trade treaties was slow in the seventeenth century, as each country battled for competitive advantage.[29]

Yet, already there were signs that Colbert's attempts to transform France into a commercial nation displeased the Sun King. Despising merchants as vulgar upstarts, Louis moved to undo many of Colbert's reforms. Rather than working to foster freer trade with England, now France's largest trading partner, Louis looked for war instead. Against Colbert's advice, he had invaded Holland in 1672.

Not satisfied with incursions abroad, Louis set out on a path of civic violence even at home. In 1685, two years after Colbert's death,

Louis revoked the Edict of Nantes, which had served to protect France's Protestant minority. More than two hundred thousand French Protestants were tortured, forced to convert, dragooned, imprisoned, or expulsed. Knowing Colbert had opposed religious oppression as bad for trade, a sadistic Louis made Colbert's son, the marquis de Seignelay, carry out the forced conversions. France's Protestant diaspora now spread from Holland, Denmark, and England to multiple points in Germany and the American colonies. It was a terrible blow to French commerce. Protestant "Huguenot" merchants and artisans took with them the expertise that Colbert had so expensively developed; glassmakers, silversmiths, cabinet-makers, and traders of all sorts were welcomed by monarchs across Europe for their skill. In fact, the edict is the reason that France has no great tradition of watchmaking, the French Protestant watch-makers having fled to Calvinist Geneva, which remains even today the center of the world watch trade.

Contrary to what economic historians have long believed, it was Louis who effectively crippled Colbertism and any hopes of ex-panded market freedom. A dynastic king presiding at the center of a splendid court of nobles, he did not see himself as a king of com-mon merchants. A myopic Louis stopped funding the navy as well, and focused less on the colonies. His eyes were now fixed on war. In 1688, he began the Nine Years' War, or King William's War, as it was called in the Americas, by aggressively crossing the Rhine to expand his borders and territorial claims. To counter Louis's aggressions, an alliance of England, the Dutch Republic, the Aus-trian Hapsburg Holy Roman Empire, Spain, Portugal, and Savoy coalesced. Coupled with the influence of Huguenots who spoke out against Louis, Protestant princes began to see the Sun King as a permanent threat. All hopes of free trade faded into a long period of war and famine.

In 1693, harvests in northern France were poor. Pressured by war taxes and food shortages, famine spiraled into a typhoid epidemic, with putrid and pestilent abdominal fevers caused by Salmonella-like bacteria. The great famine of 1693–1694 killed around 1.3 million people above normal mortality rates. Soldiers began to catch typhoid and had to fight while ill. Its finances in disarray, and with mass death stalking its population, France lived under constant threat of Louis's capricious wars and their catastrophic effects. When Louis found he could not successfully invade the Dutch Republic or England, he harassed their traders around the world, threatening English colonies and trade routes from the West Indies to India. By the time the Nine Years' War finally ended in 1697, all sides were traumatized. William III now put England on a constant war footing with France, and British merchants saw its neighbor as a threat both militarily and commercially.

It was the opposite of what Colbert had intended. Colbert's dream of balanced free trade, based on treaties and the mutual interest of trade among equals, had been replaced by violent warfare and mass death in France. In an attempt to make a break with the past, reformers blamed Colbert for Louis's senseless destruction. Those who began to advocate for reform and free markets in France used the long-dead minister as a symbol of what needed changing. Colbertism and Colbert's place in economic history became warped, tarnished by the debacle of Louis's later reign. Free market thought would develop in opposition not to Colbert's actual economic policies, but in opposition to the distorted shadow of the minister cast by Louis's bellicose, absolutist follies.

CHAPTER 8

THE NIGHTMARES OF THE SUN KING AND THE DREAM OF FREE MARKETS

Our virtues are usually vices in disguise.
—Duc de La Rochefoucauld, *Maxims*, 1665

By the end of the Nine Years' War (1688–1697), France was as exhausted as the rest of Europe, which had endured more than two decades of near-continuous conflict. Louis had terrorized the Spanish Netherlands and used his influence to chase down and persecute French Protestant refugees in neighboring states. His notably sadistic minister of war, the marquis de Louvois, pursued a reign of violence across the continent and across the globe. To keep up with war expenses, the state levied extraordinary taxes that brought widespread misery to the French, most of whom now lived in a perpetual state of hunger.

This seemingly endless cycle of violence and suffering, corresponding as it did with the rise of French industry, compelled many philosophers to look back in time for what they believed to be a freer, more peaceful and prosperous model. Inspired by Cicero and old aristocratic agrarian values, some French thinkers rejected the idea that wealth was created only by cities, innovation, and manufacturing. They tried to develop a free market model of economic growth based in agriculture and Stoic morals.

In what with hindsight might seem a great paradox, Colbert's heirs led this reform movement. At the turn of the seventeenth century, Colbert's children and nephews formed the most powerful group within the royal court. The object was to tailor Colbertism for a new age of reform. They believed that in ignoring good government management and the quest for a free market and peace, Louis XIV had undermined Colbert's most fundamental policies. The family response was to design and support a series of government policies and books that would later spark the eighteenth-century free-market movement.

IN THE SECOND half of the seventeenth century, a growing number of thinkers, perhaps not surprisingly, were coming to take a very despairing view of human nature and human society. Wars and repression led some philosophers to the cynical conclusion that self-interest dominates all else, and that truly virtuous, disinterested conduct is impossible in what is a constant earthly vale of tears. Ever since Cicero first proposed the idea that feelings of love, duty, and friendship among Rome's landed aristocrats acted as both catalyst and guarantor of market exchange, philosophers had been debating the relationship between sentiment and economics.

Christian thinkers had introduced aspiration for heavenly salvation into the market mix, insisting that individual free will and a desire to exchange earthly for heavenly treasure were the forces that kept the divine mechanism spinning. Now, philosophers looked for a more practical economic and political system that could harness the less noble passions of men to make them work for the general welfare. Rather than fighting for religious faith or aristocratic military glory, the energy of human desire could be invested into covenants of exchange: commercial agreements by which men realized their rational self-interest.[1]

The English political theorist Thomas Hobbes had already set forth the idea of self-interest as the basis of political and economic life in his 1651 work, *Leviathan*. Echoing Augustine and Machiavelli when he said that humans were bad at their very core, Hobbes saw man as "enemy to every man" in what was a constant state of quarreling brought on by an inherent want for "gain," "reputation," and "self-preservation." Natural law gave humans the right to preserve their lives and property at all cost. The only way out of this constant state of war over property was for people to make a common "covenant" in politics and to engage in peaceful commercial exchange. Like the absolutist Jean Bodin, Hobbes felt that individuals had to surrender their personal liberty to an absolute monarch who would carefully "procure the common interest."[2]

One of the most important seventeenth-century philosophers of self-interest was the illustrious French aristocrat François, duc de La Rochefoucauld. His work, which promoted the belief that individual opportunism drove commercial societies and markets, would become essential to free market thought. Skeptical of Cicero's claim that love and friendship drove exchange, La Rochefoucauld followed Saint Augustine and Hobbes in their belief that humans did not act out of benevolence but rather out of concern for themselves. And so he looked to understand how desire, and what he called "self-love" (in French, *amour propre*), influenced all human actions. He believed that under better conditions, people could find virtue through Stoic discipline. But under an absolutist and morally bankrupt king, such ethical freedom was impossible. La Rochefoucauld was particularly opposed to how Louis XIV's royal absolutism deprived the aristocrats of their ancient agrarian virtues, comparing the royal court at Versailles to "a stock exchange" of honors and privileges from which nobles now sought to profit. In Louis's world, he complained, all actions and friendships were "based on self-interest alone."[3]

Nonetheless, La Rochefoucauld saw hope. He believed that these selfish feelings, channeled properly, could serve the common good. "Self-interest, blamed for our misdeeds, often deserves credit for our good actions," he wrote, expressing an essential tenet of modern market thought. Self-interest "keeps trade going, and we pay up, not because it is right to settle our account but so that people will be more willing to extend us credit." Thus did greed and desire create a powerful force of exchange, pushing humans to be honest, if only to protect their own concerns.[4]

The leading critics of Louis XIV's repressive Catholicism were Jansenist Catholics. Like La Rochefoucauld, they looked for a system to harness self-interest and turn it to something good. Inspired by Cornelius Jansen, the early seventeenth-century bishop of Ypres, Flanders, French Jansenists searched not just for spiritual perfection, but also for a system by which to mitigate the effects of Original Sin and improve earthly life. Close readers of Saint Augustine, the Jansenists believed God had made a perfect world only to have man disturb it through sin. Exhausted by Louis's greed and narcissism, Jansenists believed that a self-sustaining commercial market offered the best possibility of channeling human sin and desire into virtue. The age of miracles, they were convinced, was over, and "God was in hiding." Aside from a small group of the chosen who were capable of receiving salvation through divine grace, God would not be coming to the rescue of humankind, leaving it instead naked and alone, prey to its own sinful instincts. Moved by Jansenist thought, a few French thinkers, such as the famous French playwright Jean Racine, withdrew from the world altogether to pursue Augustinian self-abnegation and piety alone in a cell. But this purism was not widely appealing. The vast majority of humans could not survive in society while fully avoiding sin and self-interest. Indeed, one could not fully function in Louis's France without taking part in his regime. Some now looked to find a way of at least managing a world in which human greed and self-interest ruled.[5]

An influential Jansenist expert on Roman law, Jean Domat, created a Christian version of the old Florentine ideal of commerce as a civic good that enriched the state. By dissecting the mechanics of how the market channeled and even nullified sin, Domat devised a Christian conceptual framework for free market thought that would have lasting influence. His internationally renowned compendium of Roman law, *The Civil Law in Its Natural Order* (1689–1694), expressed a clear vision of how markets worked freely in response to human desires and sentiments. Following Cicero, Domat thought that it was possible to discern immutable laws in nature that, once permitted to operate freely, would set in motion a dynamic market system that would rein in the mercenary tendencies of individuals.

Domat saw physical labor as a punishment "inflicted" by God on man outside the Garden of Eden's "State of Innocence." Man had to find a way to make good out of God's punishment by using labor to make "Things" and wealth for "Commerce." In Domat's theory, God put "common goods" on earth that "Man" could "render" into "Agriculture, Commerce, Arts, Sciences," and all that the "Wants of Life may demand." These "Things," then, became the basis for "Engagements," or contracts within society. In doing one's "duty" by trading, one's actions caused no public "disorder," instead channeling energy away from negative "engagements," such as "Infidelity, Double-dealing, Deceit, Knavery, and all other ways of doing Hurt and Wrong." The market was like a current that could sweep one toward virtue in a system of sins reliably canceling each other out through commercial exchanges. In this way, God's punishment of labor would be transmuted into the civic advantage of creating wealth and paying "Taxes and Imposts" for the public good of the state. Domat's system effectively transposed the old Christian holy market of salvation into an entirely earthly market of happiness and civic virtue. In asserting that the object of law was to allow individuals to find contentment and salvation through trade, Domat provided a religious justification for commercial society.[6]

If philosophers such as La Rochefoucauld and Domat were seeking a formula for turning individual vice to public virtue, a number of figures more directly implicated in Louis XIV's affairs of state were also searching for a recipe that might cure the country of its ingrained maladies. Pierre Le Pesant, sieur de Boisguilbert, a Jansenist tax collector from Rouen and a pioneering theorist of free markets and economic equilibrium, went so far as to present free market solutions directly to Louis's finance ministers, among them Colbert's nephew and professional heir Nicolas Desmaretz.

Boisguilbert worked as the intendant of police in one of Colbert's most successful commercial regions: the prosperous wool-manufacturing town of Rouen. Using his experience enforcing tax collection on his own noble lands as well as in his administrative bailiwick, he developed the first modern concept of a self-perpetuating market for practical application to state policy. Believing that France's economic misery was the result of human misjudgment, he began writing a work on how an economy might drive itself. His 1695 *Detail of France* is the first comprehensive book of economic thought purely concerned with explaining the mechanics of a self-sustaining market. In it, he complains that while there is money circulating in France, it is not creating wealth, because it either only serves the interests of the rich or else is eaten up by taxes. Unfair and punitive taxes on peasants paralyzed consumption, undermined agriculture, decreased the value and circulation of money, and hamstrung wealth production and the market itself.[7]

Boisguilbert was right in many ways, not least in believing that a market needed a consumer base. But he saw wealth as fundamentally grounded in agriculture. A nobleman with traditional views, Boisguilbert failed to grasp the economic power of Rouen's wool industry that so threatened English merchants. Instead, again like Cicero, he saw all wealth as originating in farming, believing that the value of money came from agricultural production. At the same time, he opposed the unfairness of the feudal economy. For the market to work, he thought, farm labor had to be better remunerated. Nor was he wrong that France's vast agricultural economy was, by this point, wrecked; Louis had taxed the peasants who made up the vast majority of France's population into starvation and misery.

Boisguilbert recommended lifting taxes on poor agricultural laborers so that money, "like blood," would move back into circulation, flowing freely throughout the body of the economy. A pioneer of tax reform for growth, Boisguilbert believed that unfair taxes on the poor created "artificial disturbances" in the natural market system. In lieu of not taxing nobles, Boisguilbert proposed a *capitation*, or a single head tax adjusted by means. In other words, he wanted to tax the rich who did not work—the nobles and rich clergy according to their respective incomes—while lowering taxes on agricultural labor. If nobles paid taxes, and the poor were spared, this would surely set off a virtuous circle of consumption and growth, boosting living standards and improving the work and productive capacities of the peasants.[8]

In describing the market as an apparatus that, if properly balanced, produced wealth on its own, Boisguilbert echoed Jean Domat's early economic equilibrium theory. He pointed out that the best way to ease taxes was to cease war. Boisguilbert was the first to explicitly connect pacifism with free market thought, contending that war created famine, destroyed agriculture, pushed up taxes, and undermined trade and healthy market mechanisms. Were the state to make peace and stop taxing farming, he argued, the natural market system might function on its own. Boisguilbert's pioneering and idealistic free-market plan was, in a sense, an upside-down version of Cicero's: he sought to free farming in order to create wealth for the poor, which would then create wealth for everyone.[9]

Boisguilbert was not just a man of abstraction. As a high-level tax collector, he was in direct communication with the Ministry of Finance and Colbert's nephew, Nicolas Desmaretz. The meeting of the first systematic free-market economic theorist with Colbert's literal heir in the Ministry of Finance shows that, contrary to some of the biggest clichés of economic history, Colbert's legacy was relatively open to these new ideas.

Desmaretz had worked by Colbert's side as an intendant of finance, trained with him, and took all his methods to heart. Clearly satisfied with his performance, Colbert had placed his nephew on a track to succeed him, with Desmaretz becoming director of finances in 1703, and controller-general from 1708 to 1715. Tasked with following Louis XIV's orders, as well as with protecting the industry and government regulation his uncle had created, Desmaretz espoused no particular economic ideology and was surprisingly receptive to Boisguilbert's ideas of laissez-faire. Boisguilbert first sent his writings on free market thought to a close friend of the Colbert family, the powerful controller-general of finances from 1699 to 1708 and secretary of state for war from 1701 to

1709, Michel Chamillart. Chamillart was also intendant-general of Rouen, which is perhaps why he responded to Boisguilbert with his thoughts about how to "turn theory" into "reality." Chamillart eventually shared Boisguilbert's letters with Desmaretz. These letters—studded with notes scrawled in the margins suggesting possible ways of applying Boisguilbert's theories—reveal that despite their initial skepticism, the two ministers eventually engaged with the tax collector from Rouen's laissez-faire ideas.[10]

What Desmaretz's responses make clear is the inaccuracy of modern bromides characterizing Colbertism as the antithesis of free market thought. Colbert and Desmaretz were not so-called mercantilists, as modern economic historians have characterized them. The Colbert family reform project was characterized by careful stewardship of its own self-interests, joined to a belief in market-building and bringing commercial managerial skills—such as accounting and maritime management—as well as legal and diplomatic expertise, into government.

In 1704, Boisguilbert began sending Desmaretz extracts from his *Detail of France*, hoping the minister would listen to his ideas about freeing the grain trade and reforming taxes. Were he to do so, Boisguilbert tried to explain, nature's providential system would make France's economy work. Revealingly, he called Desmaretz the "sovereign conductor of the clockwork" of the economy. For if Boisguilbert believed in a self-perpetuating market system that worked like a clock, he also believed that powerful government ministers were required to set the clock. In directing state finance, Desmaretz had the power to free the wealth of the state to reproduce more wealth and then to tax more fairly and efficiently, so that the market could work on its own. It should be noted that in the same series of letters, this early advocate of laissez-faire also asked for a state job for his son.[11]

While Desmaretz told his assistants that Boisguilbert's letters contained interesting ideas, he nonetheless complained in the margins that Boisguilbert's proposals were impractical and inapplicable, given the immediate financial needs of the state. By 1705, however, driven by desperation, Desmaretz had begun to reexamine Boisguibert's tax proposals, promising to give them serious "reflection." Clearly torn, Desmaretz in the end took part of Boisguilbert's advice only to undermine the spirit of the project. In the midst of France's catastrophic war finances, Desmaretz was able to institute a short-term universal tax, the *dixième*. The only problem was that he added it to all the other existing taxes. This meant that the rich now paid some taxes, while the poor paid even more. But with Louis's wars sucking up every sou he could find, Desmaretz explained to Boisguilbert, there was no margin for idealism. As much as Colbert's nephew wanted to try laissez-faire reforms, they would have to wait.[12]

THIS EXAMPLE OF free market philosophies at work within the policies of Colbert's direct heirs was not a lone incident. Indeed, at the end of the seventeenth century, the Colbert family found themselves in the very vanguard of free market thought. Desmaretz was not the only relative to collaborate with others on free market reforms. Colbert's sons-in-law worked closely with the archbishop of Cambrai, François de Salignac de la Mothe-Fénelon, an ardent laissez-faire theorist and one of the most influential writers of his day.

As tutor to the young duc de Bourgogne, Louis XIV's presumptive heir, from 1689 to 1697, Fénelon was part of the royal household and had regular access to the king, his family, and his ministers. In addition to being a gifted religious orator, Fénelon would become the most widely read seventeenth-century author to propose a vision of laissez-faire. He was the protégé of Louis's principal theologian, Jacques-Bénigne Bossuet, an advocate not only of religious absolutist political theory but of religious intolerance, who preached at the royal chapel in Versailles. After the Revocation of the Edict of Nantes in 1685, Louis sent Bossuet and Fénelon on a state mission to convert Protestants around the city of La Rochelle, on the southwestern Atlantic coast of France. There, Fénelon became disenchanted with the violent military methods used for religious conversion, as well as with Louis's political and economic policies.

Remarkably well connected at court, Fénelon had become close to Colbert's son-in-law Paul de Beauvilliers, 2nd duc de Saint-Aignan, and, by association, to Desmaretz. Another close friend of Beauvilliers and a rising power in the court was one of Colbert's other sons-in-law, Charles-Honoré d'Albert, duc de Luynes, known as the duc de Chevreuse from another family title. With the Colbert sons-in-law Beauvilliers and Chevreuse in positions of power at court, Desmaretz at the Ministry of Finance, and Colbert's other nephew, Jean-Baptiste Colbert, marquis de Torcy (or Colbert de Torcy), named minister of foreign affairs in 1696, the family now constituted an unbeatable lobby within Louis XIV's court and at the top of government. Their letters show they worked as a family unit, furthering their fortunes even as they supported Fénelon's ideas. Led by Beauvilliers and Desmaretz, this powerful group strategized together to figure out a way to bring back Colbert's good government administration to build freer markets.[13]

Beauvilliers was also governor to the royal children, which lent him immense influence within the royal family. Aware that they worked as a team, Louis XIV would call official meetings of leading members of the Colbert governmental group: Colbert de Torcy, Beauvilliers, and Desmaretz. He had them name Fénelon as the tutor of Louis's seven-year-old grandson, the eventual heir to the throne, the duc de Bourgogne. Beauvilliers and Fénelon believed the path to reform—not to mention to their own power—was through this young prince. Their idea was to create a program of study for the young duke based on Colbert's approach to government. In 1697, Beauvilliers and Fénelon started their project for the duc de Bourgogne, commissioning a huge set of statistical books, *The Tables of Chaulnes*, which were meant to show the heir how to expand France's population and commerce through a set of government reforms to free the economy. It focused on market-building through Colbert's old statistical method of counting, measuring, and mapping all the riches and jurisdictions of the kingdom. It was also a plan for better taxation: every form of taxable wealth was to be documented.[14]

In 1699, the Colbert family closely supported Fénelon's writing of a novel, *The Adventures of Telemachus*, for the education of the duc de Bourgogne. The clearest and most influential statement of agrarian free-market thought of the period, *Telemachus* also became an eighteenth-century best seller, inspiring major figures, from Mozart to Adam Smith. Fénelon's novel fills in a missing section of Homer's *Odyssey* with the story of the adventures and education of Odysseus's son Telemachus. Throughout the story, Telemachus is accompanied by a wise tutor, Mentor, who Fénelon reveals is, in fact, the goddess of wisdom, Minerva, in disguise.[15]

Rather than praising Louis, the work is an indictment of his reign and the court at Versailles as well as a call to free trade. It describes how Telemachus learns to be a good king by being the opposite of Louis. Fénelon's ideal monarch rejects war, courtiers, luxuries, changing fashions, and grandiose buildings with no practical purpose. He upholds justice and is kind and generous to his subjects. Echoing Cicero, he believes that "virtue" and good exchange are found in friendship and faithfulness. The king himself should inspire the Christian Stoic values of "love of justice… fidelity, moderation, and disinterestedness." He should push his people to focus on "sober" agricultural work.[16]

Virtuous monarchs, according to Fénelon, value "the liberty of all citizens." The most "absolute" rulers, he warned, are the weakest. He said that those who rule by fear are like "plagues of the human race": they place themselves "so far above the rest of mankind" that they "cannot see the truth with their own eyes," surrounding themselves with "flattery." In the end, the duty of a good king is to avoid war.[17]

Telemachus mixed Fénelon's Ciceronian vision of royal virtue with some general Colbertian economic nostrums. Like Colbert, Fénelon spoke of the need to develop good commerce backed by "navigation," well-stocked "arsenals," and "an empire of the sea." In reference to Colbert's commercial laws, he evoked the necessity of good "regulations" to limit "bankruptcies" and audits for the account books of merchants. "Penalties," he said, would keep merchants from risking the wealth of others in dishonest ventures. However, Fénelon was against an industrial economy based on luxury goods. After all the follies of the court, he forcefully demanded that kings prohibit "luxury and effeminacy," "music," "parties," and palaces. The population, both high and low, was to be kept close to the soil, hardworking and tough. He did not want Frenchmen spending their money on the "stuffs" of "foreign manufacture," such as "costly embroideries, in gold and silver plate," and on "liquors and perfumes." "Luxury poisons a whole nation," Fénelon warned, separating the rich from the poor until "vice" is "extolled as virtue."[18]

Fénelon envisioned a laissez-faire economy with "simple and explicit" rules. Above all, he said, individuals must be free to pursue trade as they choose. This freedom would attract foreigners and more wealth to France. Specially trained state magistrates would maintain free trade and help establish "companies" for projects that were too complicated for merchants without the requisite knowledge. It was the job of a good king to guarantee liberty and the natural creation of wealth for all.[19]

In a line that might have sprung from the Roman conservative agrarian writer Cato, Fénelon exhorted the ruler never to neglect his lands or to tax too much. Landowners must be free to direct all their funds to improving crop yields, while their strong, large families must work the land in health, attend public schools, and partake in "physical exercise." The unhealthy "artificial wealth" of manufacturing and trade was to be despised. Farming, in short, was the basis of a rich nation, Fénelon stressed, noting that "a well-cultivated field is a real treasure."[20]

Needless to say, Louis XIV heeded neither Fénelon nor any other member of the Colbert family. None of the free market reforms that Fénelon recommended saw the light of day. If anything, Louis's later reign can be seen as a destruction of the true ambitions of Colbert and his heirs. Furious at Fénelon's criticisms, Louis banished him from court in 1699 and pursued the War of Spanish Succession (1701–1714). It was the very nightmare Fénelon had warned against. Louis's wars pitted France against the Grand Alliance of England, the Dutch Republic, the Archduchy of Austria, and later Spain and Savoy. Military historians estimate that between 700,000 and 1.2 million died from the fighting—this, after some 1.2 million French people had already died in the Great Famine of 1693–1694. During the Great Frost of 1709, a cold snap caused by a sunspot, another 600,000 died in France. Weakened, hungry, and hopeless, the population declined by several million.

The well-educated duc de Bourgogne died in 1712 of measles contracted from his wife, infected while refusing to leave her side.

By then, he had already spread the disease to two of his three sons, who also died. A wet nurse kept the duke's youngest son locked away, and this survivor became Louis XV, who was just five in 1715, when his great-grandfather Louis XIV died from gangrene of the leg. Louis's health was a metaphor for his regime: his dynasty had rotted from the inside, and he had left France traumatized, starving, and bankrupt. No one mourned Louis, and on the day of his funeral procession the streets were empty. Some privately celebrated.

Louis had trampled Colbert's legacy, and with it any hopes of commercial liberty or economic growth. Yet, in all these debacles, some of Colbert's most important reforms held. Although France remained an agrarian society, ruled by nobles and an absolute monarchy, French industries continued to produce and compete with the English on the global stage of commerce. France not only remained one of the two great scientific powers of the world, but became the very cradle of the European Enlightenment: a complex movement of science and ideas of progress that would prove central to modern philosophies of free market thought. French economic thinkers would seek a permanent way to peace and prosperity through what the philosopher Charles-Louis de Secondat, baron de Montesquieu, would call "gentle" commerce, which would replace warring instincts of self-love with the mutual self-interest of trade. Free trade, in other words, was the antidote to jealousy, war, and poverty. In this, France would have a profound effect on British economic philosophy. For in both countries, there remained a persistent belief that if humankind could properly tap into nature by freeing agricultural markets, then the market, left in peace to work its wonders, would produce endless wealth.[21]

CHAPTER 9

THE MOVEMENT OF THE PLANETS AND THE NEW WORLD OF ENGLISH FREE TRADE

Trade is in its Nature Free, finds its own Channel, and best directeth its own Course: and all Laws to give it Rules, and Directions, and to Limit, and Circumscribe it, may serve the particular Ends of Private Men, but are seldom Advantageous to the Publick.

—CHARLES DAVENANT, *An Essay on the East India Trade*, 1696

IN THE EARLY 1500s, the Polish mathematician and astronomer Nicolaus Copernicus created a new heliocentric model for understanding the universe, explaining that planets revolved around the sun according to set laws of motion. The twentieth-century philosopher Ludwig Wittgenstein called Copernicus's discovery "a new point of view" about the way nature works; if the planets moved in circles, according to set patterns of what looked like intelligent design, then this must also be true of society and economics. It was an exciting idea in a world that had seen nature as a divine mystery. Looking for a force that could bring a planet-like equilibrium to human affairs and thereby establish earthly peace and prosperity, seventeenth-century philosophers fixated on the study of self-perpetuating systems. They now saw perpetual motion everywhere: in the stars, in nature's seasons, in the human body, and in human laws and economic markets.[1]

IN THE FIRST decades of the seventeenth century, the Florentine gentleman astronomer Galileo Galilei continued Copernicus's research, insisting that basic physics could be applied to the planets via rigorous, objective mathematical laws. Galileo sought to understand planetary movement through the power of inertia, which allowed planets to resist changes to direction and thereby remain in constant motion around the sun. Galileo's discoveries had great influence in the early part of the century, but he was not the only leading scientific figure working on dynamics. In 1628, the English physician William Harvey published his *Anatomical Account of the Motion of the Heart and Blood*, showing that the heart pushed the blood throughout the body in a self-perpetuating loop; the human body mirrored the stars in being an organic machine of movement and flow. The works of Galileo and Harvey inspired the French philosopher René Descartes's work *The World* (1633), which showed how matter followed its own natural course, propelled by the interaction of things rather than by mystical propulsion. He thought that the dynamics of movement came not from God, but from the mechanical interaction between small bodies, or *corpuscules*.[2]

The English natural philosopher, mathematician, and astronomer Isaac Newton argued that nature worked predictably, according to self-perpetuating laws of physics. This led Newton to devise a new vision of divine action with God as a superintendent of, rather than a direct actor in, the workings of nature. For example, God did not create lightning and storms as punishment, and comets were not omens; rather, these were moving parts in the great machine of nature. Newton insisted that natural phenomena worked according to constant physical laws that humans could understand through mathematics. Even more, he thought that what was true for planets was also true for society and markets. They, too, could work predictably if one understood the mechanism that moved them.[3]

Newton believed that if humans could understand nature's processes, they could then access the secrets of creating an infinite supply of gold and silver. Following the long, mystical tradition of alchemy, he theorized that the earth worked through the power of a "vegetable spirit" and was itself a "great animal" that breathed, sought "refreshment," and maintained its own life. Newton was convinced that the earth had a secret energy within it that came from the "philosopher's stone" of sulfur-mercury. This was not all magical thinking. Newton's paradigmatic work, the *Principia mathematica* of 1687, showed the mathematical principles of the gravitational movement of the planets and heliocentrism, and was meant to put to rest atheistic claims that universal chaos showed there was no divine plan. The system was a fundamentally mechanical one based on clear patterns that Newton believed showed God's hand in creation.[4]

Working at the same time as Newton, the German Protestant philosopher Gottfried Wilhelm von Leibniz was also on the hunt for the driving powers of the universe. A polymath who helped invent calculus and modern physics, Leibniz subscribed to the idea that God created human life and nature to work like a complex clock with infinite possibilities of movement. The German word for the balance of a clock, he noted, was *Unruhe*, which might be translated as "disquiet" or "restlessness." This restlessness, according to Leibniz, is what creates movement. The universe was the infinite sum of all things circulating in "a system of Pre-established Harmony." He eloquently characterized the difficulty of understanding ceaseless movement as "the labyrinth of the composition of the continuum."[5]

SEVENTEENTH-CENTURY PHILOSOPHERS SURMISED that, just as gravity moved planets, so free human moral choice created social and economic movement. The idea that individual actions could drive earthly mechanisms would become fundamental to free market thought. In his famous book of economic and social statistics, *Political Arithmetick* (1672), the English philosopher William Petty outlined a new conception of how individuals affect the economy as a whole. One of Petty's principal ideas was that wealth could be calculated as the product of the efficiency of human labor and the value of natural resources. Proposing that the work of certain people created greater wealth for the society, he used the economic productivity of various segments of England's population to calculate a rudimentary balance sheet of national net worth.[6]

Petty argued that those who worried that England suffered from a negative trade balance with France fundamentally misunderstood national wealth. England's economy was not to be understood by total output, or what we might roughly call gross domestic product, or GDP, today, but rather by the net worth of what England produced per capita. For while the value of England's output was less than that of France, Petty showed that its population was in fact more productive. He compared the two countries by counting trade numbers, output per capita by profession, and tax income statistics to prove his theory. France still posed a commercial threat to England, and, until the Seven Years' War (1756–1763), outpaced it in total economic output, especially in manufacturing.

However, Petty rightly perceived that on its current course, England's economy would one day surpass France's in volume.[7]

France's economic weakness, Petty suggested, was tied to Catholicism, which he believed undermined individual labor productivity. Using an old anti-Catholic argument, he insisted that the Church—with its powerful economic role and large population of priests, monks, and nuns—sucked up assets without creating commercial riches, effectively hampering per capita efficiency and the French economy as a whole. According to Petty, religious freedom in France would support Protestantism and thus lower the number of inefficient clergymen, thereby boosting productivity. Removing limits on lending and lowering taxes for the most economically successful professions would also spur industry.[8]

While Petty had faith in market efficiency and recommended a version of laissez-faire policies, he also believed that if the clockwork of society and of economy did not function on its own, humans—and more often than not, the state—would have to set it accordingly. Because man had fallen from the Garden of Eden and was incapable of perfection, tapping into God's system of nature would always be conditional on human behavior. If the Irish were not productive enough, as Petty felt was the case, then they forfeited their right to ownership, and the English state had a moral prerogative to conquer them and take their land. Distributing Irish Catholics' property to the more productive Anglican Englishmen would, he asserted, make Ireland richer. He took part in Oliver Cromwell's conquest of Ireland (1649–1653), when the English army confiscated Irish lands and brutally subjugated its people into poverty. Presenting Ireland as a seventeenth-century laboratory for colonial conquest, Petty handed out land parcels to English military settlers and made an economic survey of the confiscated estates and their potential productivity, claiming that his economic data were essential for governing the country. These statistical tools, however, proved perhaps most useful in justifying his own landgrabs. It was not through free trade that Petty made his fortune, but through plunder. He eventually acquired fifty thousand acres, making him, the son of a clothier, into a wealthy landed gentleman and a celebrated fellow and vice chancellor of Brasenose College, Oxford.[9]

The political theorist John Locke's vision of human society as organizing itself according to rational principles reflected Newton's theory of the mechanics of motion and Petty's idea that individuals could, through free choice, create economic efficiency. Locke, who was vehemently opposed to political absolutism, became the most influential theorist of constitutional politics and individual rights of his time. It was out of a deep disgust with the Stuart and Bourbon absolutist monarchies and their trampling of individual rights that Locke wrote his *Two Treatises on Government* (1689). Drawing on a mix of Ciceronian and Christian inspiration, he explained that private property was the linchpin of both political liberty and a functioning market. Adam's Fall from the Garden of Eden—where all things were shared in common—created the need for private property and human labor.[10]

For Locke, private property gave all landowners the possibility of maximizing their economic production according to personal choice. They were free to choose what to buy and whom to do business with, thus creating market conditions. At the same time, Locke believed that freedom meant doing what one wanted as long as it did not hurt others or encroach on their property. Individuals therefore had to think about the common good. Humans were subject to "the law of Nature," which gave man the power to preserve his property through elected civil government, contracts, and laws to regulate currency and exchange, but it also gave them the responsibility of maintaining good and productive stewardship. Property owners had a responsibility to produce and trade for the common good.[11]

Locke's vision of the rule of law protected political, religious, and economic freedoms but also reserved a large place for the state to regulate. Indeed, Locke saw the possibilities for a self-regulating system in society, but as a believer in Original Sin, he thought that government would have to step in where humans would inevitably fail. It was man's fallen state that created the need for government, because it meant the communal life of the Garden of Eden was lost. Government was a compact by which the "determination of the *majority*" decided laws, Locke observed: "*Compact* and Agreement *settled the Property* which Labour and Industry began." Thus, making compacts spurred the dynamics of property ownership. Locke did not rule out state intervention in the economy or in private property so long as it was done through Parliament following a constitutional representative process, which he believed was a political reflection of the laws of nature.[12]

At the same time, Locke did not believe that freedom was meant for everyone. Those societies which had not developed private property, agriculture, and trade had also failed to earn freedom. Only men who lived in Christian societies with private property, and with contracts bound by law, could fully enjoy freedoms. Societies that were not already property and contract societies would have to become part of such a society through force. This was Locke's argument to expand and spur market activity through colonialization. Though slaves and Indigenous peoples in the Americas were born with natural freedoms, and Locke thought that "the Indians" had more "decency and civility" than Europeans, he nevertheless maintained that in order to be free, they would have to create compacts and develop a property-based society. He was convinced that while Indigenous people had an abundance of land and natural resources—which "Nature hath provided in common"—they had squandered their natural wealth by failing to develop property, agriculture, and commerce for the greater good. Therefore, in North America they needed a colonial government to correct this moral and economic failure and force them to take part in the market. For this, the Christian colonial state would need a strong coercive hand, both to pacify the colonies and to guarantee private property and its efficient use by Indigenous people and Europeans alike. However, Locke never fully explained how the Indigenous peoples, whose land had been expropriated, would become property owners in their own right.[13]

LOCKE'S PHILOSOPHY WAS part of a paradoxical English school of economic thought at the end of the seventeenth century that recognized constitutional rule of law at home and colonial conquest abroad as keys to creating wealth. The Tory economist, philosopher, tax collector, and member of Parliament Charles Davenant was the most eloquent and frank defender of free trade through British individual liberties and gunboat imperialism. Davenant maintained the old view that while free trade existed through "links" and "chains" of trade, and was the most advantageous and natural approach to economics, the state still had to "take a Providential Care of the Whole" of commerce.[14]

Davenant worried that war with France had created state debt, which in turn led to corruption and the oligarchy of a professional class of creditors. Paying the national debt through colonial trade was his proposed solution for getting rid of the entrenched and parasitic financial class. Davenant hewed to an old Machiavellian vision of government by which the state needed to stay rich and avoid debt in order to uphold freedoms and transparency and ward off the constant threats of oligarchy, tyranny, and corruption.[15]

Davenant was a defender of political freedom and markets at home, but he also advocated repression abroad as a key part of his recipe for wealth creation. If Locke avoided discussing the big moral dilemmas of empire and slavery, Davenant embraced them in a brazen form of free market imperial economics. In *An Essay on the East India Trade* (1696), Davenant explained that the road to English peace, prosperity, and political liberties ran directly through slave plantations and colonial trade. He saw no conflict or irony in the idea that the liberty of the English could be purchased by the depredations of its faraway territories. He would later write a detailed account of how the good management of the African slave trade via complex joint-stock companies would be the basis of England's wealth and "National Advantage"—a point with which Adam Smith would later partially agree. And he would famously proclaim that "Trade is in its nature Free, finds its own Channel, and best dictateth its own Course."[16]

Davenant believed that England's imperial free-trade zone would lower manufacturing and consumer prices while lifting living standards. Plantations could produce essential commodities cheaply while serving as key additional markets for "manufactures" from back home. The slave plantations would thus become "an inexhaustible mine of Treasure to their Mother Kingdom." Trade in India was also necessary to the plan, not least because it lowered silk prices by 25 percent. "Garrisons" and a navy would be required to maintain this trade, so that not even the great Mughal rulers of India could "insult" the English. The Dutch and Hugo Grotius had shown that arms were necessary to maintain a free system of foreign trade. Now the English would turn this commercial strategy into the most formidable global empire the world had ever seen. From running plantations in the Caribbean to looting India and other rich colonies in a militarized free-trade zone that spanned the globe, imperial government would feed the Industrial Revolution at home.[17]

Davenant's *Essay on the East India Trade* shows how the English borrowed from Colbert's old approach. Davenant saw that government had to play an important role in freeing trade and supporting the economy. He recommended that the state use its legislative power to create workhouses to employ the indigent for low wages and bring manufacturing costs down, and thus produce cheaper goods. At the same time, he believed in free trade, and that it functioned by laws of dynamics. But Davenant's early version of general equilibrium was one-sidedly advantageous to the English. Having low prices at home while exporting expensive luxury goods would, he thought, yield the most prosperity for the nation. He also advocated the creation of inexpensive local luxury industries for England's own internal market, which would sap neither the wealth nor the virtue of the nation.

Locke's and Davenant's views fit the science and the politics of the time. Indeed, in the Glorious Revolution of 1688, William of Orange and his English wife, Mary, overthrew her brother, the absolutist-leaning James II; installed a constitutional monarchy with a bill of rights; and truly ushered in England's global commercial age. Now, the battle over global economic supremacy would be played out even more furiously between England and France. Ironically, their fight for economic dominance would be the catalyst for a new movement of economic and political thought. The more the two countries fought over commerce and industry, the more philosophers yearned to achieve their ideals of free trade by mixing Cicero's faith in farming and peace with concepts of perpetual motion and wealth creation.[18]

CHAPTER 10

ENGLAND VERSUS FRANCE

Trade War, Debt, and the Dream of Paradise Found

Thus every Part was full of Vice,
Yet the whole Mass a Paradice.
—BERNARD MANDEVILLE, *THE FABLE OF
THE BEES*, 1714

THE WAR OF Spanish Succession played an outsize role in the genesis of free market thought. Philosophers looked to end the war and find a way to establish lasting and self-perpetuating peace. They wanted to find a system to create wealth without commercial jealousy and war between nations. But more pressing than all those problems was that of public debt, which per capita was more or less the same in each country: by the end of the war, England had an unprecedented total debt of around £50 million, while France's national debt and various liabilities stood around a staggering 2.3 billion French livres (1 British pound equaled around 13 French livres), three times what it had been in 1675, representing around 70 percent of national output.[1]

Economists now set out to find a market solution to managing this overwhelming public financial challenge. By the early 1700s, leading economists in both countries looked to design instruments by which private companies would pay the public debt in return for monopolies. It might not sound like a free market solution, but in many ways it was. It was based on the assumption that if economists and entrepreneurs could properly tap what they thought was infinite American natural wealth, this new colonial market system could solve the debt problems that governments and taxes could not while driving entire economies.

BRITAIN AT THIS time was in the midst of its Financial Revolution. In 1694, William III's government needed better credit terms for England's wars with France, so it helped establish the Bank of England to loan it money at reasonable rates to manage debt, as well as to build confidence in the credit market and to fund entrepreneurial projects. As John Locke had argued, societies needed systems of belief and assent to build trust in the market. But the debt continued to grow, rising from £1 million in 1688 to over £19 million in 1697, a complex mix of 7 percent annuities, floating debts, lottery loans, and loans from the Bank of England and the South Sea and East India Companies. Even with the new bank, the national debt remained an intractable problem.[2]

Added to this, the country was in political flux. In 1707, England and Scotland formed the Union to become Great Britain. When William and Mary's daughter Queen Anne died in 1714 without an heir, it triggered the constitutional Act of Settlement of the Glorious Revolution, which stipulated that the crown go to the queen's closest living Protestant relative, which happened to be the German imperial elector of Hanover, George Louis, Duke of Brunswick-Lüneburg, or George I of Great Britain. At his accession to the throne on August 1, 1714, he also inherited the national debt.[3]

In response to the new complexities of the economy, as well as the seemingly uncontrollable growth of debt, government ministers, entrepreneurs, philosophers, alchemists, and early scientists began looking for a magic recipe to create endless wealth to solve the interminable financial crisis. They hoped that American riches would provide a solution. Inspired by the gentleman explorer Sir Walter Raleigh's description of his voyage down the Orinoco River (today in Colombia and Venezuela), the quest to find El Dorado became a major element of early eighteenth-century economic thought. Centered at Cambridge University, an international group of scholars, called the Hartlib Circle, maintained that "Alchemy and Science" had the power to "ignite hidden resources." Some sought to discover these hidden resources in America, while others believed the road to riches lay in divining the secrets of market mechanics. To this end, they studied credit, the laws of probability, and even gambling. Calculating risk and contingencies, or even the number of cards in a deck, could theoretically help the investor design insurance and reliable investment schemes.[4]

These ideas soon gained traction with the public. In 1707, there appeared in London an anonymous pamphlet with a fantastical title: *An Account of What Will DO; or, an Equivalent for Thoulon: In a Proposal for an Amicable Subscription for Improving TRADE in the South-West Part of AMERICA, and Increasing BULLION to About Three Millions per Annum, Both for the East India Trade and the Revenue of the Crown, Which by Consequence Will Be Produced if This Is Encouraged.* Arguing that America was "the only Fountain of Gold and Silver," and that whoever possessed it would have "all the *Material Treasure* in the World" and control the "Trade of the Whole Universe," the pamphlet insisted that England had to dominate the West Indies before the French did. The state should help "projectors"—meaning adventurer entrepreneurs—take America, by violent means if necessary, so that Britain could control all this wealth. Britain would then be able to build a navy superior to all others and build a global empire.[5]

In this atmosphere, the Anglo-Dutch satirist, physician, and economic philosopher Bernard Mandeville wrote *The Fable of the Bees: or, Private Vices, Public Benefits* (1714), the clearest—and also one of the most scandalous and famous—works of early free-market philosophy. It summed up the both critical and hopeful vision of British commercial society. Following the cynical view of human nature that Machiavelli, Hobbes, and La Rochefoucauld had delineated, Mandeville described a commercial culture beset by vice within the beehive of a nation where the lawyers, businessmen, clergy, and landed gentry were no different from "Sharpers, Parasites, Pimps, Players, Pick-Pockets, Coiners, Quacks, [and] Sooth-Sayers" in their venial addiction to "Fraud, Luxury, and Pride." Indeed, he rhymed that "All Trades and Places knew Some Cheat / No Calling was without Deceit." He believed that "selfishness" drove human actions.[6]

Yet Mandeville also asserted that individual vice was not wholly bad, as it drove the collective creation of wealth in the beehive: "Thus every Part was full of Vice / Yet the whole Mass a Paradice." Mandeville famously claimed that private vices were public benefits, and that vice and "tricks" came together in "harmony" like planets to create wealth and "brilliance." He believed that Britain needed a positive trade balance to grow. For this a country had to export rather than consume luxury goods. But the underlying energy that would spur market activity was greed. It was a truly scandalous opinion. Even Colbert believed that businessmen needed the decorous honesty of Cicero. But endless war and battles over

trade had jaded many. Figures such as Mandeville irreverently followed the old Jansenist beliefs that sins could produce an earthly
paradise if taken up into a system of trade.[7]

Like Britain, France was looking for a miraculous solution to
its debt and failing economic system. The country was crushed
by famine and near bankruptcy. In 1714, Colbert's nephew, the
controller-general of finances Nicolas Desmaretz, was wringing his
hands, looking for ways to manage France's de facto bankruptcy.
All reforms had stalled, and he was still trying to squeeze every cent
of tax he could from France's battered population. The country had
no national bank and a weak tax base, as the French nobles would
not pay taxes on a regular basis. Desmaretz became desperate. He
had heard of the famous Scottish economic theorist and gambler
John Law (in French, his name was pronounced like *l'as*, "the ace"),
who had proposed a scheme for a national bank and paper money
in Scotland. In 1705, Law had published an extraordinary tract,
Money and Trade Considered, that proposed that the more money a
country had, the more trade it would produce. The idea was to print
money, not as a form of wealth, but as a catalyst for creating it.[8]

Law was a visionary of modern market tools. He proposed the
creation of paper money pegged to the value of silver and land.
Banks in Amsterdam, Nuremburg, Stockholm, and London were
already issuing bills based on coin reserves. Law's theory backed
these moves. Money had to be stable, trustworthy, and plentiful to
support Britain's high rate of economic exchange and growth. Unlike precious-metal coinage, paper money could not be corrupted
or clipped; as such, Law argued, it would be more stable and create
more market confidence.[9]

After failing to create a National Bank of Scotland and a program of paper currency, Law proposed his project to the French
government. He found in Colbert's nephew a man ready for the

promise of market reform. Desmaretz wanted to present Law's plan to Louis, but the old king was sick—this was not a time for innovation. Once Louis died in 1715, however, the door opened for Law. Although Desmaretz by then had lost his job, Law had in the meantime become friends with Louis XIV's nephew, Philippe II, duc d'Orléans, who would serve as regent of the kingdom for the five-year-old heir, King Louis XV. Law proposed something even more ambitious to the regent, who, in need of funds, was willing to take a chance.[10]

The Scotsman and the French regent met in the elite gambling parlors of Paris. Law was a gambler both as someone studying probabilistic ways of making money and as an addict to risk. It was not the best mix for the man who would become France's finance minister. In 1716, Orléans gave Law permission to create a privately financed Banque Générale that could issue paper money based on its gold savings reserves. The government would accept these bills as payments for taxes. In 1718, Law's Banque Générale became the Royal Bank. It took deposits, loaned money, and also received a profitable state monopoly to run the colonial tobacco trade and sale. That same year, Law founded the new Company of the West (formerly the Mississippi Company), which he then merged with the slave-trading Senegal and Guinea Companies. In 1719, Law's company absorbed the French East India and China Companies, becoming a global financial conglomerate, the Perpetual India Company, profiting from colonial trade, including slavery. The regent's hope was that Law's monopolistic entity could manage money for the state and bring in much-needed funds.[11]

In 1720, Orléans named Law controller-general of finances—Colbert's and Desmaretz's former ministerial post. The Scottish gambler had risen to the summit of the French state. He had managed to fuse the Royal Bank and the Perpetual India Company, which now, in return for colonial monopolies, would take over the government's debt. The deal seemed to solve the state's intractable financial problems. But Law's colonial company would have to make a lot of money quickly in order to fulfill its part of the bargain. Law already had the confidence of the regent; now he needed the public to invest in his new project.

At first glance, Law's System, as it was called, looks like anything but a story of free markets. Yet Law's monetary theories and the novel idea that a company could take care of the state debt were at least conceived and advertised as a market-based response to debt management. Law the gambler, understanding the important role that imagination played in supporting credit and driving markets, started a vast propaganda campaign advertising the potential riches of America in a bid to convince the public to invest in his bank and the company's shares. The Mississippi Valley was Law's El Dorado and the French American dream. Law referenced René-Robert Cavelier, sieur de La Salle's descriptions of exploring the Mississippi, published cartographer Guillaume Delisle's extraordinary maps illustrating the vast virgin territory of Louisiana, and hired members of the Royal Academy to write books extolling the natural wealth of the French New World.[12]

The Treatise on the Creation of Infinity (ca. 1695–1715), by a French priest, Father Jean Terrasson, was a key piece of propaganda supporting Law's vision of Louisiana as a marvel of wealth. Declaring that the earth was "positively infinite," and so were its riches for those who went to America, the manuscript circulated and gained popularity in Paris. Terrasson asserted that the national economy did not need experts, financial managers, and accountants to direct it. Rather, driven simply by faith, the economy would settle into a self-regulating system. The Royal Bank would lend to all who wished to invest in Law's company, thus transforming "the

entire Nation [into] a body of Tradesmen." This national investment scheme would be backed by the guarantee of the Perpetual
India Company and the economic fuel produced by paper money.
In this way would wealth be shared and generalized, and all members of society would have a part in the equity. There would be no
risk, as any difficulties would be smoothed over by an "enlightened"
and all-powerful prince, the regent himself.[13]

Law claimed to have devised a perfect market plan driven by
credit, a constant money supply, the boundless riches of the Mississippi, and a business-friendly, absolutist royal government seeking to lower taxes. There was one major problem: it was a Ponzi
scheme. Law had overplayed his hand by issuing paper money that
exceeded the value of the bank's precious-metal reserves, while also
starting to sell shares for prices that were not supported by the
company's true value. Blinded to the scheme's fatal flaws, the ever-
faithful acolyte Terrasson published his last letter defending Law's
System on May 18, 1720. Meanwhile, Law's enemies had been
buying stock to drive up the value of what would be called "the
Mississippi Bubble," and then cashed in as much as they could in
order to drain the bank of its reserves. The attack worked. There
was more paper money than cash reserves, crashing Law's System.

On May 21, 1720, the state ordered the value of stock down
from 9,000 to 5,000 livres per share, but large stockholders rebelled.
Panic ensued and violent protests took place outside the Royal Bank
as well as in rue Quincampoix, the famous stock-trading street
in the heart of old Paris. The government annulled the value of
paper money, the Royal Bank collapsed, and in December, John
Law, inventor of the first attempted self-regulated market—and
a real-life version of the character in Stanley Kubrick's film about
an eighteenth-century gambler and adventurer, *Barry Lyndon*
(1975)—fled France in ignominy to Brussels, and then Venice,

where he lived off gambling and died in 1729. His stockholders, for their part, lost everything.[14]

In Law's wake, the regent called in a pair of state financiers and professional accountants, the Pâris brothers, to try to balance the books and manage the state's spiraling debt. Dreams of instantaneous wealth were traded for balance sheets, and they were not pretty. In a secret manuscript treatise for the regent, Claude Pâris La Montagne warned that the principles behind Law's scheme caused corruption and that the only antidote was transparency: a "solid and geometric plan" of "faithful tables" of double-entry accounting alone would provide a "General Control" of all state finance. Sound public financial management, he concluded, was the basis of "the public good." For Pâris La Montagne, a wealth-generating market system was not to be found in dreams of American gold, but in the balance of account books, which, if correctly kept, had their own form of gravity. But the public had not wanted serious balance sheets; they wanted the American dream. Even in his failure, Law had revealed something fundamental in free market thought: it was often driven by passions and desires rather than by hard evidence. Jean Domat and Bernard Mandeville were wrong when they claimed that free markets, spurred by the "private vices" of greed and self-interest, worked automatically—true, they could lead to wealth, but they could also lead to crashes and economic catastrophe.[15]

GIVEN THE SOPHISTICATION of British finance, and even of its political and commercial classes, it seems amazing that it experimented with a similar scheme to manage British public debt. But Britain was also under the spell of the promise of American wealth, and of the hope that it could prop up the credit market. Dreams of a system that would solve all financial problems were powerful.

The first lord of the treasury and chancellor of the exchequer, Robert Harley, joined forces with John Blunt—a former lottery promoter, as well as director of another stock company and bank—to found the South Sea Company in 1711. The crown would give the company a trade monopoly, in this case for the entire east coast of South America—the legendary source of wealth, from the Orinoco River to the Tierra del Fuego—as well as for the entire west coast. In 1719, copying Law, the company would offer all holders of government debt shares in the company. Thus, in England, too, government debt was magically turned into shares of the South Sea Company.[16]

The powerful Whig politician and future prime minister Robert Walpole hoped that by offering the debt through the market, investors would "make Use of the favourable Opportunity, [and] that the Publick might share in the Advantage of the flourishing State of publick Credit." The deal was heralded as a miracle of modern finance that could pay the national debt while producing dividends for investors. And, as in France, the anticipated income failed to materialize. The company had relied on false profit statements, which led to a speculative boom. Following the same Ponzi scheme logic that Law had adopted, the South Sea Company issued more stock to pay its dividends.[17]

Not surprisingly, in August 1720 the stock price plummeted and the entire system collapsed, leaving investors with enormous losses, among them great nobles and government ministers. Even Isaac Newton lost an immense sum, £20,000, speculating at the height of the scheme. The genius who discovered the system of planetary movement, who became director of England's mint, and whose work had led so many to believe that the market would function like the laws of gravity, was thus brought to earth by a scam based on the promise of a self-sustaining market that would never crash.[18]

And yet Law had been right that France needed a national bank and paper money. In spite of these unprecedented failures, a deepened understanding of and faith in market mechanics kept the hope alive that, some bright day, a perfect recipe for wealth creation might be found. Quite remarkably, or perhaps all too obviously, a philosophy of a self-sustaining free market would revive in Versailles, Louis XIV's bankrupt dreamland.

CHAPTER 11

THE FRENCH CULT OF NATURE AND THE INVENTION OF ENLIGHTENMENT ECONOMICS

The Land is the Source or Matter from which all
Wealth is Produced.
—RICHARD CANTILLON, *ESSAY ON THE NATURE OF
TRADE IN GENERAL*, CIRCA 1730

BY THE MID-EIGHTEENTH century, the two great economic powers of the world, France and Britain, had both experienced stock crashes and were still embroiled in a series of costly and destructive wars. Both felt they had lost ground to the other in what David Hume, the Scottish philosopher and mentor to Adam Smith, famously called "a jealous fear" over commerce. Remarkably, although France was the bigger loser financially and diplomatically, it continued to dominate the wool trade. Thanks to Colbert's industrial policy and the manufacturing successes of Rouen and Lyon, France was now out-exporting Britain. Even more surprising, given France's financial and diplomatic problems, not to mention its lack of a national bank, Louis XV managed to borrow at the same rate as the English government.[1]

Still, the economic outlook was not cheerful. France had lost its paper currency and its Royal Bank in the melee of Law's project. The effort to create market institutions and trust had collapsed, leaving France without the tools to build effective capital and stock markets to repay its nearly untenable debt. The rising commercial class suffered a setback as philosophers and nobles who supported the agrarian dominance of society looked to prioritize agriculture over industry. Harking back to Cicero's ancient belief that social hierarchy and the economy were simply reflections of a clockwork "causal" mechanics of nature, there emerged a group of French economists known as the physiocrats (from the Greek word *phusis*, meaning "nature"), who fervently believed that free agriculture would produce wealth only if the government taxed industry and let farmers operate with no duties or regulations.[2]

AGRARIAN FREE-MARKET THOUGHT represents a remarkable moment in the history of class consciousness. Those who still believed in the landed hierarchy and in a world dominated by agriculture saw agrarian laissez-faire as a natural remedy to the threats of absolutist government and the rise of the merchant class. With the crash of 1720, and with French economic confidence at a new low, economic philosophers led the charge not only against Law's scheme, but also against the world of finance that produced it. Distrusting the use of financial instruments such as a national bank, paper money, and early sovereign bonds, they sought to devise a self-driving economic system based on farming that was, according to them, socially virtuous. Merchants did not yet fully control France's society or economy, and early eighteenth-century free-market reformers were determined to preserve farming's economic dominance.

Supporters of Ciceronian and Newtonian cults of nature created a powerful free-market lobby in France. During the early 1730s, the Irish-French free-market economist Richard Cantillon was writing his foundational agrarian economic work, *Essay on the Nature of Trade in General*, which circulated in manuscript form and would be published posthumously in 1755. Cantillon's essay espoused a simplistic and mechanical view: that freeing agriculture from taxes and regulations would produce capital, translating into economic growth. The nineteenth- and twentieth-century economists William Stanley Jevons and Joseph Schumpeter would both credit Cantillon with being the first "systematic" economic thinker before Adam Smith. For them, systematic economics meant anything that sounded like a theory of economic equilibrium. In reality, Cantillon was one of many thinkers who misunderstood the wealth-generating potential of innovation and industry, and believed that freeing agriculture was the only way to create a wealthy society.[3]

The son of an Irish landowner, Cantillon moved to France in the early 1700s and made his money financing and outfitting armies in the War of Spanish Succession. He was an early investor in Law's scheme. Indeed, his speculation helped push the stock to its highs. He sold off his own shares just in time, making a spectacular fortune, and then claimed he had simply realized that Law's System would collapse. Others, whom he had convinced to buy the stock, were ruined. A rich man, Cantillon traveled Europe and later settled in London. Many considered him a swindler—until his death, Cantillon was hounded by lawsuits from investors and creditors, and it was even rumored that he staged his own death in a London house fire to escape his creditors.[4]

Cantillon was also a pioneer of agrarian labor theory. While the seventeenth-century economic philosopher William Petty maintained that population and productivity drove national wealth, Cantillon based his formula solely on agricultural labor, asserting that "the Land is the Source or Matter from which all Wealth is Produced." In Cantillon's formulations, farm labor cost was the basis for all other costs, prices, and values. If it were free of taxes, rules, and regulations, this primary economic driver would create wealth and produce market equilibrium. Creating economic equilibrium, for Cantillon, meant identifying the most important producers of capital and giving them a special status of total laissez-faire. His was a modernized theory of landed nobility: as leaders of the wealth-creation process, landowners were "independent" of the state, and the state dependent on them. "Lords and Proprietors" stood as almost holy figures above government authority, but also above inferior "entrepreneurs and mechanics" of commerce and industry.[5]

Cantillon's belief in free trade was limited to agriculture, and he advocated regulation for the trade of manufactured goods. This version of laissez-faire applied only to perceived economic winners. He wanted foreign buyers to pay for agricultural products in gold so that agricultural labor would be worth more than industry, driving down the value of manufactured goods in order to protect farming. Given the importance of industrial wealth in England at the time, it was an odd concept. But agrarian prejudices were hard to shed. While Cantillon theorized that ultimately all market forces were sparked by the cost of farm labor, he insisted that all market prices must be calculated starting with the rents and costs of the farmer in agricultural production. Only when agricultural prices were determined did quantity and supply come to play a role in determining value.[6]

Relying on his own less-than-scientific statistics, Cantillon calculated the net value of agricultural output according to the quantity of labor needed to make the land produce. He then accounted for how much of that produce went to the owners of the land for labor and rent and upkeep. He did not draw on commercial data or compare agricultural and manufacturing labor productivity values in tabulating his numbers. His free-market, agrarian vision ignored hundreds of years of urban history and commercial statistics. At the same time, despite its deficiencies, his early labor theory of value set the basis for a long tradition of economic thought, serving Adam Smith, David Ricardo, and Karl Marx.

Rather than showing how industry adds value to raw materials, Cantillon created an equation suggesting that raw materials determined the value of manufactured goods. "Entrepreneurs"— merchants and industrialists—were middlemen who managed the pricing of manufactured goods, mixing the intrinsic value of the agricultural product with market demand to come up with a final sales price. But their own labor and technology did not amount to anything. However important "entrepreneurs" were, Cantillon insisted, they could still only minimally affect the price of goods, which remained firmly based on the price of labor on the land. Cantillon went so far as to claim that while trade and manufacturing sectors brought agricultural products to the market and affected pricing, they actually took away from the capital of the landowner, and thus subtracted from the net worth of the economy. While it complemented agriculture, industry was also a liability; if allowed to dominate an economy, it would sap agriculture and the wealth of a nation. If the state refrained from market intervention and gave landlords free rein to farm, Cantillon mistakenly believed, the economy would grow exponentially.[7]

Cantillon's book would be influential for agrarian free-market thinkers to come. However, other contemporary economists believed in agrarian economic liberalism while still recognizing industry, commerce, and finance as central elements of economic growth. They were confounded by the idea that farming was more productive than industry. John Law's former secretary, the French economic thinker Jean-François Melon, connected Colbert's old ideas about market-building to the idea of a self-perpetuating economic system. Melon's influential *Political Essay on Commerce* (1734) reiterated the importance of paper money in helping to expand economic development and commercial action. But he also thought that markets had to be connected and smoothed out by the state—for example, by standardizing weights and measures.[8]

Melon believed in the "liberty of commerce" and said it was always better to err on the side of liberty, as merchants would in any case find a way around rules and regulations. At the same time, he expressed a vision of free commerce with elements of Cicero's and Locke's thought: liberty was not "a license for each to do as they see fit," but a mandate to work for the "general good." He warned that giving free rein to merchants was "imprudent," as merchants were prone to cheating. The government had to choose what to export and import, so that valuable natural resources, necessary for manufacturing, were not sold off overseas. In other words, Melon believed the market would work through a balance between liberty and state regulation designed to support a national economic strategy.[9]

Melon further maintained that several national monopoly companies were necessary to ensure that France dominated the European economy. The government would have to design a better version of what Law had attempted, building a system to create credit and capital to grow the economy. Finding the right balance of liberty, credit, money, interest rates, and trade was the best approach to creating more capital for France to invest. Melon hoped that government could create an economic approach "generalized and applied to all" in order to enrich France. Yet he admitted that creating such a market system was daunting, and that it was unlikely to be a one-size-fits-all universal model. France was not a "tabula rasa," he warned, but a country bound by its history and its own specific national circumstances. Designing a successful economic system would require taking France's particular context into account.[10]

Other thinkers sought a more universal economic approach that would work like the laws of gravity and planetary motion. In his influential *On the Spirit of Laws* (1748), the French philosopher Montesquieu suggested that prosperity came from peace and that societies and countries would have to manage themselves in a harmonious way. He maintained further that "the natural effect of commerce is to bring peace." By working together in trade, countries shared a common interest that made them "gentle" with each other.[11]

In 1752, during this great fomenting of Enlightenment philosophy and economic thought, the French intendant for commerce, Jacques-Claude-Marie Vincent de Gournay, decided that he would create a "circle" of economic thinkers to tackle France's commercial challenges and to develop different approaches to building market mechanisms. Born in Saint-Malo, France, Gournay had worked in international trade for his family's company in Spain. To his practical experience in business he added managerial training in the laws of commerce from the tradition of Colbert's state intendants. He, too, believed that a coherent state economic policy was the way to manage the kingdom's commerce. Gournay knew France needed reform, including more political and economic freedoms, and to that end invited a number of young economic thinkers to join his group.[12]

While Gournay did support some government intervention, his motto was "Laissez-faire, laissez-passer," or let commerce do as it pleases and happen as it pleases. Famed philosopher, economic thinker, intendant of Limoges, and future finance minister Anne-Robert-Jacques Turgot, baron de l'Aulne, wrote that Gournay's thought could be expressed by two words: "Freedom and protection, but above all freedom." Gournay also coined the term *bureaucratie* (bureaucracy) as a sarcastic joke, meaning government by desks. While he criticized heavy state regulation and secrecy, and hoped public opinion and tastes would help drive the market, he nonetheless took a stance between Colbertist development and laissez-faire.[13]

The Circle of Gournay gathered together a group of philosophers dedicated solely to economic thought. François Véron de Forbonnais, a financier from a cloth-making family who climbed to the high post of inspector general of coinage, a leading member of the group, disagreed with agrarian wealth theory. An admirer of Colbert, Forbonnais defended a liberal version of state economic oversight. He believed in liberty of commerce, and that the state should not interfere with the economy without specific goals to help the development of industry. His *Elements of Commerce* (1754) was a careful critique of Cantillon. Forbonnais made the point that wealth came from both agriculture and manufacturing, but he rightly insisted that manufacturing and commerce were the real sources of wealth creation. Like Colbert, he thought that markets could be freed once a level of trade equality had been reached.[14]

Forbonnais was skeptical that unmanaged free trade would work, believing rather that trade policy had to be designed according to the needs of each country in accordance with its strengths. He recommended that countries develop systems of equal and reciprocal exchange, where both parties benefited. He did not believe the market would do this on its own. Once states had established well-designed, mutually beneficial trade agreements, then tariffs between these states could be lifted and markets freed. If states and merchants could together design a "perfect equality of Commerce," it would then bring peace and prosperity among nations.[15]

Forbonnais noted that if agriculture fell short during a time of high industrial production, then a more developed country could follow the Dutch model to purchase agricultural products abroad. With reference to Colbert, he insisted that the most important thing a country could do was to develop the arts and sciences in order to build confidence, expertise, and manufacturing. Countering Cantillon, Forbonnais maintained that economic genius did not come from the soil; rather, it grew from a national investment in education and specific points of innovation and manufacture that had to be fostered and protected. He explained that England, for example, had become a rich and successful trading nation precisely through such careful development of the cloth trades.[16]

But there was great philosophical resistance to even this liberal Colbertist vision of national industrial development. While Gournay and Forbonnais represented what can be seen as a middle ground of laissez-faire, a strident defense of Cantillon's agricultural model emerged in the work of another member of Gournay's Circle, François Quesnay. The son of a peasant, Quesnay had gone on to become a medical doctor before founding the sect of economic thinkers known as the physiocrats. Quesnay would push Cantillon's thought to new lengths, using a mathematical approach to create an early equilibrium theory by which low taxes and free imports and exports of grain would lower prices, raise agricultural production, and provide an increasing surplus for investment back into farming. For this, Karl Marx saw Quesnay as a pioneering thinker of capitalism and surplus value, while the twentieth-century American Nobel Prize–winning economist Paul Samuelson saw him as the inventor of equilibrium theory. Along with his free trade philosophy, Quesnay was strident in his belief that agriculture was the only form of wealth and that industry and commerce were only "sterile" assistants in promoting agricultural production. Like Cantillon, he believed the value of agricultural labor set the price of manufactured goods. This meant that on his national balance sheet, commerce and industry were calculated at an economic loss, and that only agriculture could produce a surplus.[17]

Quesnay lived and worked in the Palace of Versailles and was the author of voluminous works on the medical advantages of the deadly technique of bloodletting to cure patients. His medical background informed his belief that economics could work like the circulation of blood. He was doctor to Louis XV's brilliant mistress and patron of philosophers, Madame de Pompadour, and, to his delight, he had been ennobled for these services. Both were parvenus, and both had risen to positions of great influence in Louis XIV's old palace of power. Indeed, Madame de Pompadour would help sponsor Quesnay's economic philosophy. Endowed with intellectual brilliance, fortune, and famed conversational skills, she became a glittering figure in the literary salons of Paris. She actively caught Louis XV's eye, and in 1745 became his official mistress, causing deep scandal for the king. Louis XV professed his love for this commoner, bestowed upon her the title and lands of the marquisate of Pompadour, and bought her the Hôtel d'Évreux, the finest city palace in Paris, now known as the Elysée Palace, home to the presidents of France.

A year before Madame de Pompadour rose to power, Quesnay moved into apartments in Versailles's basement. The man who was to lead the most powerful early movement of free market thinkers began composing his philosophy in the king's palace. Free market thought thus grew from within the very absolutist, pro-industrial state that so many free marketeers wanted to counter with their philosophy. This contradiction did not bother Quesnay. He was a fervent believer in the great oxymoron called legal despotism. Inspired by the philosopher Pierre-Paul Lemercier de la Rivière, he believed that the system of nature expressed itself through the will of the sovereign. It was only the king, Quesnay said, who had the power to free grain markets and create more wealth for landowners.[18]

Quesnay would travel to Madame de Pompadour's palace in Paris, where he hosted dinners for major philosophers of the time. His guests included Denis Diderot and Jean le Rond d'Alembert, principal authors of the best-selling *Encyclopédie* (1751–1772); Claude-Adrien Hélvetius, the atheistic and egalitarian philosopher and doctor to Louis XV's pious Polish queen, Marie Leszczyńska; Georges-Louis Leclerc, comte de Buffon, a famed naturalist and the head of the royal garden, the Jardin des Plantes; and the great laissez-faire economist Turgot. As the royal mistress, Madame de Pompadour could neither officially invite such figures to dine nor hold a salon of her own, so she would drop in on Quesnay's gatherings, where his guests discussed the new philosophies of metaphysics and economics in elegant surroundings. Quesnay's exalted guests enjoyed philosophical conversation about agrarian laissez-faire along with staggering luxury, culinary delights from the regal kitchens, and direct access to the king's ear through Madame de Pompadour.[19]

WHILE THE PHYSIOCRATS in Parisian salons waxed eloquent about the primacy of agrarian wealth over industry, a very different reality was unfolding across the channel. The first Industrial Revolution had begun, and it was powering the British economy. The steam engine was coming onto the scene. The Englishman Thomas Savery built a pistonless engine in 1698, and in 1712 Thomas Newcomen created a pump steam engine that could produce continuous energy and movement. In addition to steam power, by the 1700s mechanical spinning had begun. In 1733, John Kay had invented a fly shuttle to dispense spooled thread, which sped up handweaving. In 1738, Lewis Paul and John Wyatt built the spinning frame for the manufacture of wool and cotton cloth. By the 1750s and 1760s, when Quesnay and his agrarian physiocratic disciples were writing, British manufacturers had begun widely using water-powered mills in larger-scale factories. In 1750, 2.5 million pounds of raw cotton were handloomed in England. By the late 1780s, 22 million pounds of cotton had passed through English loom machines. This was a threat to the agricultural social order of Europe and noble landowners. As industry grew, a battle began over the place of commerce in France's still feudal, agrarian-dominated society. Free market thinkers would fight to bring the advantage back to farming. They believed that laissez-faire reforms for grain would unlock nature's potential, and that farming would come roaring back to dominate the economy.[20]

In 1756, the Seven Years' War broke out in North America. Raging from Europe, to North and South America, and to India and Africa, this first global conflict pitted France and Great Britain—while also pulling in the other great powers of Europe—in a struggle over the mastery of international trade. The war was a catalyst for French free-market thought, as it made clear that agricultural society was giving way to a new commercial order. For obvious reasons, the reactionary French aristocratic ruling class did not want to sit passively by and watch as merchants took over; some even suggested that aristocrats should seize the means of production and wrest it away from the industrial classes. In 1756, a French churchman and pro-industrial economic thinker, the abbé Gabriel François Coyer, wrote a subversive work called *The Commercial Nobility*, in which he attacked the aristocratic agricultural social order. A member of the Circle of Gournay, Coyer called for the nobility to give up their callings as soldiers and priests and to stop passively living on their land, trying to squeeze wealth from agriculture. France was under strain by economic competition and war, he warned, and it needed to produce trade and industrial wealth. Rather than seeing landed nobles as the drivers of the economy, Coyer characterized them as parasites. Because French feudal law forbade them from taking part in trade, Coyer charged, nobles had become economically "useless."[21]

In comparison to commerce and manufactures, Coyer believed, agriculture and its associated feudal system were dangerously unproductive. Coyer demanded a change to the status of nobles. He calculated that France would be much richer if nobles became merchants and worked, as they did in England, where the second sons of aristocrats entered into trade. This was a practical call for the overthrow of France's feudal constitution. Coyer's work was popular and was taken up in a widely circulated periodical, the *Mercure de France*, and his book went through a large number of editions and translations.[22]

The response was swift. One noble, Philippe-Auguste de Sainte-Foix, chevalier d'Arcq, immediately replied with *The Military Nobility Opposed to the Commercial Nobility, or The French Patriot* (1756), which defended the traditional order. A literary feud ensued, and the government banned the works of all who continued Coyer's call for a legal change to the status of nobles. Gournay and Forbonnais, believers in commerce and industry, continued, however, to publicly support Coyer.[23] Coyer and his followers wanted economic liberty, but they also wanted vast social change through industrialization and commerce. Landowners needed a response to this growing threat, and this response would take the form of a more full-throated philosophy of free market agrarianism.

The powerful French nobility had many privileges. Nobles not only owned the greater part of the land in France but also had the privilege of paying no taxes, except in extraordinary times of war. Boisguilbert's and Desmaretz's attempts to tax the wealthy nobles had pitted the aristocracy against the centralized royal state at the turn of the seventeenth century and produced the first economic arguments that connected the issue of taxing the rich to the need to protect not only the poor, but also the productive classes. Noble landowners still saw all attempts to tax them as furthering inequality, because they claimed they were the only people who created wealth, and that taxes on farms would undermine economic growth. They rejected the idea that a free market had to be based on fair and equal taxation.[24]

Quesnay, the leader of the free market physiocrats, bitterly opposed the rise of industry and taxes on agriculture. He labeled the business and manufacturing class of the bourgeois merchants "idiots," and called for the removal of all their privileges and freedoms. Quesnay sought to turn physiocracy into a fanatical movement that pitted those who believed in a society based on a laissez-faire agrarian economy against the classes that Colbert had sought to promote—merchants, manufacturers, high government administrators, and financiers, who thought that France's future would be in industry and trade.[25]

Quesnay's ideas are startling given the rise of industry and trade by the mid-eighteenth century. He ignored the principal argument of Diderot and d'Alembert in their famous *Encyclopédie*: that technology, practical mechanics, trade, artisanship, and industry were now so important that they deserved to be ranked as formal knowledge along with theology and philosophy. In many ways, the *Encyclopédie* was the announcement that the bourgeois commercial class was moving to the fore of society in Western Europe. And while

Quesnay was invited to write for the *Encyclopédie*, adding his free-market agrarian theories to the project's eclectic mix of economic schools and thought, such inclusion was not enough for him. He wanted his ideas to dominate.

Quesnay began looking for disciples to turn physiocracy into an ascendant ideological movement. In 1757, he invited the young Victor de Riqueti, marquis de Mirabeau, to his apartments in the basement of Versailles to discuss the work of the founding agrarian economist Richard Cantillon. From a grand aristocratic family (his father, the infamous and renowned comte de Mirabeau, would be one of the leaders of the French Revolution), Mirabeau the Younger was a friend of Montesquieu. In *The Friend of Mankind, or Treatise on Population* (1756), he had defended the property and tax rights of the nobility against government incursion. Quesnay asked the young Mirabeau to help him with his new project, the *Tableau économique* (*Economic Table*), a treatise that attempted to prove Cantillon's theory, that all wealth came from the land by means of a pseudo-scientific balance sheet of national wealth, which Colbert had undermined by developing industry. His book would become the bible of physiocracy and eighteenth-century free-market thought.[26]

Mirabeau later claimed that in his conversation with Quesnay he experienced an intellectual and spiritual "conversion" to an economic religion of nature. Blind faith in agriculture, mixed with Quesnay's self-styled scientific approach, was what was needed to stem the tide of industry and win the confidence of leading philosophers and policy makers. They immediately set out to work on Quesnay's *Table*, attempting to appeal to those who wanted to reform and expand French agriculture by advancing the simple theory that better land management would produce great riches through an agricultural surplus.[27]

In the context of the Seven Years' War, Quesnay's strange model did have the selling point of national self-sufficiency. France could survive and get richer simply by freeing and improving agriculture. Quesnay was correct that France's farms were less productive than England's. He hoped lowering taxes and removing all agricultural regulations would create a new farming ethic among the nobility, who owned huge tracts of land and had feudal rights over up to 40 percent of peasant property, but were often absentee landlords who did not invest in land improvement.[28]

Yet Quesnay's *Table* was not a practical manual of agricultural reform. Quesnay looked to make the case for free agrarian markets through a pseudo-scientific calculation of the economic product of France based on the theory that only land produces wealth. In the left-hand column of the *Table*, under revenues, Quesnay showed the productive side of the economy: agriculture, forests, grasslands, livestock, raw materials, and some manufactured commodities. In the right-hand column, under expenditures, he put the economically "destructive" nonagricultural products of the "sterile class": manufactured goods, warehousing, commercial costs, and sales. The *Table* draws zigzagging arrows between the various economic activities on each side to illustrate that only agriculture produces wealth; industry and commerce instead subtract from what Quesnay called the "net product" of the country, a number he calculated in the third edition of the text. Quesnay understood that labor value can produce wealth, and he understood the importance of capital surpluses; he just did not understand that investment in industrial production brought infinitely more added value and returns than farm produce ever could.[29]

While Quesnay preached market freedoms for landowners, he believed that only a strong state could create and maintain them.

Physiocrats wanted to make the king into a fully empowered despot who could rule alone and guarantee the economic freedoms of the landowning class. Quesnay's model was China. In his *Despotism in China* (1767), he claimed that the emperor maintained a natural patriarchal and agrarian order that produced a focus on disciplined farming by training its subjects to focus on the skills of "husbandry." Quesnay claimed that the absolute power of the Chinese emperor meant that he would never break laws or do anything contrary to the general interest, which was synonymous with his own. Thus Quesnay believed that subjects of the Chinese emperor enjoyed the pure liberty to pursue farming without hindrance.[30]

According to Quesnay, France needed its own all-powerful despot to push aside industry and rid the country of monopolies and useless regulations. Nowhere was this more important than in the colonies. Quesnay proposed abolishing colonial monopolies and granting freedoms to the planters of France's sugar and slave islands. This free, "monarchical empire" would spark the agricultural force not only of the colonialists, but also of slaves, who, according to Quesnay's plan, could become indentured and work to attain liberty. Quesnay believed that freedoms for planters and slaves alike would help regenerate France. But the planters were not about to give up their slaves. It was an idealistic and ultimately fruitless vision of absolute monarchy.[31]

Criticism mattered little to the physiocrats, even when it came from other respected members of Gournay's Circle, and even when it came with concrete questioning of Quesnay's statistics. Forbonnais was outspoken in his critique of Quesnay's faulty numbers. He showed that French agricultural production was higher than Quesnay claimed, and that many of the numbers in the *Table* were inaccurate. He could not understand how Quesnay thought that farmers were productive and merchants were not, and he found grave errors in Quesnay's calculation of national net product, and of how goods and money circulated. The final sticking point for Forbonnais was the idea that economics could be understood by the "transcendent economic truths" of Quesnay's *Table*. He did not agree with Quesnay that one universal economic model could work in all places at all times, and he concluded that his bogus statistics failed to prove the theory that the economy could work automatically through laissez-faire.[32]

In spite of these and other criticisms, Quesnay and his disciples worked tirelessly to defend and spread their vision of agrarian liberty and royal despotism. One of Quesnay's most successful disciples was Pierre-Samuel du Pont de Nemours, a passionate physiocrat, French revolutionary, and critic of slavery. Du Pont de Nemours was the son of a Protestant watchmaker, but he had run away from home to chase his ambitions in Paris, joining Mirabeau as a disciple in the cult of physiocracy. In 1765, du Pont de Nemours wrote a series of articles on "natural right" that would form the basis for his best-known work, *Physiocracy* (1768). It was here that he defended the positive natural right of labor and property, which meant that men had the right to own land and prosper from their labor on it. Du Pont repeated Locke's idea that individuals enjoyed the right to self-preservation, and should be free to enrich themselves if they did not encroach on the property, or "right of possession," of others. The role of government was to ensure individual liberty and private property. This sense of individual right led du Pont to oppose slavery, which he felt contravened the natural freedoms inherent to all humans. It should be noted that, like Quesnay, du Pont did support the principles of aristocratic feudalism. Indeed, he had enthusiastically accepted a title of nobility from Louis XV.[33]

Quesnay worked in unison with du Pont, insisting that a free international grain trade would favor farming and a system by which countries would harmoniously import only the agricultural products they needed through a natural comparative advantage. For Quesnay, free trade was not about competition, but about harmony. Nature had given each country different local agricultural riches. Thus, no rules were required: nations, he thought, would only import and export what they needed, avoiding direct competition. It was a hopeful and simplistic message, as the Seven Years' War had brought France deeper into poverty, debt, and bankruptcy while Britain forged ahead in its industrial development.[34]

IN 1763, BRITAIN won the Seven Years' War, cementing its domination of colonial markets and the slave trade. At the same moment, the country was experiencing the first Industrial Revolution (1760–1820), with inventors and manufacturers moving from hand production to the use of steam and water power for mechanized factories, chemical production, and metalworks. In practical terms, this left physiocracy with nothing more to show for itself than a series of ideals. As du Pont de Nemours's descendants—the founders of the DuPont fortunes in the New World—would find out, it was not nature that freed the American slaves, but the artillery of the industrialized and ultimately victorious Union Army.[35]

As England's industrial might became clear, the physiocrats and their followers still clung to the nostalgic notion that farming could produce economic growth. For the moment, free market thought was detached from economic reality and had little influence on the economic policies of powerful commercial nations. If anything, the dawn of the Industrial Revolution in Britain, Europe, and North America saw a rebirth of Colbert's approach, in which the state was essential in building and maintaining complex economic markets.

There were also democratic rumblings. As Britain made economic strides with constitutional monarchy and trade, in France the idea that a despotic monarch and a small agrarian noble elite could oversee the economic well-being of the entire nation was hardly convincing after a thousand years of feudalism.

CHAPTER 12

FREE MARKETS VERSUS NATURE

Man is born free, but everywhere he is in chains.
—Rousseau, *The Social Contract*, 1762

In a time of growing manufacturing, expanding overseas empires, and booming international trade, physiocracy was not a
popular economic theory. Although celebrated by modern-day free-
market thinkers, the writings of physiocratic philosophers did not
sell well in their time. Indeed, the best-selling economic books
of the eighteenth century were critical of the idea that economies
could be totally self-regulating. Those on the front line of economic
growth were looking for ways to promote industrial development
along with freer markets. This meant designing a constructive economic role for the state in addition to elements of laissez-faire.

It should not be surprising, then, that a pro-industrial reform
movement grew in Italy, the birthplace of European capitalism and
trade. Italian philosophers sought a more Colbertist path to build
markets through new legal systems and enlightened government
institutions. The erudite churchman, historian, and librarian of Milan's great Ambrosiana Library, Ludovico Antonio Muratori, took

183

inspiration from Colbert and Montesquieu in his work *On Public Happiness* (1749). Muratori's treatise explained how to make the world a "happier" place through government reforms and legislation to improve safety, education, health, and religious life. Several absolute monarchs, such as the Austrian empress Maria Theresa, followed his recommendations to support the natural sciences, religious tolerance, and expanded, albeit limited, individual and market freedoms through constitutionalism. The Italian and Austrian Enlightenment thinkers worked closely with those in Paris, London, and Scotland in a quest to build more just societies, a concept that some Italians called "socialism," a program to build societies and markets through state institutions such as modernized law courts and codes, schools, and infrastructure. (The historian István Hont called its adherents "society-ists.") It was a movement that would later influence Smith.[1]

THE MOST IMPORTANT of the Italian state market-builders was the Neapolitan political economist Antonio Genovesi, who, as a precursor to Adam Smith, saw the economy as a series of self-perpetuating market mechanisms. A visionary market thinker, he felt that governments had to build market conditions. Rather than subscribing to the idea that labor itself created prices, he believed that intangible societal and labor conditions drove prices. In his widely acclaimed *Lessons on Commerce, or On Civil Economics* (1765), he maintained that utility, personal relationships, and public trust determined labor and commodity values. The state had to free, but also carefully foster, markets. Governments had to build roads and protect them from bandits, for example. Citing Melon, Hume, and Montesquieu, Genovesi saw wealth as an interplay between productive agriculture and manufacturing. Much like Forbonnais, he believed that removing obstacles to commerce was generally good, but that merchants still had to follow regulations and pay certain tariffs. Thus, free markets were a constant and careful give-and-take between the state and merchants. There was no one single recipe, but instead a pragmatic awareness that trust and commercial freedoms had to be negotiated, built, and maintained according to local context.[2]

Italy and Austria were not as industrially developed as England. State leaders in the former believed they would have to work to spur innovation as England and Holland had done. Northern Italy would eventually become one of the richest and most industrialized places on earth by rejecting physiocracy's precepts and instead following a more Colbertist path. Early urban industrial thinkers, such as the Milanese philosopher Pietro Verri, considered the physiocrats to be reactionary agrarian hindrances to modern industrial reform. Verri warned that the physiocratic idea that industry was "sterile" was a grave economic error. If anything, industry and industrious expertise among the population were sources of "abundance."[3]

Of all the Italian economic thinkers, the greatest foe of physiocracy was a Neapolitan translator of Locke, the abbé Ferdinando Galiani. In 1759, King Charles IV of Naples sent the brilliant economist to Paris as a secretary to the embassy. There, he became a fixture on the social scene and in fashionable salons, befriending Diderot, to whom he introduced economic study. Having worked on monetary reforms in Naples, which brought him into close contact with physiocrats, Galiani had little patience for what he considered the ignorant agrarian optimism of Quesnay's group of devotees. He believed that society had to work with nature, not simply follow it. In his *Dialogues on the Commerce of Grains* (1770), Galiani maintained that only the state had enough credit to handle food shortages in times of bad harvests, famines, and wars.[4]

He agreed that nature and society functioned in systems. And he thought that manufacturing was dependent on farming. Yet he also maintained that farming remained too unreliable to allow it full control over market systems. With one bad harvest, not just agriculture, but corresponding industry would grind to a halt, and then society would find itself in an economic and fiscal disaster. Without the state warehousing and managing the grain supplies, farmers could easily find themselves "deprived of all funds" to replant. In other words, a successful agricultural system could be left neither to nature nor, Galiani thought, to the market. He insisted that nature produced disasters so large that only the state could manage them.[5]

It was during the 1770s that the Circle of Gournay's most famous and influential member, the French philosopher and state intendant Turgot, eventually became controller-general of finances. He would be the first leading politician to embrace agrarian free-market principles and to try to apply them in national policy. His attempts and failure would lead not only to mass uprisings, but also to firm philosophical resistance against the idea that markets could depend on farming without state intervention. A rich aristocrat and a government minister, Turgot was a believer in the progress of humankind and society; he adhered to a liberal vision of economics, embracing the quantity of money theory and opposing government monopolies and state regulations. He created a theory of the law of diminishing marginal returns in agriculture—the market theory that there are production capacity limits, and that adding more labor is inefficient if it cannot produce more wealth. Turgot believed that, like nature, society and economies had a natural equilibrium. The state could help tip the balance and give humans the help and liberty to create wealth.[6]

Though Turgot was a supporter of free markets, his 1757 *Encyclopédie* article on "Fairs and Markets" was subtler than Quesnay's repetitive hammering of the points of physiocracy. Turgot claimed that the large medieval fairs—which the great modern French historian Fernand Braudel would later associate with the rise of capitalism—were repressive monopolies. During the Middle Ages, fairs were situated at the meeting points of key trade routes between countries and regions, such as in Champagne in France. Here, for several weeks a year, farmers, artisans, traders, and bankers would bring their goods and skills to create the giant commercial zones that motored the medieval economy. "Convenience," Turgot said, made the fairs sedentary; it also made them into monopolies that controlled prices. Fairs with fixed participants limited competition and trade volume. Sedentary fairs also allowed the state to streamline and control the taxation of goods. He called this approach "irrational," as it benefited taxation over wealth creation.[7]

What was needed, Turgot asserted, were not annual fairs in a specific place, but constant free trade wherever demand brought it, without taxes. This economic freedom would allow society to progress. If there were no privileges or rules, trade would flourish; the prince would lose some tax revenue, but society as a whole would get richer. Turgot valued merchants more than the physiocrats did. He thought that with a greater volume of transactions, trade would become more efficient and create a marginal benefit by bringing down prices and spurring consumption and production. Turgot claimed that in Holland, there were no fair days; instead, trade happened everywhere, all the time, and the Dutch were much richer for it. Perhaps Turgot was unaware not only that Holland had abandoned agriculture as its economic base for trade and industry, but that its government had taken an active role in this policy as well as in commercial regulation.[8]

In Turgot's eyes, the market was not driven by the individual property owner, but by the rural laborer. In his *Reflections on the*

Formation and Distribution of Wealth (1766), on which he collaborated with du Pont de Nemours, Turgot advanced a revolutionary modern defense of feudal aristocracy through a utilitarian labor concept in which landowners were not productive, but legitimately inactive. In his defense of noble property, he claimed that proprietors were socially necessary to the economy, writing, "The Cultivator needs the Proprietor only by virtue of human conventions, and those of civil laws." Echoing Cicero, Locke, and Montesquieu, Turgot claimed that landowners, while not active themselves, were vital to the balance of the system as a whole, as they produced an elite endowed with the moral capacities to master the law and the liberal arts and sciences as well as to lead society and farming.[9]

At the same time, Turgot used his utilitarian agricultural labor theory to criticize slavery and colonialism. He insisted that liberty had to be positive, and not infringe on anyone else, and that property ownership could not apply to slavery, which was a product of "violent men" depriving laborers of their natural part in the "products" they "raise[d]." Turgot went further, criticizing the colonial economy as a theft that could not last. He felt the same way about feudalism and advocated a rudimentary version of the division of labor by which free workers would specialize and become more productive. These were revolutionary ideas for an aristocrat, an advocate of the agrarian economy, and a royal government minister.[10]

Unlike the physiocrats, who presented their labor theories in salons and apartments in Versailles, Turgot went out into France as a state intendant and actually tried to apply his free market theories in the real world. From 1761 to 1774, he was intendant of Limoges, a poor city in central western France. There, as the direct agent of the crown, he worked on alleviating the region's poverty through tax and grain-market reform. Unlike the physiocrats, whose defense of farming focused simply on augmenting production and circulation in the grain market, Turgot looked to spread wealth to the poor, so that the grain market could bring economic development to society as a whole.[11]

The physiocrats criticized Turgot's reliance on the state, but Turgot held to the Colbertist idea that the market could not work to its potential unless the state made extensive reforms first. Turgot believed that before freeing markets, one had to first protect the poor from the immediate market shock of liberalization, and that the state would have to step in to help those with no work and no food. He forced landowners to support the poor, and worked to end the feudal forced road-building labor of the *corvées*, by developing a tax for building highways. He proposed establishing state-supported "Charity Offices and Workshops" to provide employment for the poor, and even for women to do "public works." The most important projects were road-building, as they would facilitate the free circulation of grain and other products. Turgot even tried to import food to sustain his impoverished region and to provide for those who could not work. In the spirit of Colbert, he then employed his state powers to help found the now famous Limoges porcelain industry. Turgot's unorthodox and highly pragmatic mix of Colbertian and physiocratic reforms produced modest success and whetted his appetite for more ambitious plans.[12]

Turgot would get his chance to try out his policies more extensively in 1774, when he attained Colbert's powerful office of controller-general of finances. His first moves as minister were highly successful. He insisted on halting state borrowing, and he managed to lower interest rates. However, Turgot's attempts to liberalize the grain trade were a fiasco. As soon as he took down price controls and government subsidies, dismantling France's complex, ancient distribution system for flour and bread, there was a bad harvest. Shortages, chaos, speculation, rising prices, and famine led to the uprisings known as the Flour Wars in April and May 1775. Galiani used the opportunity to repeat his point that in times of natural disaster, the government had to step in. Deregulation without poor aid had ended in disaster. Turgot had forgotten his own rules of market development.[13]

At the very height of the Flour Wars, Jacques Necker published *On the Legislation and the Commerce of Grain* (1775), an attack on Turgot and the physiocrats. Necker was a highly successful Swiss Protestant banker, financier, and philosopher who lived in Paris, and who loaned the French state great sums of money. As an economic thinker, he agreed that liberty was preferable to regulation, and that, generally, freedom of trade was to be desired. One should have the right to do with one's own money, labor, and industry what one wants, he exclaimed. Following Colbert, Necker insisted that the state legislator had to make "prohibitive laws" so that the "abuse of liberty" in the grain trade did not cause famines. He agreed with Galiani that one could not simply leave grain to market forces—nature was too fickle, and society too fragile. Like Galiani, he felt that sensitive food supplies needed government guardrails. Thus, Necker made the old argument that while market freedoms were key, they were best suited to nonessential products.[14]

In spite of this criticism, Turgot persisted in his liberalizing reforms. He tried to break feudal forced peasant labor and guild privileges. In doing so, he managed to alienate everyone—from the peasants to the merchants to the nobles. Turgot's reforms and court intrigue aligned all government factions against him. In May 1776, King Louis XVI ordered his resignation. His grand liberal experiment in agricultural laissez-faire was deemed a spectacular failure. Many of his other modernizing reforms were also lost in the melee of his humiliating defeat.[15]

TURGOT'S FAILURES ONLY hardened opposition to the idea that free markets would work automatically without government intervention. Some radical philosophers thought feudal society and culture needed not reform, but revolutionary change. As government ministers failed to produce results under the monarchy, philosophers turned back to La Rochefoucauld's and Mandeville's ideas about feelings being the principal drivers of markets. They looked to understand how these human sentiments could create a more just market society.

The Swiss-born philosopher Jean-Jacques Rousseau came up with some of the most powerful ideas about human feelings in relation to economics. While he, too, believed in the economic primacy of agriculture, unlike Turgot he was opposed to a social system dominated by aristocratic landowners. He envisioned a democratic and egalitarian rural society based on an original state of nature in which property was commonly managed and the fruits of the earth shared. Rousseau reached back to La Rochefoucauld for his vision of how the market worked. He did not believe that nature spontaneously produced a healthy or harmonious social and economic order. On the contrary, "nature" and agriculture created castes in society that resulted in poverty, injustice, and inequality. He saw the refusal of nobles to pay taxes as the root of France's economic problems. Rousseau's outrage at the staggering inequality of France's society would inspire his radical *Discourse on Inequality* (1755). The book drew clear battle lines between the laissez-faire philosophy of the elite and the call for radical, republican democracy, based on the political thought of Machiavelli and Hobbes, to check the market and tax the rich. Rousseau said it was evident that a majoritarian government would have to heavily regulate wealth, commerce, and the power of landed lords. In his eyes, Ciceronian reverence for the state of nature and a society mirroring its immutable laws led to injustice. Democratic politics would have to step in and tear down this "natural" hierarchy and build a more just world.[16]

Rousseau would go on to become the most famous author of his time as well as a great leading radical whose thought would inspire Thomas Paine and other revolutionaries on both sides of the Atlantic. His political tract *The Social Contract* (1762) would shake the foundations of the European establishment and lay the framework for nationhood and democracy. This is where Rousseau famously exclaimed, "Man is born free, but everywhere he is in chains." In contrast to Hobbes and Locke, Rousseau did not think society made people good; rather, it corrupted them from their original state of goodness. The real original sins were society and property themselves. For Rousseau, inequality was the product of self-love and pride, by which individuals defined themselves solely in comparison with others. In the quest to satisfy their pride, they created unnatural "conventions" and "privileges" to distinguish and celebrate themselves in a hierarchy. Here was the anti-Locke and anti-physiocrat. The chains of mankind were private property and elite, minoritarian political and economic rule.[17]

Rousseau claimed that the most positive human value could be found in the sentiment of pity, which ran parallel to the "noble maxim of rational justice." Pity brought an instinct of empathy. When one saw suffering, one could identify with it and live the ideal of "doing unto others as you would have them do unto you." Rousseau believed that without these innate feelings of generosity, humanity would have long ceased to exist. Even more, he saw property as a corrupting vice to be fought with sympathy, empathy, and a political push for economic equality. The existence of great noble landowners and peasants only showed that modern man needed to correct tradition. Rousseau attacked Locke's Christian history of private property, in which the Fall from Eden created the laws of possession. On the contrary, Rousseau protested, the first man who found a piece of land and said "This is mine" was an "imposter," responsible for the misery and inequality of the human race. The recognition of property, he believed, was the first step on the long path toward feudalism, oligarchy, and tyranny, as humans gave up their individual rights to nobles and kings. Rousseau felt that law should not come from property, or through the use of civility and manners, but from the democratic, communal decisions of the majority of society: "It is manifestly contrary to the law of nature... that a handful of people should gorge themselves with superfluities while the hungry multitude goes in want of necessities."[18]

Rousseau's writings posed a terrible problem for economists of all sorts by making a passionate case against an interest-driven market and in favor of market intervention and egalitarianism via radical democracy. Unlike earlier economic theorists, such as Machiavelli, Mandeville, and Domat, who saw human passions as powerful drivers of market exchange, Rousseau roundly rejected the idea that exchange driven by private vice (or sin, in Domat's Christian vocabulary) could ever result in public good. Rather, the majority had to consciously reject the vices of pride and self-love and instead mobilize the human sentiments of pity and empathy in order to create a happier, more equal, and more just society.

Rousseau's philosophy was a direct threat to all the powers of his time: monarchy, clergy, aristocracy, and businessmen and financiers, whose wealth was beginning to rival that of the old nobility. It was a call for popular sovereignty in all things, especially farming, and could be seen as an extreme form of the Machiavellian idea that no one person or group of oligarchs should be richer than the state. It was an affront to Cicero's beliefs in decorum and a hierarchical society as reflective of natural order. Through his incredibly popular writings, Rousseau demanded a democratization of agriculture and convinced the public that they should have a legislative say in economic matters.

Rousseau was not only a pioneer of egalitarian political radicalism. His analysis of human sentiments and economics would be a major inspiration for Adam Smith. Smith saw in Rousseau a way to think about, and ironically, ultimately justify, free markets. But Smith would flip Rousseau's equation on its head: Where Rousseau saw the higher human sentiments of pity and empathy as antidotes to the market-driving passions of greed, pride, and self-love, Smith said that it was not simply greed that drove the market—the human virtues of empathy and moral duty were themselves market drivers. Where Rousseau believed that radical democracy fueled by empathy was the path to a peaceful and moral society, Smith believed that traditional agrarian British parliamentarian society was naturally moral, and that, under the right circumstances, it could channel greed and hierarchy to create a benevolent free market that would work for the common good.

CHAPTER 13

ADAM SMITH AND THE BENEVOLENT FREE-TRADE SOCIETY

It is by this superior knowledge of their own interest that they [merchants and manufacturers] have frequently imposed upon his [the country gentleman's] generosity, and persuaded him to give up both his own interest and that of the public, from the very simple but honest conviction, that their interest, and not his, was the interest of the public. The interest of the dealers, however, in any particular branch of trade or manufactures, is always in some respects different from, and even opposite to, that of the public.

—ADAM SMITH, *THE WEALTH OF NATIONS*, 1776

LIKE ROUSSEAU, ADAM Smith did not like greed. He, too, was perturbed by the cynicism of Mandeville's *Fable of the Bees*. As a professor of Stoic moral philosophy at the University of Glasgow, he did not believe that vices could be virtues. Virtue was hard work, and his job was to teach it. Smith disagreed with Rousseau's vision

195

of purely innate human emotion, whether it be greed or pity, as well as with his contention that society was inherently bad. Cicero's Stoic philosophy taught that individuals could learn self-discipline and morals to make society good, and Smith believed it. If there is one clear idea to take away from Smith's economic work, it is that morality is essential for a market to function. *The Wealth of Nations* (1776) clearly shows that Smith was not a modern economic liberal, least of all a libertarian. He believed that only a moral agrarian society with a strong governing elite could create and maintain free markets.

This is not how most modern economists think of Smith. He is often associated with a defense of greed and business interests. But, as with Colbert, modern economists have caricatured Smith and warped him into something he wasn't. In 1944, for example, Friedrich August von Hayek painted Smith as a thinker opposed to all government intervention who focused on economic efficiency. Milton Friedman followed in the same vein, reading Smith's invisible-hand passage in *The Wealth of Nations* as a call for removing government from economic life altogether. Smith's "key insight," Friedman claimed, was that economic cooperation should be "strictly voluntary," with "no external force, no coercion, no violation of freedom." However, both Hayek and Friedman cherry-picked their passages, and in doing so, transformed Smith from a moral philosopher—one distrustful of merchants and corporations, who believed in a strong elitist government, colonial rule, slavery, public education, and targeted tariffs—into a libertarian defender of modern corporations.[1]

To be fair, reading Smith's nearly one-thousand-page *Wealth of Nations* can be daunting, and many of his quotes make it look like he advocated total laissez-faire. He warned that it was folly for the government to "attempt to direct private people in what manner they ought to employ their capitals." He criticized government interference in an individual's direct economic decisions: "In the great chess-board of human society, every single piece has a principle of motion of its own, altogether different from that which the legislature might choose to impress upon it." And, although he was a future tax collector, he mused about the misery of taxes: "There is no art which one government sooner learns of another than that of draining money from the pockets of the people." Smith believed that production and consumption had to be free of any government hindrance: "Consumption is the sole end and purpose of all production; and the interest of the producer ought to be attended to, only so far as it may be necessary for promoting that of the consumer." Certain of Smith's writings can make him appear to be a proponent of totally free markets: "[Without trade restrictions] the obvious and simple system of natural liberty establishes itself of its own accord. Every man...is left perfectly free to pursue his own interest in his own way."[2]

However, if one reads Smith's quotes on market freedoms in their historical context, it becomes clear how far his vision was from that of modern free-market thinkers. *The Wealth of Nations* was a remarkably ambitious attempt to reconcile the agrarian oligarchy of the time and a vision of a self-regulating market with the rise of commerce and empire. Smith believed that trade would only flourish in a society where agriculture was dominant, under a landowning, governing elite that could limit the interests of merchants and promote learning and Stoic virtue. As a professor of Roman moral philosophy, Smith was in a good position to help lead this Ciceronian moral regeneration.

THE CONTINUING CONFLICT between Britain and France dashed physiocratic hopes for a return to agriculture, free markets, and peace between the nations. Both countries pursued protective strategies to grow their home industries in a battle for world market dominance. In the first half of the eighteenth century, Britain was in an economic slump. France's cloth manufacturing was biting into the British economy. The French tightly controlled Mediterranean markets, hindering British trade with Turkey and Spain. The French also dominated the sugar market, and their total volume of national exports equaled or surpassed that of the British. By the 1740s, French overseas trade had grown at a rate three times that of Britain. Between 1720 and the 1750s, French exports grew 3 to 5 percent annually, whereas British exports grew 1.5 percent. The global Franco-British proxy war, the War of Austrian Succession (1740–1748), would pit the two powers against each other on an imperial stage, and the Seven Years' War (1756–1763) would prove an even greater global struggle over commercial and imperial hegemony. The fight spanned from Europe to the Americas, India, and West Africa. Some settlement was needed, and many economic thinkers believed that free markets could bring peace.[3]

An academic himself, Smith thought that international scholarly interaction proved that free exchange was mutually beneficial. While France and Britain fought each other militarily, intellectual and scientific collaboration between the two countries remained remarkably free. Rooted in a long tradition of leading thinkers crossing the channel to study and work, France and Britain had developed together, in conflict as well as in friendship and learning. Thomas Hobbes was educated in France in the 1630s, and he fled there again in 1640 to escape political strife at the beginning of the English Civil War. It was there that he wrote his *Leviathan* (1651). The exchange worked both ways. The French philosopher Voltaire went to London in exile and wrote about English philosophy, politics, and life. By the mid-eighteenth century, intellectuals from all over Europe and the Americas were flocking to the salons of Paris, where philosophers debated science, politics, and the possible solutions to endless global conflict as well as to the challenges of markets. This long tradition of Franco-British intellectual exchange was essential to Smith's free market theories.[4]

Smith also depended socially and intellectually on his mentor, the Scottish philosopher David Hume, whose French intellectual roots and essays on free market thought paved the way for *The Wealth of Nations*. Hume's work was a blueprint for that of Smith. A child prodigy and impoverished nobleman with a degree from the University of Edinburgh, Hume had continued his education in France to "improve" his "talents in literature." From 1734 to 1739, Hume studied in Anjou in the Loire Valley at the Jesuit college of La Flèche, famous for its former pupil René Descartes. Many of the resident Jesuits were former missionaries, and they regaled the young Scotsman with tales of their voyages in Asia and South America, instilling in Hume a deep fascination with the comparison of societies and peoples. He made ample use of the college library's extensive holdings in Greek and Continental philosophy as well as French historical, moral, and economic thought.[5]

It was at La Flèche that Hume wrote his pioneering *Essay on Human Understanding*, which he would publish on his return to London in 1738. Hume's book was a fundamental work of Enlightenment epistemology—a study of how humans learn and know things. Hume believed that through an understanding of ethics, one could build a moral economic system and society. He described how the Greek Stoic and Epicurean philosophers had established durable principles of natural movement and behavior, and compared that to how Ptolemy and Copernicus had developed their understanding of the movements of planets and stars. He believed that mixing Stoicism and astronomy provided insight into human behavior and economics. It was an approach that would deeply inform Smith's own economic thinking.[6]

A religious skeptic, Hume thought that humanity advanced not through the quest to understand God, but through its capacity to know and understand nature and society through observation. He called for any religious work of philosophy that did not adopt rational, scientific methods of understanding to be "committed" to the "flames." Hume never declared himself an atheist, but he rejected all supernatural or miraculous explanations. Everything, he claimed, has a natural and probabilistic cause.[7]

Based on his study of history, Hume contended that man could avoid a failed society through free thought, education, the arts and sciences, and free trade. Rather than seeing life through the lens of Christian sin, Hume drew on Cicero, the emperor Marcus Aurelius, and the Greek Stoic philosopher Epictetus to create an optimistic vision of virtue based in earthly forms of duty to justice and charity, which led to happiness and prosperity. Marcus Aurelius had devised a philosophical approach to civil peace by considering the "viewpoint of the wrongdoer." To do so, he argued, tempered individual vanity and fostered benevolence. Following Plato and Cicero, Marcus Aurelius claimed that the path to perfecting humanity was through the "arts and sciences." The only way to have successful learning was through free government and "a polite and learned society" that would act as a bulwark against "the tyranny" of one's fellow citizens. Following these ancient Stoic recipes, Hume hoped that British leaders, ideally, would produce good legislation that embraced moral, agrarian-led free trade.[8]

If free trade and commerce were to flourish, Hume proposed, Britain would have to overcome its "jealous fear with regard to the balance of trade" with France. He declared that such "hatred" of France was "without bounds" and undermined happiness and prosperity. Colbert and Montesquieu had hoped for this as well. Once commercial society reached maturity, Hume predicted, free trade would bring peace and the benefits of commercial wealth. Speaking from his own positive experiences in France, he said he believed that rather than seeking a favorable balance of trade or a world without luxury, pursuing "open commerce" with the French would bring harmony, or a comparative advantage in which each country would benefit.[9]

Hume and Smith were writing in the period following the Act of Union of 1707, by which England and Scotland became Great Britain. Union opened Scottish access to English and colonial markets. Edinburgh and Glasgow became rich imperial trading cities and gained leverage in negotiating advantageous treaties and contracts. Both Hume and Smith witnessed this economic expansion and benefited from it. In 1747, the city of Glasgow negotiated an agreement of monopoly on the importation of tobacco from the French colonies. The river Clyde became a hub for tobacco and manufactured goods, which Scottish merchants exchanged for slaves in a circle of trade that Glaswegians could not have imagined fifty years before. Tobacco, slaves, cotton, sugar, and rum made Scottish merchants rich, and academies and great universities prospered. Scotland was finally tasting wealth, and it was heady and seductive. It was clearly this concrete promise of imperial free trade and its opulence that led David Hume and his protégé Adam Smith to support the Union and a broad vision of free trade and empire.[10]

Adam Smith came of age during this period of conflict, economic expansion, and intellectual ambition. He was born in Scotland in 1723, in the ancient commercial manufacturing town of Kirkaldy, across the Firth of Forth from Edinburgh. His father (who died when he was two months old) was a lawyer and comptroller of customs. His mother came from landed gentry, and Smith attended the town's excellent Burgh School, where he received a rich classical education and a firm grounding in Latin. A prodigy, he attended the University of Glasgow at age fourteen, studying with the famous moral philosopher Francis Hutcheson. With Hutcheson's charismatic encouragement Smith developed a taste for the Enlightenment mores of the day, which valued Roman ethics, science, free speech, and Locke's ideas of liberty. In 1740, Smith won a scholarship to undertake postgraduate studies at Balliol College, Oxford. Smith hated the place, finding it corrupt and intellectually unchallenging. He read widely on his own, but suffered from nervous shaking fits. He left Oxford in 1746, before his scholarship ran out. In 1748, Smith began lecturing at the University of Edinburgh, and in 1750 he became a professor at Glasgow, teaching classical rhetoric, moral philosophy, law, and belles lettres.

Smith's career as a writer began in 1756 with a letter to the *Edinburgh Review*, in which he critiqued Rousseau's theories of inequality and empathy. Smith rejected Rousseau's idea that man's morality was inherent, based only on pity. As a Stoic, Smith believed that morality came from education, society, property, learned philosophical exchange, and personal discipline. In his judgment, Rousseau's cynical view of society created a nihilistic "indifference for good and evil." While recognizing that commercial society had bad and greedy tendencies, Smith countered this by arguing that leading citizens had to be landowning, wealthy, law-abiding, educated, rational men of goodwill and "compassion." Otherwise, Smith suggested, the world would fall to war and "despair."[11]

In 1759, Smith published his *Theory of Moral Sentiments*, in which he advanced his core idea: that through Stoic moral philosophy, one could build a moral society. Rather than the innate and savage origin of sentiments described by Hobbes and Rousseau, Smith followed the Stoic ideal that moral sentiments could be cultivated to create a good society. Smith felt that the "bitter and painful emotions of grief and resentment more strongly require the healing consolation of sympathy." Writing in the context of the conflict with France in the late 1750s, he sought a philosophical recipe to escape the grip of war, which he saw as a product of human moral failings.[12]

Drawing on Epictetus, Smith created a philosophy that rejected greed. For society and markets to work well, moral individuals had to control passions such as anger and desire. It was essential never "to be angry with those who fall into error." Instead, one must be an "impartial spectator," and show them the error of their ways and "how to amend their faults." If Smith could find a method to channel this personal Stoic ideal of self-control and impartiality and infuse it into his own society, he hoped to make a better world.[13]

While Smith's writings had a Christian tone, they contain no references to the Bible. His language was decidedly deist. He described God as "the All-Wise Author of Nature," who created man as "his viceregent upon earth to superintend the behavior of his brethren." Smith also called God the "Superintendent of the Universe." But this deity was not a moral judge. Instead, humans had to be the judges of others' conduct. It was through morality, as well as through Newtonian concepts of causality, that Smith hoped to build a self-regulating society. In his 1773 manuscript essay *The History of Astronomy*, he would later write that "a chain of invisible objects join together two events that occur in an order familiar to all the world." Newton had shown "a system" in which an "invisible hand" set a rational clockwork equilibrium in motion.[14]

In Smith's eyes, human moral actions, love, and cooperation were the levers that kept the mechanism of society in balance and in perpetual motion. He believed that trade, conducted freely, morally, and focused on agriculture, was an essential piece of machinery in the division of labor: the efficient assignment of different, cooperative manufacturing and trading activities that allowed men to work together to create wealth peacefully. Channeling Cicero, Smith wrote that commerce "ought to be, among nations, among individuals, a bond of union and friendship." Smith's great insight was that if men and nations could cooperate economically, it would create wealth for all.[15]

Yet Smith's ideal of a benevolent, cooperative, self-regulating society would not materialize on its own; it required leaders and legislators, and for Smith, these could only be educated, rich aristocratic landowners. Smith had long noted that few people actually understood the legal principles of how to govern, even imperfectly. Evoking Aristotle and Cicero, he described the ideal legislator as finely educated, polite, and benevolent, partial only to the law itself. Only such men could practice the necessary self-restraint and "science" of the civil law.[16]

Moral, aristocratic government would bring the freedom and riches that Louis XIV's great critic Fénelon had described in *Telemachus*. Smith declared that although France might have been richer than Britain, it lacked the moral society necessary to be a leading commercial nation, as it did not have a free parliamentarian government to maintain "the safe, respectable, and happy situation of our fellow citizens." The French monarchy was intolerant and despotic, and this lack of political and social virtue rendered the society incapable of true benevolence. Smith believed that elite, representative government, as practiced in Britain since the Glorious Revolution of 1688, was the only way to avoid "foreign war and civil faction" and create a happy, opulent country. It was also the only path toward a free market. Remarkably, Smith's theory failed to account for the fact that Britain had been at war with France for nearly a century, and had not passed free market laws. But he seemed optimistic that Britain had the moral foundations to make the progress in which he so fervently believed.[17]

ADAM SMITH'S PHILOSOPHY cannot be divorced from his personal life or from the material circumstances that helped make his first book, *The Theory of Moral Sentiments*, a great popular success. With the aid of Hume, Smith assiduously built a network of powerful friends to bolster his fortunes and promote his work. When Smith's *Theory of Moral Sentiments* was first published in 1759, Hume and his friends at the *Edinburgh Review* made sure that Smith's publisher, Andrew Millar, sent copies to the great Scottish aristocrats who wielded power and influence: the royal favorite and prime minister, the Earl of Bute, as well as to the Duke of Argyll, Lord Mansfield, the Earl of Shelburne, and Charles Townshend, stepfather to the Duke of Buccleuch. According to Hume's well-placed contacts, *The Theory of Moral Sentiments* was "in the hands of all the persons of the best fashion." These powerful hands would shape Smith's career and the reception of his work.[18]

In the summer of 1759, Smith became the tutor of Thomas Fitzmaurice, the younger son of the 1st Earl of Shelbourne. This was the beginning of an exciting period of teaching the sons of the great Scottish peers. He was their guide to ancient philosophy, the law, and Roman aristocratic virtue. A perennial academic bachelor, Smith liked luxury and would gain a taste for expensive clothes. He lived in what has been called Britain's "Age of Oligarchy," a society dominated by "independent country gentlemen," who often served as the Tories and conservative Whigs who dominated the House of Commons. These hereditary aristocratic chieftains rose to a nearly unprecedented level of parliamentary power. Though

Smith critiqued arbitrary social hierarchy, he had ably climbed his way to the top of Scottish landed society and was quite happy there. It was perhaps not by chance that his economic vision would be tailor-made for his patrons.[19]

It was in part because of the gift of a copy of *The Theory of Moral Sentiments* that Smith would later be hired as a tutor and traveling companion to the young Duke of Buccleuch. The duke's stepfather would pay Smith a salary of £500 per annum (over $100,000 today) for tutoring, and afterward gave Smith a £300 per annum stipend for life. On top of these emoluments, the Buccleuch family would eventually help Smith acquire the lucrative government post of commissioner of customs.[20]

As always, Hume prepared the terrain for his protégé and made sure that he shared his success. In 1763, the Earl of Hertford invited Hume to become secretary to the British embassy in Paris, an advantageous posting. Hume wrote to Smith that the invitation was "accompany'd with great prospects and expectations." France was in a depressed state after the losses of the Seven Years' War. In spite of this, Hume found social life there so rich that he scarcely had time to "open a book," and occupied himself with socializing with other famous philosophers. Smith followed Hume to Europe in 1764, under the rich patronage of Townshend. He noted that he used the opportunity to begin "to write a little book to pass away the time." It is thought that this book was *The Wealth of Nations*.[21]

With Hume's introduction, Smith met France's most influential economic thinkers and discussed the major ideas of the day. In Geneva, he met Voltaire. In Paris, Hume introduced him to the famed Franco-German atheist philosopher Paul-Henri Thiry, baron d'Holbach, who welcomed him into his circle, as did Quesnay and the physiocrats. Smith's social success was impressive given that he was one of the few educated men of his time who could not speak fluent French, the lingua franca of the European elite. He became a habitué of the leading salons and cut a dashing figure at the opera in his new Parisian clothes. It was the first time in history that one could travel to the great cities of Europe and find social groups of economic philosophers. Smith felt most at home with the physiocrats, who gave him manuscripts and early editions of their most important works. Quesnay, du Pont de Nemours, and Mirabeau introduced Smith to their main argument: that land was the only source of a nation's wealth. With the physiocrats, Smith felt he had found kindred intellectual spirits.[22]

In 1766, the tour ended and he returned to Scotland; a year later, his health forced him to move back to Kirkaldy to live with his mother. It was there that he wrote *The Wealth of Nations*. Smith's muse was Britain and its empire, and, rhetorically at least, absolutist France was its antithesis. Smith's idea of free markets had a distinctively national and imperial tone to it. When he spoke of free markets, he spoke specifically of Britain and its colonies. What was possible in Britain, with its constitutional monarchy and Bill of Rights, he believed, was not possible in other countries on the Continent with different social and political systems.

In *The Wealth of Nations*, Smith developed his own version of physiocratic economics, beginning with the old refrain that wealth comes from agriculture. Smith agreed with Quesnay that farm labor was the source of all wealth and that the surplus of agricultural goods was the basis of industrial wealth production. Industry did not produce wealth; it only spread the value of surplus farm products. For Smith, Quesnay's *Economic Table* was "the great discovery of our age," because it showed how agricultural products fed commerce, leading to economic growth and "opulence." Like Hume, Smith believed that agriculture should not be taxed, in order to protect its productive capacity. Nor did he believe in investing in industry. In a healthy, natural system, even nonagricultural commercial and industrial profits should be directed back into farming, for "no equal capital puts into motion a greater quantity of productive labor than that of the farmer." Smith studied flow and how economies achieved mythic equilibrium, but he did not understand that capital investment in technology and industry, not agriculture, was the only way to create exponential wealth.[23]

Smith was deeply suspicious of industry and private corporations as potential enemies of society, charging that both companies and trade guilds led not only to monopolies, but also to the poor treatment of workers. *The Wealth of Nations* spends a considerable number of pages warning against how "corporations" and "masters" undermine the wages, honesty, and labor of "workmen," who are more productive dealing directly with "customers." Smith thought corporations were parasitic middlemen who brought down wages. It was not inventors, companies, and investors who encouraged industry, he said, but rather the workmen themselves. If workers were free from companies, he thought, it would lead to an overall rise in wages and a progressive state of society.[24]

Quoting Quesnay, Smith insisted that merchants and manufacturers were economically "sterile": "The labor of artificers and manufacturers," he asserted, "never adds anything to the value of the whole annual amount of the rude produce of the land." Members of the commercial class could only "augment the revenue and wealth of their society" by reinvesting capital in agriculture. For Smith, only if the farming sector got richer would commerce expand, industry grow, and the salaries of even the "industrious poor" and their families provide a "wholesome" diet, good clothing, and comfortable lodging. For these reasons, Smith proposed that if one freed agricultural production and let landowners dominate society, it would create a benevolent, virtuous society with an "invisible hand" that would bring commerce into the moral fold of farming.[25]

Smith's use of the analogy of the invisible hand appears three times in his writings: once in *The Theory of Moral Sentiments*, once in his *History of Astronomy*, and once in *The Wealth of Nations*. Each time, he uses it rather ambiguously, even critically, to the point that historian Emma Rothschild has hypothesized that he was using the metaphor "ironically." Smith did not like the idea of a system moving humans around like chess pieces. Rather, people moved themselves within society, and morality helped them do it in ways that were collectively beneficial. However, Smith did not believe that merchants could make good moral economic choices if left to their own devices, either. He thought they were selfish, and when a merchant did something good, it was because he was "led by an invisible hand to promote an end which was no part of his intention." The "invisible hand" that pulled merchants away from their instinctive greed was society, led by a not-so-invisible landowning governing elite that, through a carefully designed tax system to support farming over industry, would free nature to create national wealth. Only farmers and those laborers closely related to farming did not need the moral nudge of society; in agricultural production, they were already working according to a division of labor that came not from wisdom but from something Smith did feel was innate: the "propensity in human nature" for utilitarian exchange. The leaders of society had to create economic equilibrium by politically supporting the agricultural sector. It was in this way, he suggested, that they could emulate the virtue of Cicero's Rome.[26]

The leaders of society had to make sure merchants did not control politics. If they did, they would create monopolies and undermine the market. Smith believed Colbert had erred by giving too much power to merchants and industrialists. It was their influence, Smith erroneously thought, that had led Colbert to pass too many government regulations, and, even more egregiously, to overvalue the "industry of the towns" while undervaluing agriculture. Smith was the first to use the term "mercantile system," by which he meant a government run by and for the benefit of merchants. The merchant class's monopolizing tendencies posed the greatest danger to the morals and freedoms of the market, Smith insisted, and therefore the state had to provide a counterforce. The role of government was to free nature and hinder the destructive, monopolistic tendencies of merchants by allowing the moral market to pull them back to the farm, the source of all wealth.[27]

And yet, for all his criticism, Smith's ideas shared much in common with those of Colbert, whose "great abilities" and "probity" he lauded. Far from opposing the economic nationalism now associated with Colbert and mercantilism, Smith sounds much like Colbert in certain sections of *The Wealth of Nations*, particularly where he describes how to build an imperial trade zone. Part of the task of the invisible hand, Smith explained, was to guide merchants to support "domestick" over "foreign industry," thus producing "the greatest value." He lauded the protectionist Navigation Act of 1651 as, "perhaps, the wisest of all the commercial regulations in England," because it aimed to keep foreign merchants from undermining British trade and supported the expansion of internal and imperial markets.[28]

By modern standards, the British society Smith lauded was no liberal paradise. Eighteenth-century aristocrats retained coercive feudal powers over those who lived on their lands. They controlled judges, police, militias, and all civic and much private life in their fiefs. And the state was no more gentle: this was the age of the press gang that scooped up poor boys and men off the roads and conscripted them without consent into a life in the navy.

In 1723, Britain had established the Bloody Code, a list of two hundred crimes—such as stealing a sheep or a rabbit or cutting down trees without permission—that were punishable by death. The hangman's noose loomed large at the time, and criminals were commonly branded. Smith was no Rousseau. He did not want to transform Britain. But he did hope that expanding national wealth would bring moderate social progress. By this he meant decent living standards for workmen so that they and their families would have enough to eat, decent lodging, and warm clothes.[29]

The invisible hand of British society was tasked with bringing its civilizing forces to the colonies, which meant educating those populations that, by dint of living so far from the metropole, needed time to develop into fully mature commercial societies. Smith used the example of Americans to make his point about merchants being ill-suited to govern, as they still considered only their own interests in decision-making. Failing to mention that John Locke himself had created Maryland's tobacco monopoly, Smith complained that "by a strange absurdity," businessmen saw the "character of the sovereign as but an appendix" to their trade and interests, seeking only to bar competition. The civilizing influence of an elite, Lockean, enlightened government would have to step in to guide the hand of nature in places where an advanced commercial society was still in the process of forming. Smith was writing at the time of the American War of Independence (1775–1783), and while he was opposed to the American colonies breaking free of the British Empire, he hoped that if it did happen, the two countries would form a free trade alliance. In fact, the new United States of America did the opposite and in 1783 imposed tariffs on all foreign goods to protect its fragile developing economy.[30]

Because Smith believed in stages of societal progress and in the British agrarian Lockean compact society, he enthusiastically supported both colonial conquest and slavery. The British Empire would bring agricultural society to the "savage nations of hunters and fishers," who could then create a surplus and progress toward the civilized "conveniences" of commercial society. Smith also believed it was possible for better laws to improve slavery. Clearly unaware of the torture, rape, and dismemberment that were common practices in the French colonies, Smith somehow thought that French slavery was a "gentle usage" that made those in bondage more loyal and productive, and also increased their "intelligence" so that they would associate their interests with those of their masters as they progressed to being "free servants." Smith viewed freedom as he viewed economies: as part of a continuum with stages of progress. The invisible hand could work for slaves, but only once they evolved to his vision of a higher moral and societal plane.[31]

Smith ignored not only the physiocratic objection to human bondage, seeing no fundamental problem with slavery, but also the economic potential of the first Industrial Revolution, which was radically changing the world before his very eyes. He knew James Watt, the inventor of the industrial steam engine, and had helped him find a place for a laboratory at the University of Glasgow. Yet there is no evidence that Smith understood the true economic significance of industrial looms and factories or even the transformative power of Watt's steam engine.[32]

Pioneering industrial inventors such as Watt knew that wealth came from value-added, innovative manufacturing and industry, not from agriculture. In 1775, Matthew Boulton and Watt founded their engine-making company, and by 1781 they had begun building large-scale industrial spinning mills in the English Midlands. Smith was alive, well, and collecting taxes while this was happening. Inventiveness, the natural sciences, entrepreneurial creation, industry, coal deposits, and pro-industrial and pro-colonial government policies would give Britain's economy its upper hand. Smith would publish four re-edited editions of *The Wealth of Nations*, in 1778, 1784, 1786, and 1789, changing passages on Stoicism and other key topics, without ever mentioning the technological advances and changes to labor that took place throughout these years. It was a bit like writing a book about economics in San Francisco in the year 2000 and not mentioning the wealth-creating capacities of tech or software. In any case, in yet another great and revealing irony of history, the father of the most influential book on free market economics spent the later years of his life rewriting his works on Roman morals and economic liberty while living as a well-paid state bureaucrat: a tax collector with connections in high places.[33]

SMITH'S THOUGHT SEEMS contradictory today. It envisioned a market sustained by morals and exchange. It was Colbertist in that it sought protectionism and empire to aid internal development and to keep investment capital within the nation. It was physiocratic in that it saw farming as the motor of wealth. Contrary to economists today who paint Smith as a social libertarian, he advocated a propertied oligarchy ruling a Lockean, limited, representative government that would, in certain cases, correct the self-serving tendencies of merchants.[34]

Smith was instrumental in advancing the fledgling science of economics. He understood the importance of the division of labor—or the cooperation of specialized industries—in a commercial, manufacturing society. He recognized the key role of government legislation in discouraging monopolies in order to guarantee free competition and rising wages. He foresaw forms of Keynesian stimulus, when the rich spend in times of dearth to maintain employment. And he, too, believed in a form of general equilibrium theory by which agricultural labor, supply and demand, representative government, and a moral society were supposed to maintain a functioning market and pricing system without too much government intervention or encroachment on individual property and consumer rights.[35]

In the end, Smith's central project was a reworking of ancient morality for a new commercial age. Once landowners were liberated from poorly designed taxes and other economic "prohibitions," free agricultural trade would continue to bring Britain opulence, order, and benevolence. It would also bring peace. As Cicero had promised, and as Smith had explained in *The Theory of Moral Sentiments*, freedom and agriculture brought healthy friendship. Smith insisted that rather than a source of discord and animosity, commerce could be "a bond of union and friendship" for both individuals and countries.[36]

Even more crucially, Smith had solved the ancient moral problem of the Garden of Eden that had driven Ambrose, Augustine, and Saint Francis to such severe religious and material austerity. In the Christian tradition, humans were fallen creatures who could not progress outside the quest for Christian salvation. Smith found a novel way around Original Sin and Rousseau's Augustinian, Calvinist pessimism about humans and civil society. Adam and Eve's mistake was to break the rules of the Garden of Eden. This act had led to their expulsion, and they became the progenitors of a fallen human world. Through Stoic moral discipline and good government, Smith optimistically believed, humans could return to something close to an earthly agrarian paradise. If they embraced nature, then even commerce could be ethical and part of human secular progress. God, or nature (depending on one's theology, and Smith was never fully clear on his), wanted this earthly opulence and progress to be attained. Hume and Smith, along with so many other leading thinkers of the Enlightenment, saw progress as a part of nature, waiting to be fulfilled through human liberty, education, science, benevolent sentiments, farming, and commerce. Smith's philosophy allowed humankind to benefit from progress in spite of itself and, as Voltaire had put it, to create "the best of all possible worlds."[37]

In Smith's later years, he commented on neither the triumphs nor the challenges brought about by the rise of industry. Matthew Boulton, James Watt, Josiah Wedgwood, and other inventors had by then become fabulously rich industrialists, proving that the future path of wealth lay through industry. But although manufacturing created untold riches for many, it also created terrible working and living conditions for others. All ships and wages did not rise in equilibrium with the tide of commercial society and its market freedoms. In some ways, Smith's fears about industry came true. Even Watt and Wedgwood had begun to realize the deadly toll that pollution exacted on their workers, themselves, and their own families.

This vast new wealth and economic development posed other challenges, too. It did not bring peace or an agrarian utopia. By the late 1770s and 1780s, Britain had become the richest, most industrialized nation on earth and the great imperial power on the world stage. Yet it was still fighting the French over North American independence and colonial domination of the Indian Ocean. World peace, supposedly to be garnered through "gentle commerce," had failed to materialize. Still, Smith's legacy was the hope that commercial society could aspire to be something moral and good in the future, an aspiration that is still central to so much economic thought today. This new secular ideal of the market would have a powerful influence on Victorian Britain. For a country that was to dominate trade, industry, and innovation for around eighty years, enjoying a competitive advantage above all others, the free market conviction that wealth was latent and there for the taking was very appealing.

The British masters of the world would, incredibly, transform Smith into a supporter of manufacturing and companies. Most of all, they would apply free market thought to their age of industrial and imperial might. The problem was that free market thought, partially by Smith's design, was a philosophy for the economic victors and the "viceregents upon earth." Thus, even those thinkers who fully embraced free markets still looked for a way to make their philosophy work for those to whom wealth had not come naturally.

CHAPTER 14

FREE MARKET EMPIRE

> How can protection, think you, add to the wealth of
> a country? Can you by legislation add one farthing to
> the wealth of the country? You may, by legislation, in
> one evening, destroy the fruits and accumulation of a
> century of labour; but I defy you to show me how, by
> the legislation of this House, you can add one farthing
> to the wealth of the country. That springs from the in-
> dustry and intelligence; you cannot do better than leave
> it to its own instincts.
>
> —RICHARD COBDEN, SPEECH TO THE
> HOUSE OF COMMONS, 1846

DURING THE NINETEENTH century, free market thought un-
derwent a fundamental change. The most influential part of the
movement centered on Britain and its industry. Free market theorists believed that if the government removed tariffs and regulations on manufacturing, the nation would thrive. This approach
would raise living standards and create a market equilibrium based
in manufacturing and consumerism. But the economic theorists of

the industrial age faced an age-old problem: the state still played an important role in maintaining market equilibrium.

HEIRS TO ADAM Smith, the most important market thinkers of the late eighteenth and early nineteenth centuries were Jeremy Bentham, Thomas Malthus, and David Ricardo. All three wrestled with the concept of a self-perpetuating, wealth-creating market, building on Smith's visions of labor and value while at the same time seeking to amend and even contest many of Smith's views. They, too, sought to design their own versions of Smith's "magnificent dynamics" of morals and economics. But the political mood had shifted, and Smith's immediate philosophical followers would struggle to maintain his optimism about happy outcomes for the market.[1]

A British jurist, reformer, and founder of utilitarian philosophy, Bentham was perhaps the most sanguine of Smith's heirs, proposing that human sentiments drove economic activity to produce happiness for the greatest number of people. Bentham adopted Greek Epicurean philosophy's belief that the pursuit of happiness is moral and good. According to Bentham's notion of "felicific calculus," humans choose their actions depending on the balance of pleasure and pain they produce. Bentham's *Principles of Morals and Legislation* (1781) explained how sensations of pleasure and pain determine what is most useful for society. In Bentham's ideal world, the richer one became, the less pleasure incremental wealth produced, giving more weight to the pleasures of higher intellectual achievement and social progress. According to his calculus, the diminishing pleasure of acquisition would act as a natural curb on greed, leading wealth creators to seek the moral rewards of investing back in the community.[2]

Bentham believed that individual desire and freedoms would drive the economy and lead to economic and social progress. He was an early advocate of individual freedom, defending women's rights, homosexual liberties, and sexual nonconformity. However, his felicific calculus sometimes required government tinkering to keep the economy functioning smoothly. Bentham was convinced that when markets driven through pleasure and pain failed to produce good outcomes, the government had to intervene. The government, for example, should foster social well-being and happiness by reforming prisons, improving public schools, and prohibiting emigration. It should also sponsor the immigration of productive workers, expand cities as needed, and ensure the provision of health services.[3]

Bentham's relatively optimistic vision of markets was not shared by all. With the descent of the French Revolution into violence and the ensuing global Napoleonic Wars, some economic thinkers expressed pessimism about the capacity of a free market to produce happy outcomes. In opposition to the physiocrats and Smith, the dour but brilliant Cambridge University don Thomas Malthus believed in market forces while at the same time warning of their dangers. An Anglican cleric who viewed humankind as flawed by Original Sin, Malthus rejected the Enlightenment faith in a natural system of human progress, as well as the virtue of individual choice. Although he agreed with other economists that human desire moved the market system, he did not see this as producing progress. For Malthus, lust drove the market, and it would destroy the world. Rather than seeing working men as potentially decent, as Smith did, he saw them as a terrifying mass of hungry, hopeless beings, driven only by the animal compulsion of sexual desire. His early writings adopted Smith's idea of a self-perpetuating system but gave it a new, more menacing spin: Humans were primitives and sinners, whose innate lust pushed them to unsustainably procreate. Overpopulation would eventually consume the riches of the earth, and humans would fall out of nature's equilibrium and wipe themselves out.

Malthus's theory of overpopulation was based on the old physiocratic and recent Smithian concept that all wealth was agricultural and that markets were driven by feelings, but he rejected their idea that wealth could grow to create permanent human opulence and benevolence. Instead, Malthus believed increased wealth would trigger an exponential population boom, and that the "ratio of increase" would quickly outpace the capacity of the earth to provide subsistence. In *The Wealth of Nations*, Smith had made a similar claim, saying that "every species of animals naturally multiplies in proportion to the means of their subsistence." While Smith believed that expanding wealth brought better living conditions for poor workers—such as better clothes and food—he, too, feared their reproduction rates. Smith the academic bachelor proclaimed that "a half-starved Highland woman frequently bears more than twenty children, while a pampered fine lady is often incapable of bearing any."[4]

Smith, of course, had no expertise in reproductive questions, and Malthus knew little of the productive possibilities of a larger population in an industrial economy. Malthus nonetheless echoed Smith's fears about the reproductive capacities of the poor, contending that poor laws and charity had done nothing to "alleviate a little the intensity of individual misfortune." Foreseeing the horrors of Victorian working-class misery, but completely ignoring the possibilities of innovation and industry to improve living standards, Malthus predicted that large, poor, urban populations would be wracked by disease and suffering. Deadly epidemics would lead to famine, "the last, the most dreadful resource of nature," and the final grim market turn that alone could cull the population and control it. Like Galiani, the Italian critic of the physiocrats,

Malthus warned that nature was cruel. He criticized Smith's belief in human goodness and the "perfectibility of man," countering that Christian faith alone could bring hope of salvation in a cruel and uncertain world. In later life he came to believe that earthly regulations might play a useful role in checking human impulses, and that government-mandated population limits could increase economic and social stability.[5]

The most influential of Smith's early followers, David Ricardo, echoed his predecessor's belief in a self-regulating natural market system. Like Smith, he also believed that the base of all wealth was agricultural. While free market theorists ranged from Catholics and Protestants to deists and atheists, Ricardo was the first notable free-market economist of Jewish descent. However, he renounced Judaism and, in 1793, at the age of twenty-one, married a Quaker and converted to Unitarian Christian deism. This brought him one step closer to the beliefs of Smith. He took an early interest in free market thought and corresponded with both Bentham and Malthus. Ricardo made his wealth by designing a fraudulent scheme to manipulate the sovereign bond market. In 1815, upon receiving reliable information that Napoleon was losing his final war of the Hundred Days, Ricardo spread rumors of the opposite—that Napoleon was actually winning—spurring many British debt holders to sell their bonds. When the debt market collapsed, he bought up all the bonds and, with Britain's eventual victory over Napoleon, he made a fortune off the hapless investors who had reacted to his false news.

Once he became rich, he established himself as a country gentleman and continued writing economic philosophy with an eye to making agriculture more productive. He became the owner of Gatcombe Park, high sheriff of Gloucestershire, and a member of Parliament. From his landed and titled perch, he paradoxically battled against landed interests to bring down agricultural prices for what he thought would be the greatest good of the greatest number.

Ricardo shaped and defended Smith's legacy at the beginning of the nineteenth century, also insisting that wealth came from agriculture. Unlike Smith, however, he thought wealth was limited. In *On the Principles of Political Economy and Taxation* (1809), he developed his Law of Rent, based on the idea that the soil's fertility determines the value of labor. Demand played no role in setting prices and salaries, which rose and fell according to the land's productive capacities. Influenced by Malthus, Ricardo developed his Iron Law of Wages, by which the income of the poor always dropped to the lowest sustainable level. Once farmworkers were paid, they would have more children and only become poorer, undoing any wage increases. The only way to boost salaries was to free the international grain markets to create competition, so that British landowners would invest in their farms and boost productivity, wages, and, possibly, living standards. However, Ricardo warned that if landowners paid high wages to workers from their fixed sum of capital, they would not have the money to reinvest in their farms, which would again depress wages.[6]

If Ricardo was pessimistic about wages, he was optimistic that for economically dominant Britain, free international trade would lower prices, create more commerce, and raise living standards. Given Britain's dominant position in the world economy, Ricardo was right: the country would win in an open economic contest. He also promoted the old idea of comparative advantage, a version of the division of labor by which each country would produce and sell what the other did not, resulting in national efficiencies, widened markets, and, possibly, improved living conditions. In Ricardo's view, free global trade made the world richer for everyone who was allowed to benefit from it.[7]

Both Smith and Ricardo pointed to British-Portuguese trade and the Methuen Treaty of 1703 as an example where both countries benefited from free trade agreements, regardless of their different economic capacities. Smith argued that even if trade favored one nation above the other, it would still spur latent wealth creation as a result of increased competition. In Smith's and Ricardo's thought, completely opening markets between the two countries helped the Portuguese wine industry (owned in great part by British port makers) and the British cloth industry, as well as the two countries' economies in general. Their claim was more true in theory than in fact, however. Flooded by cheaper and higher-quality British goods, Portugal's economy floundered, and it was never able to develop its own industries to the point where they could compete with Britain. It is now generally accepted as obvious that this asymmetrical bargain granted a competitive advantage to Britain while gravely undermining Portuguese industrial development. In any case, Ricardo designed his economic theories for Britain and its continuing economic dominance.[8]

By the early nineteenth century, Britain was unquestionably the workshop of the world—the leading industrial and colonial nation. It also was a leading producer of grain. Ricardo's great project as a parliamentarian was pro–free trade. He supported abolition of the Corn Laws, the protectionist grain tariffs that had been implemented in 1815 at the end of the Napoleonic Wars to shield British landowners from cheaper foreign grain. Drawing on Smith's Newtonian belief in the self-regulating nature of free trade, Ricardo argued that landowners simply used the tariffs to create national monopolies on grain and push up its price. Although he did not live to see it, the repeal of the country's Corn Laws in 1846, under pressure from the laissez-faire advocates of the Anti–Corn Law League led by Richard Cobden, an industrialist and member of Parliament from the manufacturing hub of Manchester, represented the beginning of what historians have called Britain's era as a "free trade nation."[9]

The end of the Corn Laws was not only the beginning of liberal Britain; it also marked the beginning of free-market political mythologies. Under the banner of universally applicable market laws, free trade boosters sacrificed Britain's agricultural elite—which Smith had so cherished—to vested manufacturing interests, who required cheaper foreign grain in order to keep down bread prices for workers. The liberal pro-manufacturing Whig Party built a successful economic narrative around free market thought and its aspirational qualities. Whig politicians lauded the success of the Anti–Corn Law League as a victory of the common man over corruption and aristocracy. It also, however, represented the rise of the Victorian social order and its wealth.[10]

Yet even with world market dominance, Britain still faced intractable problems of poverty and wealth inequality. As Malthus had warned, the market, left to its own devices, would not solve them. The economic and political philosopher John Stuart Mill saw that free trade was a double-edged sword, celebrating its liberalism while recognizing its failure to deliver higher living standards for the poor. In many ways, Mill is the thinker who best represents the internal contradictions of early nineteenth-century free-market thought—a belief in the productive capacities of free markets balanced by acknowledgment of the state's role in pursuing social reforms to create a more just economic system.

Born in 1806, Mill was raised by his father—a follower of Bentham's utilitarian teachings—to be a political economist. In another great irony of economic history, Mill, the great liberal thinker, worked for the state monopoly East India Company until it was privatized and he was fired, and he never stopped defending either the company or imperialism. Mill followed Smith in his belief that a free market would produce wealth and societal progress. He imagined international trade working as a self-regulating system, driving British prices down and increasing production, capital wealth, and development. This system would produce a "surplus" of goods, which, along with low prices on imported products, would improve social and economic conditions. "Laissez faire," Mill wrote, should be the "general practice"; to depart from it was "a certain evil."[11]

However, Mill added a caveat to Smith's system of progress and Ricardo's confidence in the market. Eschewing his predecessors' belief in a deist, wealth-creating "Superintendent of the Universe," Mill placed his faith instead in a democratic version of Ciceronian and Lockean politics. The best government was not to be found in oligarchy, but in common citizens, who, dutifully educated, would rise to be moral legislators. Mill accepted Malthus's claim that while the economy could work mechanically, it would eventually reach natural limits, and not all would prosper by it. And while Mill believed that both workers and investing capitalists created value together, he presaged industrial diminishing marginal utility, insisting that the increasing quantity of manufactured goods would drive down prices and average working wages, leading, as Malthus had predicted, to lower "rewards of labor."[12]

Like Smith, Mill naively thought there was a market cap, where the rich accumulated enough money to satisfy themselves. Once a high enough standard of living had been met for the upper classes, they would eschew moneymaking and naturally move toward leisure and the pursuit of learning. The result would be a "stationary state" of the economy capable of producing a regular and constant stream of wealth. At this point, the state would have to implement "socialist" reforms to help the poor and the "working men" who were stuck in a Malthusian wage trap.[13]

Mill also saw a competition between the owners of capital and the workers and their trade unions as bettering society. Ideally, the state would help workers obtain property, which would allow them to exit poverty and enter into a moral, utilitarian state of ownership and competition. Mill mixed Locke's faith in property, Smith's deist optimism, Bentham's utilitarianism, and Malthus's Augustinian pessimism to arrive at the doorstep of social democracy.[14]

Mill wrote his *Chapters on Socialism* in 1869, ten years after the publication of Charles Darwin's *The Origin of Species* (1859). Darwin thought about biology through the lens of commerce, and his theory of evolution would leave a profound mark on free market thought. According to his theory, evolution looked like a sort of positive, amoral version of Smith's idealistic progress mixed with Malthus's harsh vision of nature as a culler of the weak. While he cited the "ever memorable" work of Malthus in *The Descent of Man, and Selection in Relation to Sex* (1871), Darwin broke with Malthus's Christian morality. No longer framed by the biblical creation story of the Old Testament, Darwin's nature worked only according to its own brutal logic. There was no high-minded Ciceronian or Christian ethic in natural selection, in which only the fittest survived and reproduced.[15]

Darwin's theory of natural selection informed the philosophy of Karl Marx, his contemporary, the German journalist and revolutionary inventor of communist economics. Marx studied the "classical economics" of Smith and Ricardo and, although he rejected much of Smith, he believed part of his theory of rent to be theoretically correct. Though an atheist, Marx agreed with Smith that economics could be a self-perpetuating system. But Marx followed Malthus in his belief that the market moved toward negative ends. Smith had formulated his theories about the division of labor and capital in a historical vacuum, Marx charged, and Smith's claim that a benevolent nature god drove human progress and the economy was little more than "a childish misunderstanding." Where Smith saw capital as a "natural" element existing in nature, and even Mill had understood the poverty of the laboring classes as inherent in market mechanics, Marx saw all of these economic phenomena as the historical product of unequal social power. In Marx's vision, the owners of capital used tools such as stock, the division of labor, and machinery to steal the surplus labor of the working class. Market mechanisms did not create wealth and were, quite simply, a system devised by the property-owning classes to cheat the proletariat. Against such a power differential, Mill's theories of social reform would be useless, Marx thought. Only a proletarian revolution could change the course of the market and history.[16]

Marx was not the only critic of capitalism and free markets. Foreign detractors emerged who saw Britain's free market policies as an attempt to further its competitive advantage and to destroy international competition. The fastest-growing nations of the late nineteenth century—the United States, Prussia, and Japan—rejected totalizing free-market approaches, instead following seventeenth-century English and Colbertist development strategies. America's first secretary of the treasury, Alexander Hamilton, instituted economic policies that closely resembled Colbert's model of market-building; the United States would follow this course for over a century, resisting laissez-faire economics until the 1930s. The new commercial republic embraced the opposite of Ricardian comparative advantage and free trade. An economy built on protectionism, increasing national returns, and a reliance on immigration, slavery, and state-made improvements, the United States turned Britain's laissez-faire dogmas upside down.[17]

Hamilton admired Colbert's success in turning rural France into an industrial powerhouse with centralized taxation, uniform weights and measures, and state-subsidized communication routes. France had found prosperity, and moved from agriculture to manufacturing, he wrote, because of the "abilities and indefatigable endeavors of the great COLBERT." The daring and even reckless Hamilton was a skilled government manager, and he possessed a clear economic vision for the young country. He believed that if America opened its markets to ultra-developed Great Britain and France, it would be inundated by cheap goods, and its manufacturing base would collapse. Laissez-faire was out of the question, as America's massive debts and weak navy put it in a fragile position. Rather, the new state would have to shepherd the development of its relatively primitive economy just as the English had done in the early seventeenth century.[18]

Hamilton was convinced that republics had to be built by strong governments. He insisted that the state be run by a series of powerful ministers, "as those in France," who—as he would later insist, in the *Federalist Papers* no. 35—were experts in their respective fields, such as finance. In his 1791 "Report to the Congress on the Subject of Manufactures," Hamilton insisted that the government of a nation in its infancy had to focus on developing industry over agriculture. While necessary for life, agriculture was not the basis of wealth creation as the physiocrats, Hume, and Smith had claimed. Indeed, Hamilton felt strongly that this idea had to be publicly challenged, and made clear that it was the industrial "cotton mill," not farming, that had been responsible for Britain's "immense progress."[19]

Following Colbert, Hamilton believed that the government would have to protect the country's markets and attract talent via immigration to build its infant industries. The government would also have to provide "inducements" for investment. A believer in self-sufficiency, Hamilton concluded that as a result of its "extreme embarrassment" in "supplying itself" during the Revolutionary War, America had to "encourage manufactures" before it could open its markets.

The United States followed this infant industry development model under the aegis of Henry Clay, the powerful senator and secretary of state whose "American System" promoted tariffs, a national commerce bank, and subsidies for industry. Attacking free trade theory as "British colonialism," Clay argued that in protecting itself from Britain, the early republic would prosper. America's exports grew from $20 million in 1790 to $108 million in 1807, and the nation continued moving toward a positive trade balance until 1870.[20]

The German economist Friedrich List would also take inspiration from Hamilton and Clay's American System. Moving to Pennsylvania in 1825, he was inspired by America's internal free-trade zone, protected by exterior tariffs, to advocate the creation of a German *Zollverein*, a coalition of German states that incorporated aspects of economic union. In his *National System of Political Economy* (1827), List explained how trade treaties were needed between German states to support German domestic industries. Tariffs would protect them from outside competition so that they could develop and become internationally competitive. List's ideas were also popular in France. They reflected the sentiment that internal free trade worked and could be facilitated by internal customs unions, and that strategic protectionism could spur development in the face of the British industrial juggernaut.

American defenders of free trade were most often agrarian slaveholders, such as the seventh vice president of the United States, John Calhoun, who sought easier ways to export cotton. But cotton and slavery were not the future. Like Hamilton, List promoted industry over agriculture, denouncing slavery as "a public calamity" that signaled the weakness of a country. List was certain that it was only an industrial development strategy, not brutal agrarian free trade, that could generate wealth. Germany eventually did adopt List's national development model with its traditional Colbertist approach, and in the last decades of the nineteenth century, both the United States and Germany would overtake Britain's economy. Then as now, careful market-building was a successful response to the laissez-faire policies of a dominant competitor nation.

Such criticisms of and countermodels to free trade did not dampen the enthusiasm of British nineteenth-century liberal economic thinkers, however. With its economy and empire riding high on its competitive advantage, Britain and its free market thinkers felt themselves immune to competition. Richard Cobden, founder of the Anti–Corn Law League, led the Manchester School of free trade doctrine. However, Cobden transformed the idea of free trade by embracing industry and the relationship between manufacturing wealth and market freedoms. The old agrarian argument of free trade as holding a mirror up to nature was still important, but free trade supporters had to pick an economic winner, and in industrial Britain, that was obviously manufacturing.[21]

Cobden also took up an old free-market theme in supporting the view that free trade was the key to ending war. A passionate pacifist, abolitionist, and believer in women's rights, as well as a critic of the cost of imperialism (he wanted funds spent at home), Cobden followed Smith in the conviction that freeing trade would bring peace and benefit workers and humanity in general. In an 1843 speech in Covent Garden, he framed the repeal of grain tariffs as an almost religious crusade: "We believe commercial freedom will develop intellectual and moral freedom," he exclaimed, "teaching the different classes their dependence on each other, uniting nations in bonds of brotherhood." Cobden attacked slavery as immoral and demanded a boycott of Brazilian sugar. In 1849, he went one step further, claiming that free trade would bring peace among nations and relieve the colonies of the need for defense; along with adopting free trade laws, Cobden urged countries to disarm. It is notable that Cobden's pacifist vision did not always extend to colonialized peoples. He believed that colonialism should be maintained peacefully and inexpensively, out of a sense of mutual benefit. However, he also believed that colonialists should retain policing powers, in order to put down local "barbarous tribes" when necessary.[22]

Nonetheless, in Cobden's context, his liberalism was radical. For him, free trade meant pacifism, political liberty, a certain degree of tolerance, and social progress. It also meant freedom of the press, and that almost unthinkable thing: friendship with France. Insisting that it was necessary to "believe there is something of honor and honesty in other countries," he was certain that joining economies through free trade would lead to world peace. He convinced the British government and the French emperor Napoleon III to agree to the historic Cobden-Chevalier Treaty of 1860, which in many ways realized Colbert's dream of free trade and brought peace between the two ancient foes. With duties on manufactured goods reduced to 30 percent, British exports to France doubled, and French wine exports doubled in turn. The quest for this elusive peace had been the engine behind free market thought for over two centuries. Alas, it was only to last thirty-two years. Sensing that British competition was undermining French industry and manufacturing jobs, France introduced the Méline Tariff on British goods in 1892 to staunch perceived losses. Nonetheless, the Cobden-Chevalier Treaty sparked a new European network of liberal trade treaties, moving toward the eventual creation of the more advanced free-trade zone that now exists within the European Union.[23]

In Britain, however, belief in free trade and empire carried the day. British economic thinkers began to mix free market economic theory with religion, drawing on a spirit of religious revival to create a powerful and unique national movement. Smith's old beliefs in a deist nature god were replaced by evangelical Christianity. Rather than focusing on Stoic morals, British evangelicals were convinced that, along with faith and free trade, "economy, frugality, professionalism, and financial rectitude" could unleash God's natural energy to improve society.[24]

The sunny optimism of this evangelical free-market movement contrasted poorly with the realities of working life in Victorian Britain. Living standards in England had improved with industrialization, but, as the novelist and social reformer Charles Dickens observed, this hardly meant that the British economy was free and fair, or that personal drive was all that was required in order to better one's economic situation. Industrial misery, child labor, low wages, poor living conditions, trade union activity, and working-class rage fueled the rise of socialism and communism. The Victorian age, decidedly, did not live up to Smith's or Cobden's moral standards. The free trade debate thus was not only a matter of discussion among economists and politicians but also came under attack from trade unionists, Chartist workingmen's associations, and anti-industrial Luddites. The plight of the working class was cause for some pessimism as well among certain British liberals, including the influential journalist and editor of *The Economist*, Walter Bagehot. Social and economic discontent with laissez-faire was an impetus behind the founding of the British Labour Party in 1900.

In spite of the shortcomings of free market policies, however, British free-market thinkers continued to embrace political and economic liberalism's focus on low taxes, limited government, self-help, and individual freedoms. The Christian Unitarian economist

William Stanley Jevons allowed neither the successes of Colbertist America, Germany, and Japan nor the suffering of the working classes to dampen his faith in free market orthodoxy. Jevons followed the scientific approach of his time, insisting that mathematics be used for economic analysis. In his *Political Economy* (1871), he echoed Bentham in theorizing that all human actions came from the "springs" of "pleasure and pain," but that "quantitative methods" would be necessary to understand and collate "individual data." There was no high-minded Ciceronian moral philosophy here. Jevons maintained that this data-driven economics was like a hard natural science and compared it to geology. He insisted that economics was simple and straightforward: it required not literary skills of interpretation, like those of Ricardo and Mill, but efficient mathematical studies and graphs—for example, the quantification of "wealth" and "human utility."[25]

Jevons used quantitative methods to attack the labor value approach of Smith and Ricardo. He believed that a thing's "value depends entirely upon utility," not on how much it was worth in farm labor. Jevons took Bentham's pleasure principle and turned it into a consumer utility principle. In his eyes, happiness was maximized by buying something at the lowest possible price with the greatest possible ease. This train of logic led him to develop his marginal utility theory. If an object was cheap, people would want it, because it was a good deal. But once an object reached its real market value, fewer would buy it, because the margin of the deal would have suddenly grown smaller. If an object went above its market price, the margin changed again, and the pleasure and utility of buying the object started to disappear. According to Jevons, the relationships among desire, utility, availability, and quantity all drove prices. All this he worked out according to mathematical principles, putting to rest the labor value theory and helping to revolutionize economics.[26]

Although there was a Darwinist element to Jevons's utilitarian theories, he was also a believer in a reformist society. He supported trade unions, for example, in the belief that they could help workers express their needs by negotiating with owners to improve working conditions, wages, and even the efficiency of work and technology. He saw industrial cooperation as the key to a wealthy and moral economy, noting that it would "remedy" the "evils" of inequality by bringing "labor and capital into harmony with each other." More optimistic than Malthus and Mill, Jevons was convinced that industrial and labor cooperation would free capitalists to pay a fair wage, and that workers would then gain "rewards" for their excellence. Where Smith had advanced a role for the "impartial spectator," Jevons envisioned official "conciliators" between capitalists and the working classes, who would help the parties understand their shared interests and recognize how they could both benefit from "voluntary bargains." Rather than a pure reflection of the market, he thought negotiation would help capitalists calculate how to best share profits with workers. Needless to say, Jevons's model enjoyed limited success in Victorian Britain, where working-class living conditions festered. Many began to believe that only the new radical political movements could adequately represent the interests of the working class.[27]

Jevons's faith in rational and sustainable management extended to the husbanding of natural goods such as coal, which he predicted would be exhausted by economic growth and demand.[28] His answer to Malthusian overconsumption and limits to growth was good management and a firm belief in the human capacity to cooperate around such essential issues as fair wages, self-regulation, and alternative forms of energy. Thus, Jevons thought that industry and society would have to constantly adapt by, for example, finding new power sources. He did not believe in a market free-for-all, but rather in utilitarian cooperation. Yet Jevons did not yet have a sophisticated understanding of the complexity of government and the political stakes in energy politics. Then as now, the market would never have a fully free hand over energy. The European powers and the United States were beginning their struggle over coal and oil fields, and governments were still helping companies fight over natural resources in far-flung locations, from Alsace-Lorraine—the rich coal territory contested by France and Germany in three wars—to the great oil fields of Baku, Azerbaijan, in the former Russian Empire.[29]

IT SEEMS REMARKABLE that at the very moment the great protectionist economic powers of the United States, Germany, and Japan were catching up with Britain in growth, Cambridge University philosopher Alfred Marshall continued to wave the flag for doctrinaire free trade. It was as if Cambridge were cut off from the rest of the world. Marshall's *Principles of Economics* (1890) unseated Mill's *Principles of Political Economy* as the preeminent British economics textbook, and Marshall became the leading economic thinker at Cambridge. He developed concepts by Jevons, such as marginal utility, and came up with new concepts, such as price elasticity, the relation of demand to pricing, and partial equilibrium theory, that would be important in later thinking. By examining the supply-and-demand flow of a single market—for example, of wool—he provided fine-grained analyses of the workings of particular areas of the economy, rather than a general view of the economy as a whole. Marshall saw supply and demand operating like a machine that created a "continuous chain" of economic activity, and said it was this machine that determined prices. The machine could bring "equilibrium" to the market so that it would function on its own, creating constant returns.[30]

Like Smith, Marshall was a professor of moral philosophy. While his focus was on aggregate quantities and marginal utility value, he still sought economic "laws" in nature, which he believed made economics resemble the natural sciences, such as astronomy. Thus Marshall looked to understand Smith's universal driving economic system from analogies with astronomy and physics. He wanted the "individual student" of economics to be able to "speak with the authority of his science." For Marshall, wealth creation and economic activity had to be understood as a complex mixture of industrial production price, quantity, efficiency, and "gradations of demand" and competition that worked in tandem to create growth.[31]

Though he was perplexed by persistent poverty, Marshall believed that the market alone would solve economic problems, and that eventually, wages would rise and living standards improve. What he could not see was that his great economic machine was about to break down. He died in 1924, five years before the Wall Street crash of 1929 and the onset of the Great Depression. Marshall kept finding new market mechanisms, and never thought the market would collapse. Some twentieth-century free-market thinkers would follow him—Captain Ahab–like in their fixation on the market, clinging more and more to the orthodoxy that it worked on its own and that government had almost no place in economic affairs.

CHAPTER 15

THE END OF VIRTUE

Liberalism and Libertarianism

The man of system, on the contrary, is apt to be very
wise in his own conceit; and is often so enamored with
the supposed beauty of his own ideal plan of government, that he cannot suffer the smallest deviation from
any part of it.

—ADAM SMITH, *THE THEORY OF MORAL
SENTIMENTS*, 1759

IF THE NINETEENTH century saw free market thought shift to
embrace industrial economies, along with British imperial aspirations, the twentieth century would give classical economics an even
broader political role on the world stage. With the rise of the Soviet Union and Communist China, free market thinkers saw themselves as defenders of individual liberties against totalitarian states.
Economists were not just academics; they were also crusading Cold
War warriors with little patience for nuance or for contradictions
in their own thought. Like politics, economics became an either/or

237

battle between good free-market nations and what President Ronald Reagan called state-run, socialist "evil empires."

To read twentieth-century free-market thinkers, from Friedrich Hayek to Milton Friedman, with the hindsight of history is partly to credit them. They constituted a powerful, conservative force that foresaw the authoritarian and totalitarian dangers—on the left and the right—that lay ahead for Europe and even the United States. And yet, along with the great moral achievements and economic insights of free market thinkers came a very particular form of paranoia, ideological obsession, and myopia. Gone was Adam Smith's vision of progress through benevolent moral discipline, education, radical science, and a worship of agriculture. Twentieth-century orthodox free-market economists believed that pure individual desire and agency were the catalyst for all societal and economic good. In their eyes, any system that deviated from this view became suspect. It was not so much an academic position as an article of faith.

IN 1905, WILLIAM Cunningham, Alfred Marshall's colleague at Cambridge, published an indictment of orthodox free-market thought titled *The Rise and Decline of the Free Trade Movement*. In this attack on British economic orthodoxy, Cunningham declared that the tradition begun by Turgot and Smith, in which "economics treats society as a mechanism," gives "valuable truth, so far as it goes; but it is never the whole truth." Cunningham's point was that if economics wanted to be treated like a science, it would have to admit that much human economic activity does not work like a mechanism. Using Darwinian language, he said that society was instead an "organism with powers of self-adaptation to its environment." As such, markets were only a partial machine that often broke down. To keep the machine going, it would have to be "tested over and over again," and even then, the great mechanical truths of free market thought might not work.[1]

Cunningham believed that economics made for "dreary reading" and that one could get through it by replacing it with neat principles, such as supply and demand. He saw the appeal of "the principle of Free Trade," by which there were no restrictions on the exchange of goods and services, and by which consumers were able to freely choose products to seek comfort and efficiency. With eloquent sarcasm, Cunningham claimed that he sympathized "entirely and heartily with the objects which the Free Trade advocate assumes," but if he went to New York and asked an American, who lived in a wealthy, protectionist country, one would find a very different attitude about free trade doctrine.[2]

Britain in 1900 was still a free trade nation, where the idea was almost a cult: the consumer was king, and the free trade crusader Richard Cobden was treated like a national hero, with statues and monuments in his honor. But Cunningham nonetheless declared the ideology bankrupt. From deep within the dank and cosseted enclaves of the Cambridge colleges, a shoot of criticism grew. Cunningham warned that the "Colbertist" reforms of Europe and the fledgling United States had made them great rivals to Britain. He noted that Friedrich List's development model had worked in those places, and that it was the only proven approach by which countries could reach an advanced state capable of free trade. Even more, Cobden's hopes of peace and disarmament had never materialized. Cunningham remarked prophetically that militarism had only grown in Europe and the United States, and as the prime imperial power, England remained reliant on its own naval and military repressive might. Imperial competition had continued to spark colonial conflict, such as the Boer War in South Africa in 1899.[3]

This "great divide" between Britain and the other industrial powers of the world, Cunningham believed, was a danger for both peace and Britain's economy. Free traders, he warned with some disdain, had become like "Rabbinical commentators," going over the Old Testament again and again in search of further truths to support their orthodoxy. Free trade was no longer a practical doctrine but had become an old and binding religion of consumerism, dooming Britain to follow "a strict rule from which there is no departure."[4]

England was about to plateau economically, while Germany, the United States, and Japan were experiencing exponential economic growth in spite of rejecting some of the central precepts of free trade. The industrial expansion and burgeoning populations of Germany and the United States, Cunningham believed, afforded them greater and more efficient potential for growth. England, on the contrary, faced a possible decline in population and looming fuel shortages. Echoing Smith, Cunningham warned that while there had been "a time when the principle of laissez faire" enabled "enterprising" men to build in the interest of the nation, it had now "become a mere subterfuge" under which greed and "indifference" to the common good "cloaked themselves." The internal market of the British Empire had created a "jealousy" of imperial trade among other nations that coveted the riches of the British Empire; worse, Cunningham charged, the imperial free-trade policies of Cobden and the "Manchester Men" had in fact caused the world to arm against Britain. Current laissez-faire principles had become "decadent lassitude," and the British disadvantages could be "fatal" to the nation and empire if policies based on them were continued.[5]

Cunningham used Adam Smith to make his indictment of the British free-trade empire. Smith, he said, would never have been so brittle and uncritical in his thought. And his economic philosophy was far more open to the role of government than that of his ultra-orthodox heirs. Claiming that the "speculations" of Cobden and Jevons had not brought the desired effects, Cunningham felt it was necessary to "look back to Kirkaldy" in order to understand the way forward. Cunningham rightfully explained that Smith had understood that the path to free trade and economic growth was through state involvement in development as enshrined in the Navigation Act of 1651. Cunningham underlined that Smith clearly said it was sometimes necessary to give "temporary monopolies" to spur industry and development. He reminded his readers that Smith had warned against the selfish motives of businessmen and traders who sold out national interests. And he noted that in *The Theory of Moral Sentiments*, Smith had recommended following the teachings of Cicero and Plato, so that legislators might learn from the example of other countries.[6]

Much like Mill, Cunningham cited Smith in seeing the "well-being of the community as overriding individual interests." If individual prosperity did not bring national prosperity for citizens in general, then the system wasn't working and would have to adapt and change. Cunningham believed that nineteenth-century free-market thinkers had ignored Smith's nuances and warnings. Thus, he read Smith as dispensing guidance to legislators, not as laying down economic precepts "as the materials of a sort of political mechanics." Cunningham suggested that Smith was not trying to create a vision of a self-regulating system, and that he would have been pragmatic enough to recognize that protectionist rules were necessary in the great Machiavellian game of imperial power in 1905.[7]

Cunningham could not have predicted what Smith would have done more than a century after his death. But he was right in pointing out that Smith had rejected the closed systems and doctrines that characterized the evangelical, triumphalist new free-market thought. Cunningham's depiction of Britain's "one-sided" free trade in an imperial system was apt in 1905. Germany and Japan had armed and set their sights on the British Empire. In 1898 and 1900, Germany had enacted the first in a series of Fleet Acts to build a German navy to counter British imperial might. In the 1904–1905 Russo-Japanese War, the modern Japanese fleet had handily destroyed its antiquated Russian counterpart, marking an epochal shift in military technology capable of a new level of "total war." Cunningham's fears were well-founded. World War I loomed, and the collapse of the British Empire and of British commercial supremacy had begun.

The modern age of warfare heralded a grave setback for Cobdenite free-market evangelism and pacifism. Cunningham's vision of Smith as a moral and social pragmatist, and a believer in developmental protectionism, is one of many legitimate ways to interpret Adam Smith. It is just not the most typical one. In any case, the tide had turned for the kind of faith that even Alfred Marshall had in free trade. World War I temporarily closed the hopes that an international self-regulating economic system would bring peace.

ALFRED MARSHALL'S OWN students began an interwar assault on the concept of a totally self-regulating market system. The Cambridge economist John Maynard Keynes supported free markets—in the 1920s, he warned of a battle between communism and individualistic laissez-faire, which laissez-faire had to win. But Keynes felt that there were holes in free market theory, and for it to survive and fight communism, it needed to recognize its weaknesses. Keynes differentiated himself from his mentor Marshall by looking for ways to protect the free market, which he believed the market itself, if left alone, could not do. His fundamental economic discovery, presented in his *General Theory of Employment, Interest, and Money* (1936), was that wages were not regulated naturally through market mechanisms. In the midst of the Great Depression, Keynes declared that it was only through "bargains" between government, companies, and labor that the market would create full employment. What the Great Depression showed was that if spending in the economy—or "aggregate demand"—dropped precipitously, as it had following the stock market crash of 1929 and the ensuing Depression, then employment would drop, too, leading to a vicious cycle of decreasing aggregate demand. Even worse, marginal theories of value could turn against the market and devour it. If the marginal efficiency of capital (the return on an investment greater than interest, so that the investment is profitable over time with inflation) cannot be earned, then the market gives no incentive to invest, further undermining hopes for growth and employment. Consumers by themselves could not fully support aggregate demand, as President Herbert Hoover tragically found out when his market approach to the Depression only made it worse.[8]

This meant that an economic crisis could feed itself, creating more job and wealth loss, unless the government aided aggregate demand through spending and promoting liquidity in the markets. In a case like the Great Depression, rich people alone did not have the means to increase spending to a level that would stop the vicious cycle of economic crisis. Only the state had the resources to catalyze the mechanisms of employment and the economy as a whole, through aggregate spending. In short, in a large-scale financial or economic crisis, aggregate demand had to be sparked by the visible hand of government. No invisible market force could do it. The state would have to take "an even greater responsibility for directly organizing investment." Keynes was criticizing free market "classical economics" and Marshall's idea that supply and demand could regulate itself.[9]

Along with Keynes, another of Marshall's famous students, Joan Robinson, would weigh in, showing how all supposedly self-regulating market systems can fail. A Cambridge professor and one of the first leading female economists, Robinson remains an enigma for her support of Chinese Communist Party chairman Mao Zedong during his terrifying and economically catastrophic Cultural Revolution (1966–1976). However misguided, her support of Mao's violent state intervention in society and economics was based on her belief that poor countries could not compete with rich ones economically and needed a shock stimulus. Robinson became a founder of development economics and spurred a new interest in the works of Marx. Development economics sought a path to wealth for countries without large commercial and industrial bases. It had its roots in the so-called mercantilist writings of the seventeenth century and in the policies of Colbert and Alexander Hamilton. In the twentieth century, the theory emerged in relation to economically underdeveloped, or "third world," countries that were unable to make the structural economic changes necessary to modernize and build a competitive commercial and industrial base.

Robinson led the charge on the argument that undeveloped economies could not realistically compete with advanced economies, and that disadvantaged people could not compete against entrenched foreign companies or individuals. Her *Economics of Imperfect Competition* (1933) created the concept of "monopsony," in which a single, powerful buyer controls the pricing of goods that are sold to other buyers, so that market prices are perverted by a sort of buyer's monopoly on wages—such as in a company town where one firm controls all wages and economic life. Monopsony undermined the logic of marginal utility. A buyer's monopoly was not based on market forces, but simply on the decisions or prejudices of a few buyers who could drive down wages to less than their marginal value. Monopsony explained why women were paid less than men, and minorities less than others. If one employer, for example, lowers wages for women simply out of prejudice, then it has helped to set a given market value; other firms can then follow this trend, and women's wages are weakened overall.[10]

In 1956, Robinson published *The Accumulation of Capital*, which continued the Keynesian tradition by showing that in some undeveloped economies, there are only capitalists and workers. The workers make just enough to survive, and the capitalists consume little in a primitive production economy, thus saving their money for foreign goods and undermining the development of a local consumer society that creates wealth. Her model critiqued the applicability of supply-and-demand-driven economic models in poorer nations. Not only would there be little growth, but capital would be pulled toward more developed markets, further weakening internal development.[11]

Once the home of evangelical free-market economics, Cambridge became the center of Keynesianism. If equilibrium-focused free-market thought had lost its ascendancy in Britain, it would find its most powerful new adherents in Austria. It was there that the modern libertarian economic tradition began before moving to the United States, where it would have great influence in the World War II era. The lawyer, journalist, and founder of the Austrian school of economics, Carl Menger, attacked Smith's labor theory of value and replaced it with a theory of marginal utility, which said that economies are driven by mutually beneficial exchanges. His liberal thought was a simplified version of Smith's and Bentham's ideas about human progress materializing through the realization of market-driven human wants. In 1871, the same year that Jevons published his *Political Economy*, Menger published *Principles of Economics*. Menger saw clearly that Smith's and Ricardo's labor theory of value did not work. Harking back to Mandeville's *Fable of the Bees*, he declared that there was only one thing that drove economies: the want of goods. Rather than positing that vices could create virtues, Menger painted a stark and simplistic economic system driven only by the "cause and effect" of "want" that structured social and economic relationships. He did not think that socialists, democratic or otherwise, could plan economic relations. Humans want things, and this demand creates supply in a continual cycle that develops constantly into a more complex commercial and industrial society.[12]

The ennobled economist and scholar Ludwig von Mises, a Jewish free-market thinker who had converted to Christianity in accordance with his economic ideology, was part of this intellectually rich, cosmopolitan Viennese world. Free market thought had moved away from its deist roots and closer to Christian movements. Like Cobden, von Mises opposed government intervention in the economy and condemned war and its horrific subordination of the individual to a nihilistic cause. In 1920, von Mises applied his beliefs with remarkable prescience by attacking national central economic planning in a "socialist commonwealth." He believed that central planning as it existed in the Soviet Union could not predict the value of goods as accurately and efficiently as the natural process of supply and demand. Well before the spectacular economic failures of the Soviet Union became visible, von Mises saw that socialist, centrally planned economies could not effectively choose which industries to favor and argued that only the free market could do this.[13]

Von Mises also believed that money had no intrinsic value outside market exchange. To him, even the quantity of money theory made no sense. Money's value was determined only by its value relative to goods. Therefore, the value of money changed according to the marginal utility of things. This seemingly simple principle would prove to be one of the greatest stumbling blocks for planned communist economies. The Soviet government could declare the value of its currency, or of a loaf of bread, but supply and demand were still decisive in creating values, which even the totalitarian state could not fully control.[14]

The Austrian school was marked by its constant vigilance against authoritarianism. Von Mises saw its specter in communism. He was convinced that the "mercantile" Colbertist statism of List and modern socialist welfare planning would lead to authoritarian government. He failed to note that American democracy was born in and grew through Hamilton's and Clay's "mercantile system." Although von Mises was terrified of socialist autocracy, it was, ironically, the right-wing Nazis who forced his flight to the United States in 1940. Not surprisingly, he came to insist that free markets were not only necessary for wealth creation—they were also necessary for liberal democracy. Yet, in his historical vision, economic liberalism was more important than political liberty. This view would have dangerous repercussions in the modern age.[15]

As the leading proponent of Austrian free-market thought in Britain and the United States, the Austrian economist Friedrich Hayek was influential in creating the new Chicago school of free market thought. He brought with him the deep traumas of World War II and a fanatical anti-statism. Hayek came from a wealthy, academic, agrarian family. He had managed to live through the fin de siècle, both world wars, and the Cold War, and in the 1980s he became the paragon of American neoliberal economic thought. His moral authority was forged in the traumas of dictatorships and war, as well as during the unique period of peace and prosperity that Western and industrialized populations mostly experienced in the postwar period. He lived to see the rise and fall of the Soviet

Union and the beginnings of economic deregulation under Margaret Thatcher and Ronald Reagan, as well as the beginnings of the liberalization of the Chinese economy.

Hayek's 1944 book *The Road to Serfdom* would become the handbook of postwar free-market and libertarian economics. One of the best-selling books of economic philosophy ever, with more than two million copies sold, *The Road to Serfdom* was less a work of economic theory than a declaration of total libertarian faith in individuals, in their leading role in market mechanisms, and in the absolute dangers of any and all government involvement in the economy. With hindsight and a knowledge of the role of government in economic growth since the end of World War II, the book stands out for its total lack of engagement with the realities of the postwar growth period and its fanatical vision of the state as a force of evil.[16]

Where Smith saw the free market as the product of a peaceful and even gentlemanly process of social and economic progress, Hayek saw market freedoms in a combative light, emerging from a struggle between good and evil. One either chose economic liberalism with no government, or one would be enslaved. Hayek's urgency and fear were understandable. In 1944, the war was not yet won. What he saw in Germany and Austria was a terrifying example of what happened when an authoritarian political regime used a state apparatus for civil terror, war, and genocide. But his vision was limited. Hayek must have known something about the leading role that German private industry played in supporting Hitler from the beginning to the end of his nightmare rule. The economics of Nazism fit into the anti-corporate suspicions of Smith. Leading industrialists from the United States and Europe had worked closely with Hitler's powerful German business supporter, Fritz Thyssen. In any case, Hayek chose to forget that Hitler could neither have taken nor held power without the concerted support of German capitalists, who saw fascism as an attractive answer to trade unions, communism, and even social democracy.[17]

Hayek began *The Road to Serfdom* ominously by citing David Hume: "It is seldom that liberty of any kind is lost all at once." Hayek showed great humanity in his condemnations of racism and authoritarianism. But he did not share the moderate and open-minded sensibilities of the Scottish philosophers of the eighteenth century, who hoped to build good institutions and were proud to work for the government. Hayek warned that any and all social planning was a form of totalitarianism. Without explaining how private monopolies worked, he associated them not with oligarchic cartels, but with union "syndicalism" and the state. Any corporatist movement, or anything that undermined his pure vision of competition and individualism, was a form of monopoly. According to Hayek's paranoid logic, any collective state goal led to fascism or communism—in wanting to "organize the whole of society and all its resources toward this unitary end," the state ended up denying individuals freedom. He believed that libertarian capitalism was the one competitive force that could counter authoritarianism. Democracy, he said, was simply a means to this economic end.[18]

Hayek had taken Carl Menger's and Ludwig von Mises's suspicions of central government, along with his absolute belief in individual agency, and packaged it as a new, pared-down, libertarian vision of free market thought. Hayek believed that freedom meant the absence of coercion. Liberty came not from rational decisions or morality, but from the checks and balances of the free choices of others. His thought had qualities of the French Jansenist jurist Jean Domat's idea that competing acts of sin canceled each other out. It transformed Adam Smith's Stoic virtues into a belief that individual actions alone drove the market and were wholly moral unto themselves.[19]

Hayek's ideas of libertarianism were influential, but it was the Nobel Prize–winning American economist Milton Friedman who would take this brand of free market economics and make it one of the dominant ideologies of the late twentieth century. Of all the modern free-market thinkers, Friedman, the Brooklyn-born, Chicago-educated son of Hungarian Jewish immigrants, was the most brilliant, the most charismatic, and the most influential. By the force of his research, rhetoric, and personal presence, he was able to translate his academic work into the libertarian political and economic ideology of the Chicago school of economics. Friedman would partially solve the conundrum of inflation, one of the biggest problems facing the United States in the 1970s. He found specific fallacies in Keynes's widely accepted belief that the government had to tinker with the national economic engine to keep it running. In an odd mixture of economic empiricism and a near-religious faith in libertarian free markets, Friedman repeated Alfred Marshall's old belief in the self-sustaining market equilibrium, with the caveat that the government had to pursue a steady policy of annual, regular increases in monetary supply.

In many ways, Friedman typified Smith's tradition of free market thought. Like Smith, he was an open-minded professor who valued free debate and took opposing ideas seriously. He, too, was a famed and beloved university teacher. Also like Smith, he was not a conventionally religious man, claiming to be Jewish in spirit but agnostic in belief. Friedman was part of a postwar generation of economists that included Jews, who until then had been a rare presence among free market thinkers. No longer the preserve of European aristocrats, or even British evangelicals, radicals, and imperialists, free market thought was becoming more American. Friedman inherited the Enlightenment belief in unlimited optimism. But he rejected Smith's confidence in public schools, the collective action of representative government, and the class establishment. Friedman's reductive vision of a purely consumer-driven society was a far cry from Ciceronian and Stoic ideals. He and his wife and coauthor, Rose Friedman, became ardent defenders of the individual's "freedom to choose," with no serious discussion of the moral implications of these choices. He seemed unaware that following Cicero, Smith had rejected the pleasure principle as too simplistic, believing instead that moral choices could only come from serious philosophical discipline. Friedman replaced this script with a simple modern commercial calculus of desire and wealth.[20]

Friedman envisioned a very limited role for government in education, health care, and economic and social life. He also had a purely negative vision of taxation, insisting that any government tax on business was a form of coercion, and therefore tantamount to government ownership: in his eyes, taxation amounted to forcibly taking part of a private business. Yet unlike Hayek, he did not believe that economic liberalism was more important than political freedom. For Friedman, freedom came first.[21]

Like so many free market thinkers, Friedman lived a life of paradox. He started his career working for Franklin Roosevelt's New Deal, assisting with a budget study and then working for the National Bureau of Economic Research. He later approved of government job-creation programs as imperfect, but necessary under the circumstances of the Depression. However, Friedman dismissed the rest of the New Deal as a Marxist-like attempt to "control" individuals' economic lives. Looking back at Roosevelt's reforms, Friedman, avoiding shrill partisanship, lauded the president's "noble intentions" but lamented what he considered the complete failure of Social Security, welfare, public housing, and all other government programs. Smith had also warned that pro-business economic policies served only special interests. Friedman maintained that social policies did the same, claiming that government aid undermined the principle of "equality before God."[22]

Friedman's important contributions to the field of economics began in 1956 with his work on monetarism, the theory or practice of controlling the supply of money as the chief method of stabilizing the economy. His influential article "Quantity of Money Theory: A Restatement" claimed that the economy creates a stable demand for money as it grows annually. He echoed early quantity of money theorists that money's value was related to its quantity within the economy, but he sounded more like Colbert when he worried that not having a regular supply of money in an economy would slow down the velocity and quantity of economic exchange. He was interested not in the value of money, but in how the economy created a necessary demand for money that had to be fed. This meant that the government needed to provide a uniform, annual supply of money equal to the average growth of the economy. He returned to the central idea in John Law's theory of paper money by which a steady supply was necessary to build confidence, or what Friedman called the "rational expectations" of economic actors.[23]

Friedman's quantity of money theory was a critique of Keynes's idea that governments stimulate economies by spending. Aside from the military and police, all state spending was wrong, Friedman believed, and any involvement by the Federal Reserve was dangerous. In fact, he maintained that the institution should be abolished altogether and that money should simply be issued each year according to statistical growth expectations. He and coauthor Anna Schwartz's massive *Monetary History of the United States* (1963) showed that the money stock in the United States had grown consistently over time. However, during the Great Depression, the Federal Reserve had limited the money supply to try to tamp down inflation. According to Friedman, these actions exacerbated and prolonged the "great contraction" of the Depression. He and Schwartz concluded that had the Fed either done nothing or put more money into the economy, it would have contributed to growth and expansion.[24]

This monetary vision of how economies, inflation, and growth work was revolutionary. According to Friedman, the velocity, or growth in demand for money, was equal to the annual increase in gross domestic product (GDP). Friedman's theory inverted the paradigmatic Phillips curve—devised in 1958 by the New Zealand economist and inventor William Phillips—by which tight money and high interest rates were seen to cause inflation. Friedman argued that this was flawed thinking and demonstrated that monetary expansion could cause temporary inflation, but the economy would eventually stabilize. Confidence in the economy would then grow, owing to the "rational expectations" of individuals who expected more money in the economy. Monetarism played a part in halting inflation in the United States in the 1970s and 1980s, but in Britain, where Margaret Thatcher implemented it, it was accompanied by massive rises in unemployment and a national economic contraction. Friedman didn't want to admit it, but proof of general economic equilibrium remained elusive.[25]

In 1974, Friedman's friend and colleague Friedrich Hayek won the Nobel Prize in Economics, but he had to share it with Gunnar Myrdal, a Swedish economist and a leading advocate of the modern welfare state. Hayek had won for showing how state-controlled low interest rates led to inflation. In attempting to stimulate investment with low interest rates before the Great Depression, he had said, the state had encouraged too much borrowing, leading to booms that would bust. This was Hayek's powerful business cycle theory, a brilliant insight for the inflationary crisis of the 1970s.

At the same time, the Nobel Committee awarded Myrdal the prize for showing how Black Americans had been left behind by the market in the United States' meteoric postwar economic rise. The committee brilliantly made Galiani's and Necker's old point: the market was the best policy until it failed, and it was failing American minorities. The message the committee wanted to give was that free marketeers and government interventionists had both discovered economic truths, and they would do best by working together. However, Hayek and Friedman seemed unable to find economic middle ground, and they were certainly unwilling to address the market's failure to correct economic and racial inequality. In 1976, the Nobel Committee once again showed its interest in understanding market mechanisms by awarding Friedman the Nobel Prize in Economics for his work on monetary theory and stabilization. The committee still did not fully embrace a universal idea of market equilibrium, however.

Monetarism became a basic tenet of modern government. Friedman's new ideas retained some basic elements of Keynesian spending. Every time a major crisis arose, the government stepped in to manage the money supply. In spite of Friedman's insistence that only steady, incremental monetary injection is necessary and that there is no need for government tinkering in the timing and the amount, government central banks now design their monetary policies for specific contexts—whether one agrees with them or not—and, as an arm of the state, they remain more central to economic life than ever.

Friedman was an idealist and a great believer in American exceptionalism. For him, aside from minimal money supplies, free markets meant that government had no role in economic growth. He did not believe that underdeveloped economies and zones needed government investment. He also insisted that unfettered capitalism helped racial minorities and made up for the failings of representative government. Friedman rejected Myrdal's work and data, blaming inequality instead on government programs, and warning that minorities could never hope that political majorities would defend their interests. He came up with the nihilistic and even possibly anti-democratic libertarian concept that "all bad things come from governments."[26]

Ignoring his own outsized role in government, and that of publicly funded research in growth and innovation (the private University of Chicago ran, and still runs, in part, on significant federal research funding), Friedman believed that only individuals, shareholders, and private and publicly traded corporations could create wealth. He recommended the legalization of all drugs, and he was a pioneering advocate of school choice. He saw immigration as the engine of US economic growth. Friedman believed that one of his greatest achievements in terms of protecting individual liberties was his role in ending conscription and helping to create an all-volunteer military. He spoke out against intolerance and was also a defender of gay rights. But as Friedman sat at the summit of influence in the 1980s, he seemed strangely unresponsive to the failings of the market, and to free market advocates—such as the Chilean dictator Augusto Pinochet—who rejected his core beliefs in individual freedom and democracy. Indeed, Friedman called Pinochet's repressive military dictatorship and economic policy "a miracle" without expressing serious qualms about its political tortures and murders, and he was silent on Chile's long history of successful commercial development before Pinochet's violent coup.[27]

THE IDEALISTIC ANTI-STATE libertarianism of Hayek and Friedman found a welcome home within older, more complicated, and often troubling libertarian traditions in the United States. Even before World War II, a movement of anti-state, free-market thought had taken hold in US industry, in the evangelical Christian movement, and in the neo-Confederate states' rights movement in the South.

Although Smith and his nineteenth-century heirs were radical reformers, many of the supporters of free markets in the United States harbored profoundly reactionary beliefs. In 1934, thoroughly disgusted with Roosevelt's New Deal, the three du Pont brothers, Pierre, Irénée, and Lammot, began writing of their fear of creeping socialism in the United States. The industrialist brothers were descendants of the physiocrat Pierre-Samuel du Pont de Nemours, one of Quesnay's most loyal followers and a champion of the abolition of slavery. A believer in agricultural wealth, du Pont had helped lead the French Revolution—that great state intervention against an abusive, archaic society—before moving from Paris to Delaware.[28]

The du Pont brothers had been upset with Prohibition, passed as the Eighteenth Amendment under President Herbert Hoover. In the New Deal era, they were also upset that the government was trying to ban child labor: "No Federal law or constitutional amendment will abolish child labor unless the parents in the community are convinced that child labor should not exist," Pierre du Pont wrote to Hugh Johnson, head of the National Recovery Administration from 1933 to 1935. The brothers did not believe that the state should step in even in the face of abusive practices against children. For them, a nebulous concept of "society" had to manage child labor without legal intervention. If the duly elected government of the country abolished child labor, it was a democratic decision, but the du Pont brothers objected to this.[29]

The new generations of the du Pont family lacked the moral clarity of their French *philosophe* ancestor. By the 1930s, the DuPont Company had become one of the largest industrial firms in the world. Its chemicals and plastics defined the modern age and spurred industrial development, innovation, and wealth, but were, and remain, notorious for pollution. It was an odd turn that the heirs of a physiocrat would found a multinational industrial chemicals firm that made its fortune from nylon. It was a far cry from physiocratic agrarian religion and the radical politics of their deist ancestor.

The du Pont brothers were part of a movement in the United States to protect companies from government interference and to stop New Deal social, educational, and welfare programs. They worked to repeal Roosevelt's policies with one of many industrialist-supported pro-free-market groups, the American Liberty League. To do that, they needed an ideology. By the late 1940s, there was also a conservative Christian reaction against the New Deal, which evangelicals believed was an attempt to shift faith away from Christianity toward the secular state.[30]

The partnership between large US firms and corporate free-market ideology; conservative, evangelical Christians; and anti-civil-rights politicians from the American South and Southwest would become one of the more unusual and reactionary chapters in the history of free market thought. What had been a radical, deist, atheist movement, aligned with the early French Revolution and hailed by abolitionists, pacifists, and women's rights advocates, as well as by utilitarian socialists such as John Stuart Mill, was becoming the new gospel of American archconservatives and neo-Confederate segregationist racists. At one level, it made sense. The rise of the Soviet Union, mixed with Roosevelt's unprecedented expansion of the federal government, was a shock—and a relief—to a country reeling from the Great Depression and World War II. Soviet communism was a threat to both American democracy and free enterprise. After World War II, which FDR had all but won, his big state economic policies continued and led to great economic expansion. Business groups, evangelicals, and anti-integrationist politicians saw this new active state as a threat, and they began to see the idealistic new free-market thinkers—figures such as Hayek—as allies in their particularly American anti-government cause.

In the 1940s, the Southern Baptist evangelical leader Billy Graham espoused a pro-free-market discourse mixed with anti-communist rhetoric, warning that organized labor and sexual promiscuity would lead to Armageddon. In the 1950s, companies such as Ford, General Electric, Mobil, and US Steel created pro-business, pro-libertarian groups, such as the American Enterprise Association (later the American Enterprise Institute) and the Foundation for Economic Education, to advocate for their interests. The companies also recruited economists such as Milton Friedman to write for them, and moved closer to conservative Republican leaders, such as William F. Buckley and his *National Review*, as well as his political allies, neo-Confederate segregationists such as Strom Thurmond and Jesse Helms. In the 1960s, the ambitious politician Barry Goldwater wrote *The Conscience of a Conservative*. In it, Goldwater, who was looking to overthrow the more moderate Republican establishment, defended the neo-Confederate cause of states' rights and popularized the work of Hayek and von Mises. Goldwater attacked all forms of union activity and decried government involvement in the economy as "an evil" that deprived Americans of the right to decide how to spend their own money. Not surprisingly, the Ku Klux Klan supported Goldwater's failed 1964 presidential bid against Lyndon Johnson. However, Goldwater had an old liberal bent. He would later embrace a southwestern form of libertarianism, advocating for free markets, gay rights, abortion rights, and the legalization of marijuana, and thus setting the stage for the ever-popular social liberalism of the western states.[31]

Around the same time that Goldwater lost his bid for the presidency, the TV evangelicals Pat Robertson and Jerry Falwell joined the libertarian, far-right wing of the Republican Party. They called for free markets and cited Hayek and Friedman to protest government bureaucrats, while also issuing daily denunciations of rock music, homosexuals, abortion, civil rights, and pornography. Hard-right evangelicals were among the most influential leaders of the new free-market movement. The Republican Party became an ideological mix of the mainline northeastern establishment, American Baptist puritanism, racism and bigotry, and a Friedman-esque and American Southwest individualist libertarianism and permissiveness—all held together by a near-religious reverence for the multinational conglomerate firm and the sanctity of capital-holding shareholders.[32]

Add to this American free-market kaleidoscope the case of the Russian Jewish libertarian author and free-market pop theorist Ayn Rand. More than any economist, her accessible and incredibly popular fictional works created a narrative around the hyper-individualist, anti-collective theories of Hayek. The protagonist of her 1943 best-selling novel, *The Fountainhead*, is the hard-driven entrepreneurial architect Howard Roark, who valiantly fights collectivists and "do-nothing" bureaucrats so that innovation and progress can come about by pure individual will. The message was that entrepreneurs—like modern Nietzschean supermen—were "Randian heroes," physically superior men who needed to break the shackles of government to realize their greatness and advance the good of humankind. Influential economists such as Alan Greenspan—a chairman of the Federal Reserve and a member of the Ayn Rand Collective—as well as countless business leaders and politicians, embraced her work in the United States. In 1991, at the fall of the

Berlin Wall, *The Fountainhead* polled as the second most influential book for US congressmen after the Bible.[33]

Friedman's American corporate libertarianism and the Randian ideal clashed with Smith's old warning against merchant entrepreneurs—"projectors"—and his hope that the market would temper their greed. Rand's ultra-individualist characters had much in common with the aristocratic, landed elite that the physiocrats had hoped to free from state tyranny. Rand's and Friedman's thought mirrored the old physiocratic idea that certain wealth-producing people should have a special status in society. Free market thinkers believed that producers of wealth, whether they were eighteenth-century farmers or twentieth-century builders, entrepreneurs, or wealthy shareholders, should not be taxed. Society had to liberate their inherent capacity to create wealth with the simple precept of laissez-faire.

TODAY, AS CRITICS from all sides attack Friedman's free market thought, we are left to wonder: Which versions of free market thought are still useful? And as China, Singapore, and, indeed, all advanced economies show, no one economic model dominates. No one model ever has. We are in constant flux according to circumstances. One thing is certain: the orthodox libertarian free-market model does not exist, and has never existed, outside of places with no government, such as the ultra-violent "frontier economies," such as South Sudan. Most advanced industrial economies follow a relatively similar recipe of liberal social democracy with general free-market mechanisms and wide government oversight and participation in the economy. Most private companies produce and sell goods and services according to market mechanisms of supply and demand, but also with private national monopolies (think Boeing and Airbus), as well as considerable state support through government contracts (think IBM and Microsoft) and through state-subsidized companies and social welfare programs (think Amazon's early use of the United States Postal Service and Walmart's and McDonald's reliance on Medicaid as part of their low-wage strategies).[34]

Each country, according to circumstances, has a very specific approach and path to development that defies pure economic models. It is therefore impossible to compare Singapore to China, to Germany, or to the United States, the latter with its huge, diverse internal markets. The United States has most of the world's largest companies, but Asia has a far superior growth rate, for now. And all have different strengths and strategies. Trying to compare the United States and China is a bit like trying to compare England and France in 1700. Both needed an array of different economic policies to develop their economies and effectively compete.[35]

AUTHORITARIAN CAPITALISM, DEMOCRACY, AND FREE MARKET THOUGHT

Even as free market economists offered brilliant insights into the workings of the market—through their understanding of marginal utility, for example—they formed an overarching, utopian belief that economies could only work well through a form of pure equilibrium. They insisted that simply by generating growth through supply and demand, market systems would magically sustain themselves in the absence of any but the most minimal role for government. This model, however, no longer seems realistic or relevant. After decades of deregulation and expanding free trade, the world has experienced regular cycles of economic crashes and government bailouts, along with burgeoning wealth inequality, wars, and climate and health disasters. Equilibrium eludes us.

If anything, the state remains a powerful economic driver, with China's rise as the world's second-largest economy only adding to the free market conundrum. In 1978, the leader of the People's Republic of China, Deng Xiaoping, announced the "reform and opening-up of China," through which the Communist Party began to introduce incremental market reforms into Chinese society.

In 1988, the party invited the most vocal defender of a totalizing vision of free markets, Milton Friedman, to make an official visit. Unsurprisingly, Friedman stated that for China, "there is no really satisfactory substitute for full-scale use of a free market." Sitting down with the Communist Party general secretary, Zhao Ziyang, Friedman insisted that, like the "principles of physics, the principles of economics applied equally to all nations," and that the only path to wealth was the expansion of "private property" and state deregulation of industry. Without political freedom, he told Zhao, Chinese markets could not work. In other words, if China did not move to a free political system, it could never be rich.[1]

Deng Xiaoping nevertheless decided in 1989 that a mixture of planned and market economies was possible, and that market economies could develop within what he called "socialism." So Deng and other Chinese leaders set out to create a "socialist market economy," drawing on Friedman's ideas about private property and incentives while leaving China's authoritarian regime in place. The Chinese leadership now looked to reduce central planning and lift constraints on private ownership while maintaining state control of key companies and huge sovereign wealth funds.[2]

In the 1990s, a leading deputy of the State Commission for Economic System Reform, Jiang Chunze, compiled a review of planned versus market-oriented economies. One of the most influential women in the history of free market reforms, Jiang recognized that market economies were superior in terms of "productive forces." Yet she also noted that successful market economies were not purely laissez-faire. A certain degree of state intervention was required. And so Jiang recommended a mixture of government intervention and private property with individual profit incentives.[3]

It worked. With the state overseeing private enterprise, property, wealth incentives, and private companies, and investing in and creating state-owned capitalist companies, China went on to become the second-richest country in the world. Playing by some free market rules but not others, it successfully disproved the well-worn free-market nostrum that there was no economic liberty or growth without political liberty.[4]

The Chinese were, in fact, using an old development model rooted in the seventeenth-century approach of Jean-Baptiste Colbert. Like their forerunners, the Chinese leadership understood something that Friedman missed—namely, that free market ideas of varying degrees of private property, efficiency, and even energetic entrepreneurialism could flourish in tandem with state control. Even more surprisingly, China discovered that certain elements of free market doctrine could actually produce prosperity in the context of authoritarianism. The Chinese socialist market economy looked like nothing so much as a more efficient version of Colbert's absolutist capitalism, with all the advantages, risks, and horrors of political despotism.[5]

FREE MARKET THOUGHT now faces difficult choices. Will it be the ally of those who reject science and open societies, and who rally against democracy and individual freedoms to support dictators and kleptocrats? Or will a new version of democratic free-market pragmatism become a potent force? Adam Smith worried about the role of business in government, while Ludwig von Mises, Friedrich Hayek, and Milton Friedman worried about the dangers of government in private life. In the age of social media and personal data-mining on a massive scale, free market thinkers will have to grapple with the fact that governments and markets both have dark sides, and that, working not necessarily in conflict, but in tandem, as they so often do, they will have to be managed and even resisted when they go off the rails. One thing is certain: free market thought will need to be much more adaptable and sophisticated than it has been since World War II if we are to see our way clear of the daunting obstacles that humanity now faces.[6]

If there is a lesson to be learned here, it is that we must be suspicious of any claim that an economic system can be self-sustaining or remain in balance without significant political intervention. Even those pioneering free-market philosophers who believed in economic equilibrium considered the state essential to it. Cicero may have coveted wealth, but he gave his life to the higher cause of upholding the Roman Republic. He saw public service as literally the greatest good a human could achieve, good government and an understanding of how to live harmoniously with nature being the foundations of functioning markets. Only with civil peace and the rule of law, after all, could one make honest and productive exchanges.[7]

Christian leaders such as Saint Augustine denied the possibility of a perfect system on earth, seeking perfection only in salvation. In the Judeo-Christian tradition, God made the earth as a flawed home for fallen man, which is why Christian theorists, such as Locke, saw the need for property and government, to make sure that economic life neither collapsed nor strayed into immorality and waste. This view of humankind and nature as imperfect changed with the secular exuberance of Enlightenment philosophers, such as Quesnay, Hume, and Smith, who looked to create scientific recipes for human progress through free market philosophies of economic equilibrium. But if Smith was an optimist in some regards, he was a skeptic before all else, and uncertain whether it would ever be possible to actually attain his economic vision. *The Wealth of Nations* was not a manifesto, then, but, as Smith was the first to admit, a hypothesis.

Nineteenth-century philosophers such as John Stuart Mill found themselves, much like their eighteenth-century forebears, optimistic that free markets could create equilibrium, while confounded by those occasions when they failed, and thus convinced that the state had to keep its hand on the tiller of the economy in case it went off balance. Even the Victorian free-market apostle William Stanley Jevons, who theorized a "perfect market," believed that government had to intervene when individuals failed to create efficiency.[8]

This is not to say that government involvement in the economy is always ideal or efficient. But the historical record shows that, as economies grow in complexity, so governments grow in response, for better or for worse. Free markets, individual ambitions, and entrepreneurialism are essential, leading to many of humanity's greatest achievements. But the fact is that government is not going away, and to assert that the state is always an economic negative is as lazy as it is misleading. Many who roundly condemn the government's role in business are perfectly aware of how great a role the state plays in economies, which is, of course, why they covet political power and pay dearly for access to it.

If we are to reclaim free market thought and make it truly relevant again, we must redesign it, not only as a democratically oriented philosophy, but as one which accepts that the state is embedded in the market and vice versa. Neither governments nor markets will ever be perfect; nor will the market—or nature, for that matter—march according to best-laid human plans. Free individual action is essential to the dynamism of the market, but it alone does not guarantee the economy's steady functioning. In the end, we would do well, then, to return to the old books of Cicero, not to find a perfect market mechanism, but to learn the lessons that have attracted readers for more than two thousand years. Wealth was only good, Cicero thought, insofar as it could be used to support constitutional government, civil peace, and decorum. More important to him than riches were the principles of living in harmony with nature, cultivating learning and friendship, and doing the hard work of ethical stewardship. Faith in the market alone will not save us, but hewing to these old virtues just might.

ACKNOWLEDGMENTS

First I would like to thank Lara Heimert, my editor at Basic Books, who helped me conceive of the scope of this book and worked tirelessly to support the project, keeping the faith during the long process of its completion. She's the smartest person in publishing and I feel lucky to work with her. The editorial team at Basic—Conor Guy, Claire Potter, Roger Labrie, and Kathy Streckfus—is simply the best. I am grateful to all of them. As always, my agent, Rob McQuilkin, played a key role at every stage of this book and has my gratitude.

I am grateful as well for support from Dornsife College at the University of Southern California (USC) and the Leventhal School of Accounting (USC), which made this book possible. Special thanks go to the National Endowment for the Humanities for a Public Scholar Fellowship and to the Charles and Agnes Kazarian Foundation for its continued support.

Thanks also to the USC Department of Philosophy, the Early Modern Studies Institute, my own Martens Economic History Forum at USC, and the students in my course on free market thought, along with seminar groups at Stanford, Yale, the University of Tokyo, Harvard Business School, the Clark Library at the University of California–Los Angeles (UCLA), the University of Naples Federico II, the Deutsches Historisches Institut Paris, and the *William and Mary Quarterly* for constructive exchange, criticism, and input, without which intellectual endeavor is impossible.

I was aided at different stages of this project by the Archives Nationales de France, Bibliothèque Nationale de France, Biblioteca Nazionale Centrale di Firenze, and librarians at USC and UCLA.

Scholarship depends on a learned community, and mine is rich and inspiring. Hearty thanks go to Alessandro Arienzo, Keith Baker, David Bell, Paola Bertucci, Gordon Brown, Paul Cheney, Frederic Clark, Jeffrey Collins, Diane Coyle, Elizabeth Cross, Will Deringer, Sean Donahue, Dan Edelstein, Lena Foellmer, Jamie Galbraith, Arthur Goldhammer, Anthony Grafton, Colin Hamilton, Lucas Herchenroeder, Margaret Jacob, Mahmoud Jalloh, Matt Kadane, Paul Kazarian, Dan Kelemen, Naka Kondo, Antoine Lilti, Sean Macauley, Peter Mancall, Meg Musselwhite, Vanessa Ogle, Arnaud Orain, Jeff Piker, Steve Pincus, Erik Reinert, Fernanda Reinert, Sophus Reinert, Emma Rothschild, Andrew Shankman, Shim Shimoyama, Asheesh Siddique, Marcello Simonetta, Phil Stern, Allegra Stirling, Giacomo Todeschini, Frank Trentmann, Melissa Veronesi, Ellen Wayland-Smith, Patrick Weil, Arthur Weststeijn, and Koji Yamamoto.

NOTES

INTRODUCTION: A NEW ORIGINS STORY
OF FREE MARKET THOUGHT

1. Léon Walras, *Elements of Pure Economics; or, the Theory of Social Wealth*, trans. William Jaffe (London: Routledge, 1954), 153–155; Bernard Cornet, "Equilibrium Theory and Increasing Returns," *Journal of Mathematical Economics* 17 (1988): 103–118; Knud Haakonssen, *Natural Law and Moral Philosophy: From Grotius to the Scottish Enlightenment* (Cambridge: Cambridge University Press, 1996), 25–30.

2. Milton Friedman, *Capitalism and Freedom*, 3rd ed. (Chicago: University of Chicago Press, 2002), 15; Milton Friedman, *Free to Choose: A Personal Statement*, 3rd ed. (New York: Harcourt, 1990), 20, 145.

3. Anat Admati, "Anat Admati on Milton Friedman and Justice," Insights by Stanford Business, October 5, 2020, www.gsb.stanford.edu /insights/anat-admati-milton-friedman-justice; Diane Coyle, *Markets, State, and People: Economics for Public Policy* (Princeton, NJ: Princeton University Press, 2020), 98–101; Rebecca Henderson, *Reimagining Capitalism in a World on Fire* (New York: Public Affairs, 2020), 19, 67; Bonnie Kristian, "Republicans More Likely Than Democrats to Say the Free Market Is Bad for America," Foundation for Economic Education, December 9, 2016, https://fee.org/articles/republicans-more -likely-than-democrats-to-say-the-free-market-is-bad-for-america; Jonah Goldberg, "Will the Right Defend Economic Liberty?" *National Review*, May 2, 2019; Martin Wolf, "Why Rigged Capitalism Is Damaging Liberal Democracy," *Financial Times*, September 17, 2019, www.ft.com

/content/5a8ab27e-d470-11e9-8367-807ebd53ab77; Ben Riley-Smith, "The Drinks Are on Me, Declares Rishi Sunak in Budget Spending Spree," *The Telegraph*, October 27, 2021; Inu Manak, "Are Republicans Still the Party of Free Trade?," Cato Institute, May 16, 2019, www.cato .org/blog/are-republicans-still-party-free-trade; Aritz Parra, "China's Xi Defends Free Markets as Key to World Prosperity," Associated Press, November 28, 2018.

4. Erik S. Reinert, *How Rich Countries Got Rich, and Why Poor Countries Stay Poor* (London: Public Affairs, 2007); Ciara Linnane, "China's Middle Class Is Now Bigger Than America's Middle Class," Market-Watch, October 17, 2015, www.marketwatch.com/story/chinese-middle -class-is-now-bigger-than-the-us-middle-class-2015-10-15; Javier C. Hernández and Quoctrung Bui, "The American Dream Is Alive. In China," *New York Times*, November 8, 2018; Karl Polanyi, *The Great Transformation: The Political and Economic Origins of Our Time* (Boston: Beacon Press, 1957), 267–268; Fred Block and Margaret R. Somers, *The Power of Market Fundamentalism: Karl Polanyi's Critique* (Cambridge, MA: Harvard University Press, 2014), 2; David Sainsbury, *Windows of Opportunity: How Nations Create Wealth* (London: Profile Books, 2020).

5. Martin Wolf, "Milton Friedman Was Wrong on the Corporation," *Financial Times*, December 8, 2020, www.ft.com/content/e969a756-922e -497b-8550-94bfb1302cdd.

6. Adam Smith, *An Inquiry into the Nature and Causes of the Wealth of Nations*, ed. Roy Harold Campbell and Andrew Skinner, 2 vols. (Indianapolis: Liberty Fund, 1981), vol. 1, bk. IV, chap. ii, para. 10; William J. Barber, *A History of Economic Thought* (London: Penguin, 1967), 17; Lars Magnusson, *The Tradition of Free Trade* (London: Routledge, 2004), 16.

7. Joseph A. Schumpeter, *History of Economic Analysis* (London: Allen and Unwin, 1954), 185.

8. Smith, *Wealth of Nations*, vol. 2, bk. IV, chap. ix, para. 3.

9. D. C. Coleman, ed., *Revisions in Mercantilism* (London: Methuen, 1969), 91–117, at 97; William Letwin, *The Origins of Scientific Economics: English Economic Thought, 1660–1776* (London: Methuen, 1963), 43; Lars Magnusson, *Mercantilism: The Shaping of an Economic Language* (London: Routledge, 1994); Philip J. Stern, *The Company State: Corporate Sovereignty and Early Modern Foundations of the British Empire in India* (Oxford: Oxford University Press, 2011), 5–6; Rupali Mishra, *A Business of State: Commerce, Politics, and the Birth of the East India Company*

(Cambridge, MA: Harvard University Press, 2018); Philip J. Stern and Carl Wennerlind, eds., *Mercantilism Reimagined: Political Economy in Early Modern Britain and Its Empire* (Oxford: Oxford University Press, 2014), 6; Schumpeter, *History of Economic Analysis*, 94; Eli F. Heckscher, *Mercantilism*, trans. Mendel Shapiro, 2 vols. (London: George Allen and Unwin, 1935); Steve Pincus, "Rethinking Mercantilism: Political Economy, the British Empire, and the Atlantic World in the Seventeenth and Eighteenth Centuries," *William and Mary Quarterly* 69, no. 1 (2012): 3–34.

CHAPTER 1: THE DREAM OF CICERO

1. Titus Livy, *History of Rome*, trans. John C. Yardley, Loeb Classical Library (Cambridge, MA: Harvard University Press, 2017), bk. 1, chap. 8. For an online version of Livy edited by Rev. Canon Roberts, see the Perseus Digital Library, Tufts University, gen. ed. Gregory R. Crane, www.perseus.tufts.edu/hopper/text?doc=urn:cts:latinLit:phi0914.phi0011.perseus-eng3:pr.

2. Livy, *History of Rome*, bk. 23, chap. 24; bk. 1, chap. 35; Ronald Syme, *The Roman Revolution*, rev. ed. (Oxford: Oxford University Press, 2002), 15.

3. Cato, *On Agriculture*, in *Cato and Varro: On Agriculture*, trans. W. D. Hooper and H. B. Ash, Loeb Classical Library (Cambridge, MA: Harvard University Press, 1935), bk. 1, paras. 1–2.

4. Cicero, *De officiis*, trans. Walter Miller, Loeb Classical Library (Cambridge, MA: Harvard University Press, 1913), bk. 1, sec. 13, para. 41.

5. Cicero, *On the Republic*, in Cicero, *On the Republic, On the Laws*, trans. Clinton W. Keyes, Loeb Classical Library (Cambridge, MA: Harvard University Press, 1928), bk. 1, sec. 34, paras. 52–53; bk. 1, sec. 5, para. 19; bk. 1, sec. 8–9, para. 24.

6. Dan Hanchey, "Cicero, Exchange, and the Epicureans," *Phoenix* 67, no. 1–2 (2013): 119–134, at 129; Wood, *Cicero's Social and Political Thought*, 55, 81–82, 112; Cicero, *De officiis*, bk. 3, sec. 6, para. 30; bk. 1, sec. 7, para. 22.

7. Cicero, *On Ends*, trans. H. Rackham, Loeb Classical Library (Cambridge, MA: Harvard University Press, 1914), bk. 2, sec. 26, para. 83; Hanchey, "Cicero, Exchange," 23; Cicero, *De officiis*, bk. 1, sec. 13, para. 41; bk. 1, sec. 16, para. 50; bk. 1, sec. 17, paras. 53–54; Cicero, *De amicitia*, in *On Old Age, On Friendship, On Divination*, trans. W. A. Falconer, Loeb Classical Library (Cambridge, MA: Harvard University

Press, 1923), sec. 6, para. 22; sec. 7, paras. 23–24; sec. 7, paras. 23–24; sec. 14, paras. 50–52.

8. Cicero, *De officiis*, bk. 14, sec. 5, paras. 21–22; bk. 3, sec. 5, para. 23.

9. Caesar, *The Gallic War*, trans. H. J. Edwards, Loeb Classical Library (Cambridge, MA: Harvard University Press, 1917), bk. 5, para. 1. See also "Internum Mare," in William Smith, *Dictionary of Greek and Roman Geography*, 2 vols. (London: Walton and Maberly, 1856), 1:1084; Peter Brown, *Through the Eye of the Needle: Wealth, the Fall of Rome, and the Making of Christianity in the West, 350–550 AD* (Princeton, NJ: Princeton University Press, 2014), 69; Pliny, *Natural History*, trans. H. Rackham, 37 vols., Loeb Classical Library (Cambridge, MA: Harvard University Press, 1942), bk. 3.

10. Wood, *Cicero's Social and Political Thought*, 48; Cicero, *In Catilinam*, in Cicero, *Orations: In Catilinam, I–IV, Pro Murena, Pro Sulla, Pro Flacco*, trans. C. Macdonald, Loeb Classical Library (Cambridge, MA: Harvard University Press, 1977), bk. 2, para. 21.

11. Cicero, *De officiis*, bk. 1, sec. 13, para. 47; Hanchey, "Cicero, Exchange," 129; Brown, *Through the Eye of the Needle*, 253.

12. A. E. Douglas, "Cicero the Philosopher," in *Cicero*, ed. T. A. Dorey (New York: Basic Books, 1965), 135–171.

13. Douglas, "Cicero the Philosopher."

14. Cicero, *De officiis*, bk. 1, sec. 13, para. 41; bk. 1, sec. 7, para. 27.

15. Cicero, *On Ends*, bk. 1, sec. 9, para. 30; bk. 1, sec. 10, paras. 32–33.

16. Cicero, *On Ends*, bk. 1, sec. 19, para. 69; Cicero, *On the Republic*, bk. 6, sec. 24, paras. 26–28.

17. Emily Butterworth, "Defining Obscenity," in *Obscénités renaissantes*, ed. Hugh Roberts, Guillaume Peureux, and Lise Wajeman, Travaux d'humanisme et Renaissance, no. 473 (Geneva: Droz, 2011), 31–37; Cicero, *Orations: Philippics 1–6*, ed. and trans. D. R. Shackleton Bailey, rev. John T. Ramsey and Gesine Manuwald, Loeb Classical Library (Cambridge, MA: Harvard University Press, 2009), chap. 2, paras. 96–98.

CHAPTER 2: THE DIVINE ECONOMY

1. Matthew, 13:44; Luke 12:33; Hebrews 9:22; Giacomo Todeschini, *Les Marchands et le Temple: La société chrétienne et le cercle vertueux de la richesse du Moyen Âge à l'Époque Moderne* (Paris: Albin Michel, 2017). All quotations from the Bible are from the King James Version.

2. Luke 12:33; Matthew 6:19–21. See also Mark 10:25 and Luke 18:25.

3. Matthew 25:29. This concept of investment and reward would become the basis of Robert K. Merton's "Matthew Effect in Science: The Reward and Communication Systems of Science Are Reconsidered," *Science* 159, no. 3810 (1968): 56–63.

4. Proverbs 19:17. See also Matthew 25:45.

5. Matthew 19:12.

6. Clement of Alexandria, *The Rich Man's Salvation*, trans. G. W. Butterworth, rev. ed., Loeb Classical Library (Cambridge, MA: Harvard University Press, 1919), 339; Todeschini, *Les Marchands et le Temple*, 28.

7. Walter T. Wilson, ed. and trans., *Sentences of Sextus* (Atlanta: Society of Biblical Literature, 2012), 33–38, 74, 261–264.

8. Wilson, *Sentences of Sextus*, 2; *The Shepherd of Hermas*, trans. J. B. Lightfoot (New York: Macmillan, 1891), Parable 2, 1[51]:5, available at Early Christian Writings, www.earlychristianwritings.com/text/shepherd -lightfoot.html; Tertullian, "On the Veiling of Virgins," trans. S. Thelwall, in *The Ante-Nicene Fathers*, ed. Alexander Roberts, James Donaldson, and A. Cleveland Coxe, vol. 4, revised for New Advent by Kevin Knight (Buffalo, NY: Christian Literature Publishing, 1885).

9. Edward Gibbon, *History of the Decline and Fall of the Roman Empire*, 6 vols. (London: Strahan, 1776–1789), vol. 1, chap. 15, n. 96.

10. Richard Finn, *Almsgiving in the Later Roman Empire: Christian Promotion and Practice, 313–450* (Oxford: Oxford University Press, 2006), 93.

11. Benedicta Ward, *The Desert Fathers: Sayings of the Early Christian Monks* (London: Penguin, 2005), 20–54; Gregory of Nyssa, *On Virginity*, ed. D. P. Curtin, trans. William Moore (Philadelphia: Dalcassian Publishing, 2018), 19.

12. John Chrysostom, "Homily 3: Concerning Almsgiving and the Ten Virgins," in *On Repentance and Almsgiving*, trans. Gus George Christo (Washington, DC: Catholic University of America Press, 1998), 28–42, at 29–31.

13. Chrysostom, "Homily 3," 32.

14. Ambrose, *On the Duties of the Clergy*, trans. A. M. Overett (Savage, MN: Lighthouse Publishing, 2013), 55, 89, 205–206; Ambrose, *De Nabuthae*, ed. and trans. Martin R. P. McGuire (Washington, DC: Catholic University of America Press, 1927), 49.

15. Ambrose, *On the Duties of the Clergy*, 55, 78, 83.

16. Ambrose, *On the Duties of the Clergy*, 122–124.

17. Ambrose, "The Sacraments of the Incarnation of the Lord," in *Theological and Dogmatic Works*, trans. Roy J. Deferrari (Washington, DC: Catholic University of America Press, 1963), 217–264, at 240.

18. Peter Brown, *Augustine of Hippo: A Biography* (Berkeley: University of California Press, 2000), 169.

19. Augustine, *On the Free Choice of the Will, On Grace and Free Choice, and Other Writings*, ed. and trans. Peter King (Cambridge: Cambridge University Press, 2010), 1; Peter Brown, "Enjoying the Saints in Late Antiquity," *Early Medieval Europe* 9, no. 1 (2000): 1–24, at 17.

20. Brown, *Augustine of Hippo*, 218–221.

21. Augustine, "Sermon 350," in *Sermons*, ed. John E. Rotelle, trans. Edmund Hill, 10 vols. (Hyde Park, NY: New City Press, 1995), 3:107–108, available at https://wesleyscholar.com/wp-content/uploads/2019/04/Augustine-Sermons-341-400.pdf; Peter Brown, *Through the Eye of a Needle: Wealth, the Fall of Rome, and the Making of Christianity in the West, 350–550 AD* (Princeton, NJ: Princeton University Press, 2014), 355; Augustine, *Letters*, vol. 2 *(83–130)*, trans. Wilfrid Parsons (Washington, DC: Catholic University of America Press, 1953), 42–48; Brown, *Augustine of Hippo*, 198.

22. Brown, *Augustine of Hippo*, 299.

23. Augustine, *City of God*, trans. Henry Bettenson (London: Penguin, 1984), bk. 1, chap. 8; bk. 1, chap. 10.

24. Augustine, *City of God*, bk. 12, chap. 23; Augustine, *Divine Providence and the Problem of Evil: A Translation of St. Augustine's de Ordine*, trans. Robert P. Russell (Whitefish, MT: Kessinger, 2010), 27–31.

25. Augustine, "Exposition of the Psalms," ed. Philip Schaff, trans. J. E. Tweed, in *Nicene and Post-Nicene Fathers*, First Series, vol. 8 (Buffalo, NY: Christian Literature Publishing, 1888), revised for New Advent by Kevin Knight, www.newadvent.org/fathers/1801.htm.

CHAPTER 3: GOD IN THE MEDIEVAL
MARKET MECHANISM

1. Michael McCormick, *Origins of the European Economy: Communications and Commerce AD 300–900* (Cambridge: Cambridge University Press, 2001), 37, 87.

2. Georges Duby, *The Early Growth of the European Economy: Warriors and Peasants from the Seventh to the Twelfth Century*, trans. Howard B.

Clarke (Ithaca, NY: Cornell University Press, 1974), 29; J. W. Hanson, S. G. Ortman, and J. Lobo, "Urbanism and the Division of Labour in the Roman Empire," *Journal of the Royal Society Interface* 14, no. 136 (2017), Interface 14, 20170367; Rosamond McKitterick, ed., *The Early Middle Ages* (Oxford: Oxford University Press, 2001), 100.

3. McCormick, *Origins of the European Economy*, 38, 40–41, 87, 101; Procopius, *The Wars of Justinian*, trans. H. B. Dewing, rev. Anthony Kaldellis (Indianapolis: Hackett Publishing, 2014), bk. 2, chaps. 22–33; Guy Bois, *La mutation de l'an mil. Lournand, village mâconnais de l'antiquité au féodalisme* (Paris: Fayard, 1989), 31.

4. Valentina Tonneato, *Les banquiers du seigneur* (Rennes, France: Presses Universitaires de Rennes, 2012), 291.

5. Tonneato, *Les banquiers du seigneur*, 315; Giacomo Todeschini, *Les Marchands et le Temple: La société chrétienne et le cercle vertueux de la richesse du Moyen Âge à l'Époque Moderne* (Paris: Albin Michel, 2017), 37.

6. Tonneato, *Les banquiers du seigneur*, 160; Alisdair Dobie, *Accounting at the Durham Cathedral Priory: Management and Control of a Major Ecclesiastical Corporation, 1083–1539* (London: Palgrave Macmillan, 2015), 145–146.

7. McKitterick, *Early Middle Ages*, 104.

8. "Customs of Saint-Omer (ca. 1100)," in *Medieval Europe*, ed. Julius Kirshner and Karl F. Morrison (Chicago: University of Chicago Press, 1986), 87–95.

9. Alan Harding, "Political Liberty in the Middle Ages," *Speculum* 55, no. 3 (1980): 423–443, at 442.

10. "Customs of Saint-Omer," 87.

11. Giacomo Todeschini, *Franciscan Wealth: From Voluntary Poverty to Market Society*, trans. Donatella Melucci (Saint Bonaventure, NY: Saint Bonaventure University, 2009), 14; Todeschini, *Les Marchands du Temple*, 70.

12. Henry Haskins, *The Renaissance of the Twelfth Century* (Cambridge, MA: Harvard University Press, 1933), 344–350; D. E. Luscumbe and G. R. Evans, "The Twelfth-Century Renaissance," in *The Cambridge History of Medieval Political Thought, c. 350–c. 1450*, ed. J. H. Burns (Cambridge: Cambridge University Press, 1988), 306–338, at 306; F. Van Steenberghen, *Aristotle in the West: The Origins of Latin Aristotelianism*, trans. L. Johnston (Leuven, Belgium: E. Nauwelaerts, 1955), 30–33.

13. Odd Langholm, *Price and Value in the Aristotelian Tradition: A Study in Scholastic Economic Sources* (Bergen, Norway: Universitetsforlaget,

1979), 29; Gratian, *The Treatise on Laws (Decretum DD. 1–20)*, trans. Augustine Thompson (Washington, DC: Catholic University of America Press, 1993), 25; Brian Tierney, *The Idea of Natural Rights: Studies on Natural Rights, Natural Law, and Church Law, 1150–1625* (Atlanta: Emory University, 1997), 56.

14. David Burr, "The *Correctorium* Controversy and the Origins of the *Usus Pauper* Controversy," *Speculum* 60, no. 2 (1985): 331–342, at 338.

15. Saint Thomas Aquinas, *Summa Theologica*, vol. 53, Question 77, Articles 1, 3; Raymond de Roover, "The Story of the Alberti Company of Florence, 1302–1348, as Revealed in Its Account Books," *Business History Review* 32, no. 1 (1958): 14–59.

16. W. M. Speelman, "The Franciscan *Usus Pauper*: Using Poverty to Put Life in the Perspective of Plenitude," *Palgrave Communications* 4, no. 77 (2018), open access: https://doi.org/10.1057/s41599-018-0134-4; Saint Bonaventure, *The Life of St. Francis of Assisi*, ed. Cardinal Manning (Charlotte, NC: TAN Books, 2010), 54–55.

17. Norman Cohn, *Pursuit of the Millennium: Revolutionary Millenarians and Mystical Anarchists of the Middle Ages* (Oxford: Oxford University Press, 1970), 148–156.

18. John Duns Scotus, *Political and Economic Philosophy*, ed. and trans. Allan B. Wolter (Saint Bonaventure, NY: Franciscan Institute Publications, 2000), 27.

19. Lawrence Landini, *The Causes of the Clericalization of the Order of Friars Minor, 1209–1260 in the Light of Early Franciscan Sources* (Rome: Pontifica Universitas, 1968); David Burr, *Olivi and Franciscan Poverty: The Origins of the Usus Pauper Controversy* (Philadelphia: University of Pennsylvania Press, 1989), 5, 9.

20. Burr, *Olivi and Franciscan Poverty*, 11–12.

21. Nicholas III, *Exiit qui seminat (Confirmation of the Rule of the Friars Minor)*, 1279, Papal Encyclicals Online, www.papalencyclicals.net/nichol03/exiit-e.htm.

22. Piron Sylvain, "Marchands et confesseurs: Le Traité des contrats d'Olivi dans son contexte (Narbonne, fin XIIIe–début XIVe siècle)," in *Actes des congrès de la Société des historiens médiévistes de l'enseignement supérieur public, 28e congrès* 28 (1997): 289–308; Pierre Jean Olivi, *De usu paupere: The quaestio and the tractatus*, ed. David Burr (Florence: Olschki, 1992), 47–48.

23. Olivi, *De usu paupere*, 48.

24. Sylvain Piron, "Censures et condemnation de Pierre de Jean Olivi: Enqûete dans les marges du Vatican," *Mélanges de l'École française de Rome—Moyen Âge* 118, no. 2 (2006): 313–373.

25. Pierre Jean Olivi, *Traité sur les contrats*, ed. and trans. Sylvain Piron (Paris: Les Belles Lettres, 2012), 103–115.

26. Peter John Olivi, "On Usury and Credit (ca. 1290)," in *University of Chicago Readings in Western Civilization*, ed. Julius Kirshner and Karl F. Morrison (Chicago: University of Chicago Press, 1987), 318–325, at 318; Langholm, *Price and Value*, 29, 52.

27. Langholm, *Price and Value*, 119, 137.

28. Tierney, *Idea of Natural Rights*, 33; William of Ockham, *On the Power of Emperors and Popes*, ed. and trans. Annabel S. Brett (Bristol: Theommes Press, 1998).

29. Tierney, *Idea of Natural Rights*, 101.

30. Tierney, *Idea of Natural Rights*, 35; Ockham, *On the Power of Emperors and Popes*, 35–37, 97.

31. Ockham, *On the Power of Emperors and Popes*, 15, 76, 79, 96.

32. Harry A. Miskimin, *The Economy of Later Renaissance Europe, 1460–1600* (Cambridge: Cambridge University Press, 1977), 11.

CHAPTER 4: FLORENTINE WEALTH AND THE MACHIAVELLIAN MARKETPLACE

1. Raymond de Roover, "The Story of the Alberti Company of Florence, 1302–1348, as Revealed in Its Account Books," *Business History Review* 32, no. 1 (1958): 14–59, at 46; Marcia L. Colish, "Cicero's *De officiis* and Machiavelli's *Prince*," *Sixteenth Century Journal* 9, no. 4 (1978): 80–93, at 82; N. E. Nelson, "Cicero's *De officiis* in Christian Thought, 300–1300," in *Essays and Studies in English and Comparative Literature*, University of Michigan Publications in Language and Literature, vol. 10 (Ann Arbor: University of Michigan Press, 1933), 59–160; Albert O. Hirschman, *The Passions and the Interests: Political Arguments for Capitalism Before Its Triumph* (Princeton, NJ: Princeton University Press, 1977), 10.

2. William M. Bowsky, *The Finance of the Commune of Siena, 1287–1355* (Oxford: Clarendon Press, 1970), 1, 209.

3. Nicolai Rubenstein, "Political Ideas in Sienese Art: The Frescoes by Ambrogio Lorenzetti and Taddeo di Bartolo in the Palazzo Pubblico," *Journal of the Warburg and Courtauld Institutes* 21, no. 3/4 (1958):

179–207; Quentin Skinner, "Ambrogio Lorenzetti's Buon Governo Frescoes: Two Old Questions, Two New Answers," *Journal of the Warburg and Courtauld Institutes* 62, no. 1 (1999): 1–28, at 6.

4. Arpad Steiner, "Petrarch's *Optimus Princeps*," *Romanic Review* 23 (1934): 99–111; Christian Bec, *Les marchands écrivains: Affaires et humanismé à Florence, 1375–1434* (Paris: École Pratique des Hautes Études, 1967), 49–51; Francesco Petrarca, "How a Ruler Ought to Govern His State," in *The Earthly Republic: Italian Humanists on Government and Society*, ed. Benjamin G. Kohl and Ronald G. Witt (Philadelphia: University of Pennsylvania Press, 1978), 35–92, at 37.

5. James Hankins, *Virtue Politics: Soulcraft and Statecraft in Renaissance Italy* (Cambridge, MA: Belknap Press of Harvard University Press, 2019), 2, 42, 46; Steiner, "Petrarch's *Optimus Princeps*," 104.

6. Raymond de Roover, "The Concept of the Just Price: Theory and Economic Policy," *Journal of Economic History* 18, no. 4 (1958): 418–434, at 425; Cicero, *De officiis*, trans. Walter Miller, Loeb Classical Library (Cambridge, MA: Harvard University Press, 1913), bk. 1, sec. 13–14, paras. 43–45.

7. Gertrude Randalph Bramlette Richards, *Florentine Merchants in the Age of the Medici: Letters and Documents from the Selfridge Collection of Medici Manuscripts* (Cambridge, MA: Harvard University Press, 1932), 5; Armando Sapori, *La crisi delle compagnie mercantili dei Bardi dei Peruzzi* (Florence: Olschki, 1926); Robert S. Lopez, *The Commercial Revolution of the Middle Ages, 950–1350* (Cambridge: Cambridge University Press, 1976), 27–36; Gino Luzzato, *Breve storia economica dell'Italia medieval* (Turin: Einaudi, 1982); Giovanni di Pagolo Morelli, *Ricordi*, ed. V. Branca (Florence: F. Le Monnier, 1956), 100–101; Matteo Palmieri, *Dell' Ottimo Cittadino: Massime tolte dal Trattato della Vita Civile* (Venice: Dalla Tipografia di Alvisopoli, 1829), 20, 66, 167–168.

8. Benedetto Cotrugli, *The Book of the Art of Trade*, ed. Carlo Carraro and Giovanni Favero, trans. John Francis Phillimore (Cham, Switzerland: Palgrave Macmillan, 2017).

9. Cotrugli, *Book of the Art of Trade*, 4.

10. Cotrugli, *Book of the Art of Trade*, 112–115.

11. Cotrugli, *Book of the Art of Trade*, 25, 30, 33.

12. Cotrugli, *Book of the Art of Trade*, 46–49, 62, 86, 112–113.

13. Felix Gilbert, *Machiavelli and Guicciardini: Politics and History in Sixteenth-Century Florence* (Princeton, NJ: Princeton University Press, 1965), 160–161.

14. Hirschman, *The Passions and the Interests*, 33; Niccolò Machiavelli, *The Prince*, ed. and trans. William J. Connell (Boston: Bedford/St. Martin's, 2005), 61–62; Colish, "Cicero's *De officiis* and Machiavelli's *Prince*," 92.

15. Jacob Soll, *Publishing* The Prince*: History, Reading, and the Birth of Political Criticism* (Ann Arbor: University of Michigan Press, 2005), 23; Niccolò Machiavelli, *The Discourses*, ed. Bernard Crick, trans. Leslie J. Walker, rev. Brian Richardson (London: Penguin, 1970), 37–39, 201.

16. Machiavelli, *The Discourses*, 39; John McCormick, *Machiavellian Democracy* (Cambridge: Cambridge University Press, 2011), 55, 201; Gilbert, *Machiavelli and Guicciardini*, 184–185; Machiavelli, *The Prince*, 61–62.

17. Machiavelli, *The Prince*, 55; Jérémie Bartas, *L'argent n'est pas le nerf de la guerre: Essai sur une prétendue erreur de Machiavel* (Rome: École Française de Rome, 2011), 32–36; McCormick, *Machiavellian Democracy*, 87; Machiavelli, *The Discourses*, 201–203.

18. McCormick, *Machiavellian Democracy*, 26; Charles Tilly, "Reflection on the History of European State-Making," in *The Formation of National States in Western Europe*, ed. Charles Tilly (Princeton, NJ: Princeton University Press, 1975), 3–83, at 52–56; Margaret Levy, *Of Rule and Revenue* (Berkeley: University of California Press, 1988), 202; Niccolò Machiavelli, *Florentine Histories*, trans. Laura F. Banfield and Harvey K. Mansfield Jr. (Princeton, NJ: Princeton University Press, 1988), 121–123.

19. Machiavelli, *Florentine Histories*, 159.

CHAPTER 5: ENGLAND'S FREE TRADE BY MEANS OF THE STATE

1. Quentin Skinner, *The Foundations of Modern Political Thought*, 2 vols. (Cambridge: Cambridge University Press, 1978), 2:5, 284.

2. Harry A. Miskimin, *The Economy of Later Renaissance Europe, 1460–1600* (Cambridge: Cambridge University Press, 1977), 36.

3. Skinner, *Foundations of Modern Political Thought*, 2:139; Francisco de Vitoria, *Political Writings*, ed. Anthony Pagden and Jeremy Lawrence (Cambridge: Cambridge University Press, 1991), xv–xix; Martín de Azpilcueta, *Commentary on the Resolution of Money (1556)*, in *Sourcebook in Late-Scholastic Monetary Theory: The Contributions of Martín de Azpilcueta, Luis de Molina, S.J., and Juan de Mariana, S.J.*, ed. Stephen J. Grabill (Lanham, MD: Lexington Books, 2007), 1–107, at 79; Martín de Azpilcueta,

On Exchange, trans. Jeannine Emery (Grand Rapids, MI: Acton Institute, 2014), 127. See also Alejandro Chafuen, *Faith and Liberty: The Economic Thought of the Late Scholastics* (Lanham, MD: Lexington Books, 2003), 54; Marjorie Grice-Hutchinson, *The School of Salamanca: Readings in Spanish Monetary Theory, 1544–1605* (Oxford: Clarendon Press, 1952), 48.

4. Raymond de Roover, *Money, Banking and Credit in Medieval Bruges* (Cambridge, MA: Medieval Academy of America, 1948), 17; Mark Koyama, "Evading the 'Taint of Usury': The Usury Prohibition as a Barrier to Entry," *Explorations in Economic History* 47, no. 4 (2010): 420–442, at 428.

5. Martin Bucer, *De Regno Christi*, in *Melancthon and Bucer*, ed. Wilhelm Pauk (Philadelphia: Westminster Press, 1969), 155–394, at 304; Steven Rowan, "Luther, Bucer, Eck on the Jews," *Sixteenth Century Journal* 16, no. 1 (1985): 79–90, at 85; Bucer, *Regno Christi*, 302; Constantin Hopf, *Martin Bucer and the English Reformation* (London: Blackwell, 1946), 124–125; Martin Greschat, *Martin Bucer: A Reformer and His Times*, trans. Stephen E. Buckwalter (Louisville, KY: Westminster John Knox Press, 2004), 236–237.

6. Jacob Soll, "Healing the Body Politic: French Royal Doctors, History and the Birth of a Nation, 1560–1634," *Renaissance Quarterly* 55, no. 4 (2002): 1259–1286.

7. Jean Bodin, *Les six livres de la République*, ed. Gérard Mairet (Paris: Livre de Poche, 1993), 428–429, 431, 485, 487, 500.

8. Louis Baeck, "Spanish Economic Thought: The School of Salamanca and the Arbitristas," *History of Political Economy* 20, no. 3 (1988): 394.

9. Henri Hauser, ed., *La vie chère au XVIe siècle: La Réponse de Jean Bodin à M. de Malestroit 1568* (Paris: Armand Colin, 1932), xxxii; J. H. Elliott, "Self-Perception and Decline in Early Seventeenth-Century Spain," *Past and Present* 74 (1977): 49–50.

10. Hauser, *La vie chère*, lviii.

11. Hauser, *La vie chère*, 499–500.

12. David Sainsbury, *Windows of Opportunity: How Nations Create Wealth* (London: Profile Books, 2020), 11.

13. Giovanni Botero, *The Reason of State* (Cambridge: Cambridge University Press, 2017), 4; Giovanni Botero, *On the Causes of the Greatness and Magnificence of Cities*, ed. and trans. Geoffrey Symcox (Toronto: University of Toronto Press, 2012), xxxiii, 39–45.

14. Botero, *On the Causes of the Greatness and Magnificence of Cities*, 43–44; Sophus A. Reinert, *Translating Empire: Emulation and the Origins of*

Political Economy (Cambridge, MA: Harvard University Press, 2011), 117; Erik S. Reinert, "Giovanni Botero (1588) and Antonio Serra (1613): Italy and the Birth of Development Economics," in *The Oxford Handbook of Industrial Policy*, ed. Arkebe Oqubay, Christopher Cramer, Ha-Joon Chang, and Richard Kozul-Wright (Oxford: Oxford University Press, 2020), 3–41.

15. Antonio Serra, *A Short Treatise on the Wealth and Poverty of Nations (1613)*, ed. Sophus A. Reinert, trans. Jonathan Hunt (New York: Anthem, 2011), 121; Jamie Trace, *Giovanni Botero and English Political Thought* (doctoral thesis, University of Cambridge, 2018).

16. Craig Muldrew, *The Economy of Obligation* (New York: Palgrave, 1998), 53.

17. Muldrew, *Economy of Obligation*, 97, 109, 138, 151; Nicolas Grimalde, *Marcus Tullius Ciceroes Thre Bokes of Duties, to Marcus His Sonne, Turned Oute of Latine into English*, ed. Gerald O'Gorman (Washington, DC: Folger Books, 1990), 207.

18. Joyce Oldham Appleby, *Economic Thought and Ideology in Seventeenth-Century England* (Princeton, NJ: Princeton University Press, 1978), 34. See also Elizabeth Lamond, ed., *A Discourse of the Common Weal of This Realm of England. First Printed in 1581 and Commonly Attributed to W.S.* (Cambridge: Cambridge University Press, 1929), 15, 59, 93; Mary Dewar, "The Authorship of the 'Discourse of the Commonweal,'" *Economic History Review* 19, no. 2 (1966): 388–400.

19. Sir Walter Raleigh, *The Discovery of the Large, Rich, and Beautiful Empire of Guiana, with a Relation of the Great and Golden City of Manoa Which the Spaniards Call El Dorado*, ed. Robert H. Schomburgk (New York: Burt Franklin, 1848), lxxix.

20. Gerard de Malynes, *Lex Mercatoria* (Memphis: General Books, 2012), 5.

21. Malynes, *Lex Mercatoria*, 27; William Eamon, *Science and the Secrets of Nature: Books and Secrets in Medieval and Early Modern Culture* (Princeton, NJ: Princeton University Press, 1994); Claire Lesage, "La Littérature des secrets et I Secreti d'Isabella Cortese," *Chroniques italiennes* 36 (1993): 145–178; Carl Wennerlind, *Casualties of Credit: The English Financial Revolution, 1620–1720* (Cambridge, MA: Harvard University Press, 2011), 48.

22. Wennerlind, *Casualties of Credit*, 79, 114, 211; Gerard de Malynes, *The Maintenance of Free Trade* (New York: Augustus Kelley, 1971), 47.

23. Malynes, *Maintenance of Free Trade*, 83, 105.

24. Appleby, *Economic Thought and Ideology*, 37; Thomas Mun, *The Complete Works: Economics and Trade*, ed. Gavin John Adams (San Bernardino, CA: Newton Page, 2013), 145.

25. Edward Misselden, *Free Trade of the Meanes to Make Trade Florish* (London: John Legatt, 1622), 20, 80, 84.

26. Lawrence A. Harper, *The English Navigation Laws: A Seventeenth-Century Experiment in Social Engineering* (New York: Octagon Books, 1960), 40.

27. Charles Henry Wilson, *England's Apprenticeship, 1603–1763* (London: Longmans, 1965), 65; Jean-Baptiste Colbert, "Mémoire touchant le commerce avec l'Angleterre, 1651," in *Lettres, instructions, et mémoires de Colbert*, ed. Pierre Clément, 10 vols. (Paris: Imprimerie Impériale, 1861–1873), vol. 2, pt. 2, pp. 405–409; Harper, *English Navigation Laws*, 16; Moritz Isenmann, "Égalité, réciprocité, souvraineté: The Role of Commercial Treaties in Colbert's Economic Policy," in *The Politics of Commercial Treaties in the Eighteenth Century: Balance of Power, Balance of Trade*, ed. Antonella Alimento and Koen Stapelbroek (London: Palgrave Macmillan, 2017), 77–104.

CHAPTER 6: FREEDOM AND WEALTH IN THE DUTCH REPUBLIC

1. M. F. Bywater and B. S. Yamey, *Historic Accounting Literature: A Companion Guide* (London: Scholar Press, 1982), 87.

2. Jacob Soll, *The Reckoning: Financial Accountability and the Rise and Fall of Nations* (New York: Basic Books, 2014), 77.

3. Maarten Prak, *The Dutch Republic in the Seventeenth Century* (Cambridge: Cambridge University Press, 2005), 29.

4. Prak, *Dutch Republic*, 102.

5. Prak, *Dutch Republic*, 91.

6. Koen Stapelbroek, "Reinventing the Dutch Republic: Franco-Dutch Commercial Treaties from Ryswick to Vienna," in *The Politics of Commercial Treaties in the Eighteenth Century: Balance of Power, Balance of Trade*, ed. Antonella Alimento and Koen Stapelbroek (Cham, Switzerland: Palgrave Macmillan, 2017), 195–215, at 199.

7. Prak, *Dutch Republic*, 105.

8. Prak, *Dutch Republic*, 96; Margaret Schotte, *Sailing School: Navigating Science and Skill, 1550–1800* (Baltimore: Johns Hopkins University Press, 2019), 42, 53.

9. J. M. de Jongh, "Shareholder Activism at the Dutch East India Company, 1622–1625," January 10, 2010, Palgrave Macmillan 2011, available at SSRN, https://ssrn.com/abstract=1496871; Jonathan Koppell, ed., *Origins of Shareholder Activism* (London: Palgrave, 2011); Alexander Bick, *Minutes of Empire: The Dutch West India Company and Mercantile Strategy, 1618–1648* (Oxford: Oxford University Press, forthcoming); Theodore K. Rabb, *Enterprise and Empire: Merchant and Gentry Investment in the Expansion of England, 1575–1630* (Cambridge, MA: Harvard University Press, 2014), 38–41.

10. Lodewijk J. Wagenaar, "Les mécanismes de la prospérité," in *Amsterdam XVIIe siècle: Marchands et philosophes. Les bénéfices de la tolérance*, ed. Henri Méchoulan (Paris: Editions Autrement, 1993), 59–81.

11. "A Translation of the Charter of the Dutch East India Company (1602)," ed. Rupert Gerritsen, trans. Peter Reynders (Canberra: Australasian Hydrographic Society, 2011), 4.

12. De Jongh, "Shareholder Activism," 39.

13. Soll, *Reckoning*, 80; Kristof Glamann, *Dutch Asiatic Trade, 1620–1740* (The Hague: Martinus Nijhoff, 1981), 245.

14. Soll, *Reckoning*, 81.

15. Hugo Grotius, *Commentary on the Law of Prize and Booty*, ed. Martine Julia van Ittersum (Indianapolis: Liberty Fund, 2006), xiii.

16. Grotius, *Commentary*, 10, 27; Hugo Grotius, *The Free Sea*, ed. David Armitage (Indianapolis: Liberty Fund, 2004), xiv, 7, 18.

17. Grotius, *Free Sea*, 5, 24–25, 32.

18. Grotius, *Free Sea*, 57; Hugo Grotius, *The Rights of War and Peace*, ed. Richard Tuck, 3 vols. (Indianapolis: Liberty Fund, 2005), 3:1750, 2:430–431.

19. Grotius, *Rights of War and Peace*, 2:556–557; Brett Rushforth, *Bonds of Alliance: Indigenous and Atlantic Slaveries in New France* (Chapel Hill: University of North Carolina Press, 2012), 90.

20. Rushforth, *Bonds of Alliance*, 93.

21. Rushforth, *Bonds of Alliance*, 70; Grotius, *Free Sea*, xii–xxiii.

22. On new attitudes of merchant virtue, see J. G. A. Pocock, *The Machiavellian Moment: Florentine Political Thought and the Atlantic Republican Tradition* (Princeton, NJ: Princeton University Press, 1975), 478.

23. Pieter de La Court, *The True Interest and Political Maxims of the Republick of Holland and West-Friesland* (London: 1702), vi, 4–6, 9.

24. De La Court, *True Interest and Political Maxims*, 24–35.

25. De La Court, *True Interest and Political Maxims*, 63, 51, 55.

26. De La Court, *True Interest and Political Maxims*, 45, 51, 55, 312, 315.

27. Prak, *Dutch Republic*, 51, 53.

28. Prak, *Dutch Republic*, 59.

CHAPTER 7: JEAN-BAPTISTE COLBERT AND THE STATE-MADE MARKET

1. Pierre Deyon, "Variations de la production textile aux XVIe et XVIIe siècles: Sources et premiers résultats," *Annales. Histoire, sciences sociales* 18, no. 5 (1963): 939–955, at 949.

2. Daniel Dessert and Jean-Louis Journet, "Le lobby Colbert," *Annales* 30, no. 6 (1975): 1303–1329; Georg Bernhard Depping, *Correspondance administrative sous le règne de Louis XIV*, 3 vols. (Paris: Imprimerie Nationale, 1852), 3:428; Philippe Minard, "The Market Economy and the French State: Myths and Legends Around Colbertism," *L'Économie politique* 1, no. 37 (2008): 77–94; Jean-Baptiste Colbert, "Mémoire sur le commerce: Prémier Conseil de Commerce Tenu par le Roy, dimanche, 3 aoust 1664," in *Lettres, instructions, et mémoires de Colbert*, ed. Pierre Clément, 10 vols. (Paris: Imprimerie Impériale, 1861–1873), vol. 2, pt. 1, p. cclxvi; Jean-Baptiste Colbert, "Mémoire touchant le commerce avec l'Angleterre," in *Lettres*, vol. 2, pt. 2, p. 407.

3. Colbert, "Mémoire touchant le commerce avec l'Angleterre," vol. 2, pt. 2, pp. cclxviii, 48, 407; D'Maris Coffman, *Excise Taxations and the Origins of Public Debt* (London: Palgrave Macmillan, 2013).

4. Colbert, "Mémoire sur le commerce, 1664," vol. 2, pt. 1, pp. cclxii–cclxxii, at cclxviii, cclxix; Jean-Baptiste Colbert, "Aux maires, échevins, et jurats des villes maritimes de l'océan, aoust 1669," in *Lettres*, vol. 2, pt. 2, p. 487; Colbert to M. Barillon, intendant at Amiens, mars 1670, in *Lettres*, vol. 2, pt. 2, pp. 520–521; Colbert to M. Bouchu, intentant at Dijon, juillet 1671, in *Lettres*, vol. 2, pt. 2, p. 627.

5. Gustav von Schmoller, *The Mercantile System and Its Historical Significance* (New York: Macmillan, 1897); Erik Grimmer-Solem, *The Rise of Historical Economics and Social Reform in Germany, 1864–1894* (Oxford: Oxford University Press, 2003). On development economics, see Erik S. Reinert, "The Role of the State in Economic Growth," *Journal of Economic Studies* 26, no. 4/5 (1999): 268–326.

6. Deyon, "Variations de la production textile," 949, 951–953; François Crouzet, "Angleterre et France au XVIIIe siècle: Essaie d'analyse comparé de deux croissances économiques," *Annales. Économies, sociétés, civilisations* 21, no. 2 (1966): 254–291, at 267.

7. Crouzet, "Angleterre et France au XVIIIe siècle," 266, 268; Eli F. Heckscher, *Mercantilism*, trans. Mendel Shapiro, 2 vols. (London: George Allen and Unwin, 1935), 1:82; Stewart L. Mims, *Colbert's West India Policy* (New Haven, CT: Yale University Press, 1912); Charles Woolsey Cole, *Colbert and a Century of French Mercantilism*, 2 vols. (New York: Columbia University Press, 1939), 1:356–532; Charles Woolsey Cole, *French Mercantilism, 1683–1700* (New York: Octagon Books, 1971); Glenn J. Ames, *Colbert, Mercantilism, and the French Quest for Asian Trade* (DeKalb: Northern Illinois University Press, 1996); Philippe Minard, *La fortune du colbertisme: État et industrie dans la France des Lumières* (Paris: Fayard, 1998).

8. Colbert, *Lettres*, vol. 2, pt. 2, p. 457.

9. Colbert, "Mémoire sur le commerce, 1664," vol. 2, pt. 1, pp. cclxii–cclxxii, at cclxviii; Colbert, "Mémoire touchant le commerce avec l'Angleterre," 405–409; Georg Bernhard Depping, *Correspondance administrative sous le règne de Louis XIV*, vol. 3 (Paris: Imprimerie Nationale, 1852), 90, 428, 498, 524, 570; Moritz Isenmann, "Égalité, réciprocité, souvraineté: The Role of Commercial Treaties in Colbert's Economic Policy," in *The Politics of Commercial Treaties in the Eighteenth Century: Balance of Power, Balance of Trade*, ed. Antonella Alimento and Koen Stapelbroek (London: Palgrave Macmillan, 2017), 79.

10. Colbert, "Mémoire touchant le commerce avec l'Angleterre," 405–409, 496, 523, 570; Lawrence A. Harper, *The English Navigation Laws: A Seventeenth-Century Experiment in Social Engineering* (New York: Octagon Books, 1964), 16; John U. Nef, *Industry and Government in France and England, 1540–1640* (repr., Ithaca, NY: Cornell University Press, 1957 [1940]), 13, 27.

11. Colbert, "Mémoire touchant le commerce avec l'Angleterre," 487; Colbert to M. du Lion, September 6, 1673, in *Lettres*, vol. 2, pt. 1, p. 57; Colbert to M. de Baas, April 9, 1670, in *Lettres*, vol. 2, pt. 2, p. 479.

12. Ames, *Colbert, Mercantilism*, 189; Mims, *Colbert's West India Policy*, 232; Mireille Zarb, *Les pivilèges de la Ville de Marseille du Xe siècle à la Révolution* (Paris: Éditions A. et J. Picard, 1961), 163, 329; Jean-Baptiste Colbert, "Mémoire touchant le commerce avec l'Angleterre," 407.

13. Jacques Saint-Germain, *La Reynie et la police au Grand Siècle: D'après de nombreux documents inédits* (Paris: Hachette, 1962), 238, 240.

14. François Charpentier, *Discours d'un fidèle sujet du roy touchant l'establissement d'une Compagnie Françoise pour le commerce des Indes Orientales; Adressé à tous les François* (Paris: 1764), 4, 8; Paul Pellisson, *Histoire de l'Académie Françoise,* 2 vols. (Paris: Coignard, 1753), 1:364.

15. Urban-Victor Chatelain, *Nicolas Foucquet, protecteur des lettres, des arts, et des sciences* (Paris: Librarie Académique Didier, 1905), 120; Pierre-Daniel Huet, *Histoire du commerce et de la navigation des anciens* (Lyon: Benoit Duplein, 1763), 1–2.

16. Huet, *Histoire du commerce et de la navigation,* cclxxii.

17. Heckscher, *Mercantilism,* 1:81–82; Jean-Baptiste Colbert, "Mémoires sur les affaires de finances de France pour servir à leur histoire, 1663," in *Lettres,* vol. 2, pt. 2, pp. 17–68; J. Schaeper, *The French Council of Commerce, 1700–1715: A Study of Mercantilism After Colbert* (Columbus: Ohio State University Press, 1983); Colbert, "Mémoire sur le commerce," 44–45.

18. François Barrême, *Le livre nécessaire pour les comptables, avocats, notaires, procureurs, négociants, et généralement à toute sorte de conditions* (Paris: D. Thierry, 1694), 3; François Barrême, *Nouveau Barrême universel: Manuel complet de tous les comptes faits* (Paris: C. Lavocat, 1837).

19. *Ordonnance du commerce du mois de mars 1673; et ordonnance de la marine, du mois d'août 1681* (Bordeaux, France: Audibert et Burkel, an VIII), 5, Art. 4.

20. Jacques Savary, *Le parfait négociant; ou, Instruction générale pour ce qui regarde le commerce des Marchandises de France, & des Païs Estrangers,* 8th ed., ed. Jacques Savary Desbruslons, 2 vols. (Amsterdam: Jansons à Waesberge, 1726), 1:25; Adam Smith, *An Inquiry into the Nature and Causes of the Wealth of Nations,* ed. Roy Harold Campbell and Andrew Skinner, 2 vols. (Indianapolis: Liberty Fund, 1981), vol. 2, bk. IV, chap. vii, pt. 2, para. 53.

21. Peter Burke, *The Fabrication of Louis XIV* (New Haven, CT: Yale University Press, 1994); Colbert, "Mémoire sur le Commerce," vol. 2, pt. 1, p. cclxiii; Alice Stroup, *A Company of Scientists: Botany, Patronage, and Community in the Seventeenth-Century Parisian Royal Academy of Sciences* (Berkeley: University of California Press, 1990), 30.

22. Colbert, *Lettres,* vol. 2, pt. 2, p. 62; vol. 5, pp. 241–242; Charles Perrault, "Autre note à Colbert sur l'établissement de l'Académie des Beaux-Arts et de l'Académie des Sciences," 1666, in Colbert, *Lettres,*

5:513–514. Also see Roger Hahn, *The Anatomy of a Scientific Institution: The Paris Academy of Sciences, 1666–1803* (Berkeley: University of California Press, 1971), 15; Lorraine Daston, "Baconian Facts, Academic Civility, and the Prehistory of Objectivity," *Annals of Scholarship* 8 (1991): 337–363; Steven Shapin, *A Social History of Truth: Civility and Science in Seventeenth-Century England* (Chicago: University of Chicago Press, 1995), 291; Michael Hunter, *Science and Society in Restoration England* (Cambridge: Cambridge University Press, 1981), 48; Anthony Grafton, *The Footnote: A Curious History* (Cambridge, MA: Harvard University Press, 1997), 202–205; Jean-Baptiste Say, *A Treatise on Political Economy*, 2 vols. (Boston: Wells and Lilly, 1821), 1:32–33; Margaret C. Jacob, *Scientific Culture and the Making of the Industrial West* (Oxford: Oxford University Press, 1997), chap. 8.

23. Perrault, "Autre note à Colbert," 5:514; Charles Perrault, "Note de Charles Perrault à Colbert pour l'établissement d'une Académie Générale, 1664," in Colbert, *Lettres*, 5:512–513.

24. Christiaan Huygens, *Oeuvres completes*, 22 vols. (The Hague: Martinus Nijhoff, 1891), 19:255–256. The bracketed notes are by Michael Mahoney, from his translation, which I am using: "[Memorandum from Christiaan Huygens to Minister Colbert Regarding the Work of the New Académie Royale des Sciences]," Princeton University, www.princeton.edu/~hos/h591/acadsci.huy.html.

25. Huygens, "Note from Huygens to Colbert, with the Observations of Colbert, 1670," in Colbert, *Lettres*, 5:524; James E. King, *Science and Rationalism in the Government of Louis XIV, 1661–1683* (Baltimore: Johns Hopkins University Press, 1949), 292; Joseph Klaits, *Printed Propaganda Under Louis XIV: Absolute Monarchy and Public Opinion* (Princeton, NJ: Princeton University Press, 1976), 74; Denis de Sallo, "To the Reader," *Journal des sçavans* (January 5, 1665): 5; Jacqueline de la Harpe, *Le Journal des Savants en Angleterre, 1702–1789* (Berkeley: University of California Press, 1941), 6, 8; Arnaud Orain and Sylvain Laubé, "Scholars Versus Practitioners? Anchor Proof Testing and the Birth of a Mixed Culture in Eighteenth-Century France," *Technology and Culture* 58, no. 1 (2017): 1–34.

26. Liliane Hilaire-Pérez, Fabien Simon, and Marie Thébaud-Sorger, *L'Europe des sciences et des techniques: Un dialogue des savoirs, xve–xviiie siècle* (Rennes, France: Presses Universitaires de Rennes, 2016); John R. Pannabecker, "Diderot, the Mechanical Arts, and the *Encyclopédie* in Search of the Heritage of Technology Education," *Journal of Technology*

Education 6, no. 1 (1994); Cynthia J. Koepp, "Advocating for Artisans: The Abbé Pluche's Spectacle de la Nature (1731–1751)," in *The Idea of Work in Europe from Antiquity to Modern Times*, ed. Josef Ehmer and Catherina Lis (Farnham, VT: Ashgate, 2009), 245–273. On the transformation of the Colbertist Société des Arts into a physiocratic institution, see Hahn, *Anatomy of a Scientific Institution*, 108–110; Robert Darnton, *The Business of Enlightenment: A Publishing History of the Encyclopédie, 1775–1800* (Cambridge, MA: Belknap Press of Harvard University Press, 1979); Kathleen Hardesty, *The Supplément to the Encyclopédie* (The Hague: Nijhoff, 1977); John Lough, *Essays on the "Encyclopédie" of Diderot and d'Alembert* (London: Oxford University Press, 1968); Dan Edelstein, *The Enlightenment: A Genealogy* (Chicago: University of Chicago Press, 2010); Jacob Soll, *The Information Master: Jean-Baptiste Colbert's Secret State Information System* (Ann Arbor: University of Michigan Press, 2009), 161; Robert Darnton, "Philosophers Trim the Tree of Knowledge: The Epistemological Strategy of the Encyclopédie," in *The Great Cat Massacre and Other Episodes in French Cultural History* (New York: Vintage, 1984), chap. 5; *Colbert, 1619–1683* (Paris: Ministère de la Culture, 1983), 168; Paola Bertucci, *Artisanal Enlightenment: Science and the Mechanical Arts in Old Regime France* (New Haven, CT: Yale University Press, 2017), 214. Also see Linn Holmberg, *The Maurist's Unfinished Encyclopedia* (Oxford: Voltaire Foundation, 2017), 175.

27. Colbert, "Mémoire touchant le commerce avec l'Angleterre," vol. 2, pt. 2, p. 405.

28. Samuel Pepys, *Naval Minutes*, ed. J. R. Tanner (London: Navy Records Society, 1926), 352–356, at 356; King, *Science and Rationalism*, 272.

29. D. G. E. Hall, "Anglo-French Trade Relations Under Charles II," *History* 7, no. 25 (1922): 17–30, at 23; Jacob Soll, "For a New Economic History of Early Modern Empire: Anglo-French Imperial Codevelopment Beyond Mercantilism and Laissez-Faire," *William and Mary Quarterly* 77, no. 4 (2020): 525–550.

CHAPTER 8: THE NIGHTMARES OF THE SUN KING AND THE DREAM OF FREE MARKETS

1. Albert O. Hirschman, *The Passions and the Interests: Political Arguments for Capitalism Before Its Triumph* (Princeton, NJ: Princeton University Press, 1977), 16.

2. Thomas Hobbes, *Leviathan*, ed. Richard Tuck (Cambridge: Cambridge University Press, 1997), pt. 1, chaps. 13–14.

3. La Rochefoucauld, *Maxims*, trans. Leonard Tancock (London: Penguin, 1959), maxims 48, 85, 112, 563; Pierre Force, *Self-Interest Before Adam Smith: A Genealogy of Economic Science* (Cambridge: Cambridge University Press, 2003), 146, 176; Norbert Elias, *The Court Society* (New York: Pantheon Books, 1983), 105.

4. La Rochefoucauld, *Maxims*, 66, 77, 223, 305.

5. David A. Bell, *The Cult of the Nation in France: Inventing Nationalism, 1680–1800* (Cambridge, MA: Harvard University Press, 2003), 28; Dan Edelstein, *On the Spirit of Rights* (Chicago: University of Chicago Press, 2019), 120; Pierre Nicole, "De la grandeur," in *Essais de morale*, 3 vols. (Paris: Desprez, 1701), 2:186; Dale van Kley and Pierre Nicole, "Jansenism, and the Morality of Self-Interest," in *Anticipations of the Enlightenment in England, France, and Germany*, ed. Alan C. Kors and Paul J. Korshin (Philadelphia: University of Pennsylvania Press, 1987), 69–85; Gilbert Faccarello, *Aux origines de l'économie politique libérale: Pierre de Boisguilbert* (Paris: Éditions Anthropos, 1985), 99.

6. Jean Domat, *The Civil Law in Its Order Together with the Publick Law*, 2 vols. (London: William Strahan, 1722), vol. 1, chap. 2, sec. 2; vol. 1, chap. 5, sec. 7; vol. 2, bk. 1, title 5; Faccarello, *Aux origines de l'économie politique libérale*, 146; Edelstein, *On the Spirit of Rights*, 120; David Grewal, "The Political Theology of *Laissez-Faire*: From *Philia* to Self-Love in Commercial Society," *Political Theology* 17, no. 5 (2016): 417–433, at 419.

7. Pierre Le Pesant de Boisguilbert, *Détail de la France* (Geneva: Institut Coppet, 2014), 18, 61–63.

8. Boisguilbert, *Détail de la France*, 77, 89, 99.

9. Faccarello, *Aux origines de l'économie politique libérale*, 115, 119.

10. Gary B. McCollim, *Louis XIV's Assault on Privilege: Nicolas Desmaretz and the Tax on Wealth* (Rochester, NY: University of Rochester Press, 2012), 106, 149; A.-M. de Boislisle, *Correspondance des contrôleurs généraux des finances*, 3 vols. (Paris: Imprimerie Nationale, 1883), 2:530.

11. Boisguilbert to Desmaretz, July 1–22, 1704, Archives Nationales de France, G7 721; Boislisle, 2:207, 543–547, 559.

12. Boislisle, *Correspondance des contrôleurs généraux*, 2:544.

13. Georges Lizerand, *Le duc de Beauvillier* (Paris: Société d'Édition-Les Belles Lettres, 1933), 43, 153.

14. Lionel Rothkrug, *Opposition to Louis XIV: The Political and Social Origins of the French Enlightenment* (Princeton, NJ: Princeton University Press, 1965), 263–269, 286–287; Louis Trénard, *Les Mémoires des intendants pour l'instruction du duc de Bourgogne* (Paris: Bibliothèque Nationale, 1975), 70–82; David Bell, *The First Total War: Napoleon's Europe and the Birth of Warfare as We Know It* (New York: Houghton Mifflin, 2007), 62; Lizerand, *Le duc de Beauvillier*, 46–77; marquis de Vogüé, *Le duc de Bourgogne et le duc de Beauvillier: Lettres inédites, 1700–1708* (Paris: Plon, 1900), 11–23; Jean-Baptiste Colbert, marquis de Torcy, *Journal Inédit*, ed. Frédéric Masson (Paris: Plon, Nourrit et Cie, 1884), 57; Louis de Rouvroy, duc de Saint-Simon, *Projets de gouvernement du duc de Bourgogne*, ed. P. Mesnard (Paris: Librarie de L. Hachette et Cie, 1860), xxxix, 13; Edmond Esmonin, "Les Mémoires des intendants pour l'instruction du duc de Bourgogne," in *Études sur la France des XVIIe et XVIIIe siècles* (Paris: Presses Universitaires de France, 1964), 113–130, at 117–119; Boislisle, *Correspondance des contrôleurs généraux*, 2:ii.

15. Georges Weulersse, *Le movement physiocratique en France de 1756 à 1770*, 2 vols. (Paris: Félix Alcan, 1910), 2, 302; François Fénelon, *Telemachus*, ed. and trans. Patrick Riley (Cambridge: Cambridge University Press, 1994), 60, 195, 325.

16. Fénelon, *Telemachus*, 195.

17. Fénelon, *Telemachus*, 16, 18, 25, 28, 60, 164, 170, 297.

18. Fénelon, *Telemachus*, 37–39, 161–162, 165, 297.

19. Fénelon, *Telemachus*, 37, 38, 105, 161, 166.

20. Fénelon, *Telemachus*, 166, 195, 260.

21. Montesquieu, *De l'Esprit des lois*, ed. Victor Goldschmidt, 2 vols. (Paris: Garnier-Flammarion, 1979), vol. 2, bk. 20, chap. 1.

CHAPTER 9: THE MOVEMENT OF THE PLANETS AND THE NEW WORLD OF ENGLISH FREE TRADE

1. Ludwig Wittgenstein, *Culture and Value*, ed. Georg Henrik Wright, Heikki Nyman, and Alois Pichler, trans. Peter Winch (London: Blackwell, 1998), 18; Richard J. Blackwell, "Descartes' Laws of Motion," *Isis* 52, no. 2 (1966): 220–234, at 220.

2. Vincenzo Ferrone, "The Epistemological Roots of the New Political Economy: Modern Science and Economy in the First Half of the Eighteenth Century," paper presented at the conference "Mobility and

Modernity: Religion, Science and Commerce in the Seventeenth and Eighteenth Centuries," University of California, Los Angeles, William Andrews Clark Memorial Library, April 13–14, 2018.

3. Margaret C. Jacob, *The Newtonians and the English Revolution, 1689–1720* (Ithaca, NY: Cornell University Press, 1976), 174; Rob Iliffe, *The Priest of Nature: The Religious Worlds of Isaac Newton* (Oxford: Oxford University Press, 2017), 6.

4. Betty Jo Teeter Dobbs and Margaret C. Jacob, *Newton and the Culture of Newtonianism* (Amherst, NY: Humanity Books, 1990), 26, 100; William R. Newman, *Newton the Alchemist: Science, Enigma, and the Quest for Nature's "Secret Fire"* (Princeton, NJ: Princeton University Press, 2019), 64, 70.

5. Dobbs and Jacob, *Newton and the Culture of Newtonianism*, 42; Gottfried Wilhelm Leibniz, *Theodicy*, ed. Austen Farrer, trans. E. M. Huggard (Charleston, SC: BiblioBazaar, 2007), 43, 158; G. W. Leibniz, "Note on Foucher's Objection (1695)," in G. W. Leibniz, *Philosophical Essays*, ed. and trans. Roger Ariew and Daniel Garber (Indianapolis: Hackett, 1989), 146; G. W. Leibniz, *The Labyrinth of the Continuum: Writings on the Continuum Problem, 1672–1686*, trans. Richard T. W. Arthur (New Haven, CT: Yale University Press, 2001), 566.

6. William Letwin, *The Origins of Scientific Economics: English Economic Thought, 1660–1776* (London: Methuen, 1963), 128.

7. François Crouzet, "Angleterre et France au XVIIIe siècle: Essaie d'analyse comparé de deux croissances économiques," *Annales. Économies, sociétés, civilisations* 21, no. 2 (1966): 254–291, at 268; T. S. Ashton, *An Economic History of England: The Eighteenth Century* (London: Methuen, 1955), 104; François Crouzet, *Britain Ascendant: Comparative Studies in Franco-British Economic History* (Cambridge: Cambridge University Press, 1991), 17–23, 73.

8. William Petty, "A Treatise of Taxes and Contributions," in William Petty, *Tracts Chiefly Relating to Ireland* (Dublin: Boulter Grierson, 1769), 1–92, at 23–26, 32.

9. William Petty, "The Political Anatomy of Ireland, 1672," in Petty, *Tracts*, 299–444, at 341.

10. John Locke, *Two Treatises of Government*, ed. Peter Laslett (Cambridge: Cambridge University Press, 1960), 171; John F. Henry, "John Locke, Property Rights, and Economic Theory," *Journal of Economic Issues* 33, no. 3 (1999): 609–624, at 615.

11. Locke, *Two Treatises*, 291, 384.

12. John O. Hancey, "John Locke and the Law of Nature," *Political Theory* 4, no. 4 (1976): 439–454, at 219, 439 (emphasis in original).

13. Holly Brewer, "Slavery, Sovereignty, and 'Inheritable Blood': Reconsidering John Locke and the Origins of American Slavery," *American Historical Review* 122, no. 4 (2017): 1038–1078; Mark Goldie, "Locke and America," in *A Companion to Locke*, ed. Matthew Stuart (Chichester: Wiley-Blackwell, 2015), 546–563; Letwin, *Origins of Scientific Economics*, 163–165; David Armitage, "John Locke, Carolina, and *The Two Treatises of Government*," *Political Theory* 32, no. 5 (2004): 602–627, at 616; J. G. A. Pocock, *The Machiavellian Moment: Florentine Political Thought and the Atlantic Republican Tradition* (Princeton, NJ: Princeton University Press, 1975), 283–285, 339.

14. Charles Davenant, *An Essay on the East India Trade* (London, 1696), 25.

15. Pocock, *Machiavellian Moment*, 437, 443.

16. Pocock, *Machiavellian Moment*, 446; Charles Davenant, *Reflections upon the Constitution and Management of the Trade to Africa* (London: John Morphew, 1709), 25, 28.

17. Davenant, *Reflections*, 27, 36, 48, 50, 58.

18. Steven Pincus, *1688: The First Modern Revolution* (New Haven, CT: Yale University Press, 2009), 308.

CHAPTER 10: ENGLAND VERSUS FRANCE: TRADE WAR, DEBT, AND THE DREAM OF PARADISE FOUND

1. Guy Rowlands, *The Financial Decline of a Great Power: War, Influence, and Money in Louis XIV's France* (Oxford: Oxford University Press, 2012), 2; Richard Dale, *The First Crash: Lessons from the South Sea Bubble* (Princeton, NJ: Princeton University Press, 2004), 77.

2. Carl Wennerlind, *Casualties of Credit: The English Financial Revolution, 1620–1720* (Cambridge, MA: Harvard University Press, 2011), 68, 89; Stephen Quinn, "The Glorious Revolution's Effect on English Private Finance: A Microhistory, 1680–1705," *Journal of Economic History* 61, no. 3 (2001): 593–615, at 593; Julian Hoppit, *Britain's Political Economies: Parliament and Economic Life, 1660–1800* (Cambridge: Cambridge University Press, 2017), 149; P. G. M. Dickson, *The Financial Revolution*

in England: A Study in the Development of Public Credit, 1688–1756 (New York: Macmillan, 1967), 80.

3. John Brewer, *The Sinews of Power: War, Money and the English State, 1688–1783* (New York: Alfred A. Knopf, 1989), 116–117.

4. Wennerlind, *Casualties of Credit*, 10; Ian Hacking, *The Emergence of Probability: A Philosophical Study of Early Ideas About Probability, Induction and Statistical Inference* (Cambridge: Cambridge University Press, 1975); Lorrain Daston, *Classical Probability in the Enlightenment* (Princeton, NJ: Princeton University Press, 1988), 164.

5. *An Account of What Will DO; or, an Equivalent for Thoulon: In a Proposal for an Amicable Subscription for Improving TRADE in the South-West Part of AMERICA, and Increasing BULLION to About Three Millions per Annum, Both for the East India Trade and the Revenue of the Crown, Which by Consequence Will Be Produced if This Is Encouraged* (London: Mary Edwards, 1707), 3.

6. Bernard Mandeville, *The Fable of the Bees*, ed. Philip Harth (London: Penguin, 1970), 64.

7. Mandeville, *Fable of the Bees*, 67–68.

8. Antoin E. Murphy, *John Law: Economic Theorist and Policy-Maker* (Oxford: Oxford University Press, 1997), 94–95.

9. John Law, *Money and Trade Considered* (Glasgow: A. Foulis, 1750), 167.

10. Arnaud Orain, *La politique du merveilleux: Une autre histoire du Système de Law (1695–1795)* (Paris: Fayard, 2018), 10; Charly Coleman, *The Spirit of French Capitalism: Economic Theology in the Age of Enlightenment* (Stanford, CA: Stanford University Press, 2021), 119.

11. Coleman, *Spirit of French Capitalism*, 119.

12. Coleman, *Spirit of French Capitalism*, 20, 81.

13. Jean Terrasson, *Lettres sur le nouveau Système des Finances*, 1720, 2–5, 29, 32, 33; Jean Terrasson, *Traité de l'infini créé*, ed. Antonella Del Prete (Paris: Honoré Champion, 2007), 225–227.

14. Orain, *La politique du merveilleux*, 13.

15. Claude Pâris La Montagne, "Traité des Administrations des Recettes et des Dépenses du Royaume," 1733, Archives Nationales, 1005, II: 3–8, 48–49, 55.

16. Norris Arthur Brisco, *The Economic Policy of Robert Walpole* (New York: Columbia University Press, 1907), 43–45; Richard Dale, *The First*

Crash: Lessons from the South Sea Bubble (Princeton, NJ: Princeton University Press, 2004), 74.

17. Cited by Dickson, *Financial Revolution in England*, 83.

18. Jacob Soll, *The Reckoning: Financial Accountability and the Rise and Fall of Nations* (New York: Basic Books, 2014), 101–116.

CHAPTER 11: THE FRENCH CULT OF NATURE AND THE INVENTION OF ENLIGHTENMENT ECONOMICS

1. Charles M. Andrews, "Anglo-French Commercial Rivalry, 1700–1750: The Western Phase, I," *American Historical Review* 20, no. 3 (1915): 539–556, at 547; David Hume, *Selected Essays*, ed. Stephen Copley and Andrew Edgar (Oxford: Oxford University Press, 1996), 189, 214.

2. Georges Weulersse, *Le mouvement physiocratique en France (de 1756 à 1770)*, 2 vols. (Paris: Félix Alcan, 1910), 1:23; Montesquieu, *De l'Esprit des lois*, ed. Victor Goldschmidt, 2 vols. (Paris: Garnier-Flammarion, 1979), vol. 2, bk. 20, chap. 2; David Hume, *An Inquiry Concerning Human Understanding, with a Supplement: An Abstract of a Treatise on Human Nature*, ed. Charles W. Hendel (Indianapolis: Liberal Arts Press, 1955), 173.

3. Robert B. Ekelund Jr. and Robert F. Hébert, *A History of Economic Theory and Method*, 6th ed. (Longrove, IL: Waveland Press, 2014), 70.

4. Tony Brewer, *Richard Cantillon: Pioneer of Economic Theory* (London: Routledge, 1992), 8.

5. Richard Cantillon, *Essai sur la nature du commerce en général*, ed. and trans. Henry Higgs (London: Macmillan, 1931), 58.

6. Cantillon, *Essai sur la nature du commerce*, 97, 123; Marian Bowley, *Studies in the History of Economic Theory Before 1870* (London: Macmillan, 1973), 95.

7. Cantillon, *Essai sur la nature du commerce*, 51–55, 85; Bowley, *Studies in the History of Economic Theory*, 96.

8. Jean-François Melon, *Essaie politique sur le commerce*, in Eugène Daire, *Économistes financiers du XVIIIe siècle* (Paris: Guillaumin, 1851), 659–777, at 671, 666.

9. Melon, *Essaie politique sur le commerce*, 673, 708.

10. Melon, *Essaie politique sur le commerce*, 683, 746, 765.

11. Paul Cheney, *Revolutionary Commerce: Globalization and the French Monarchy* (Cambridge, MA: Harvard University Press, 2010), 22; Montesquieu, *De l'esprit des lois*, bk. 20, chaps. 1–2.

12. David Kammerling-Smith, "Le discours économique du Bureau du commerce, 1700–1750," in *Le Cercle de Vincent de Gournay: Savoirs économiques et pratiques administratives en France au milieu du XVIIIe siècle*, ed. Loïc Charles, Frédéric Lefebvre, and Christine Théré (Paris: INED, 2011), 31–62, at 34.

13. R. L. Meek, *The Economics of Physiocracy* (London: Allen and Unwin, 1963), xiii.

14. François Véron de Forbonnais, *Éléments du commerce*, 3 vols. (Paris: Chaignieau, 1793–1794), 1:62.

15. Forbonnais, *Éléments du commerce*, 1:67–68, 75–76.

16. Forbonnais, *Éléments du commerce*, 1:3, 38, 45.

17. Steven L. Kaplan, *Bread, Politics, and Political Economy in the Reign of Louis XV*, 2nd ed. (New York: Anthem Press, 2012), 108; Gérard Klotz, Philippe Minard, and Arnaud Orain, eds., *Les voies de la richesse? La physiocratie en question (1760–1850)* (Rennes, France: Presses Universitaires de Rennes, 2017), 11; Gustav Schachter, "François Quesnay: Interpreters and Critics Revisited," *American Journal of Economics and Sociology* 50, no. 3 (1991): 313–322; Paul Samuelson, "Quesnay's 'Tableau Économique' as a Theorist Would Formulate It Today," in *Paul Samuelson on the History of Economic Analysis: Selected Essays*, ed. Steven J. Medema and Anthony M. C. Waterman (Cambridge: Cambridge University Press, 2015), 59–86, at 60.

18. Pierre-Paul Mercier de la Rivière, *L'ordre naturel et essentiel des sociétés politiques*, 2 vols. (London: Jean Nourse, 1767).

19. Liana Vardi, *The Physiocrats and the World of the Enlightenment* (Cambridge: Cambridge University Press, 2012), 42.

20. Vardi, *Physiocrats*, 84; David S. Landes, *Unbound Prometheus: Technological Change and Industrial Development in Western Europe from 1750 to the Present* (Cambridge: Cambridge University Press, 1969), 82.

21. Steven Pincus, *The Global British Empire to 1784*, unpublished manuscript; Gabriel François Coyer, *La noblesse commerçante* (London: Fletcher Gyles, 1756), 33–34, 45, 72.

22. Simone Meyssonnier, *La balance et l'horloge: La genèse de la pensée libérale en France au XVIIIe siècle* (Paris: Les Éditions de la Passion, 1989), 264.

23. Meyssonnier, *La balance et l'horloge*, 265.

24. Meyssonnier, *La balance et l'horloge*, 249.

25. Meyssonnier, *La balance et l'horloge*, 80–81; Coyer, *La noblesse commerçante*, 33–34, 279.

26. Le marquis de Mirabeau, *L'ami des hommes, ou traité de la population*, 2 vols. (Avignon: 1756); Meek, *Economics of Physiocracy*, 15.

27. Meek, *Economics of Physiocracy*, 18.

28. Meek, *Economics of Physiocracy*, 23; E. P. Thompson, *The Making of the English Working Class* (New York: Vintage, 1966), 218; Boaz Moselle, "Allotments, Enclosure, and Proletarianization in Early Nineteenth-Century Southern England," *English Economic History Review* 48, no. 3 (1995): 482–500.

29. Meek, *Economics of Physiocracy*, 109–114, 136.

30. François Quesnay, *Despotism in China*, trans. Lewis A. Maverick, in Lewis A. Maverick, *China: A Model for Europe*, 2 vols. (San Antonio: Paul Anderson and Company, 1946), 1:216; W. W. Davis, "China, the Confucian Ideal, and the European Age of Enlightenment," *Journal of the History of Ideas* 44, no. 4 (1983): 523–548; Stefan Gaarsmand Jacobsen, "Against the Chinese Model: The Debate on Cultural Facts and Physiocratic Epistemology," in *The Economic Turn: Recasting Political Economy in Enlightenment Europe*, ed. Steven L. Kaplan and Sophus A. Reinert (London: Anthem Press, 2019), 89–115; Cheney, *Revolutionary Commerce*, 203; Pernille Røge, *Economists and the Reinvention of Empire: France in the Americas and Africa, c. 1750–1802* (Cambridge: Cambridge University Press, 2019), 10.

31. Quesnay, *Despotism in China*, 11; Røge, *Economists and the Reinvention of Empire*, 88.

32. Loïc Charles and Arnaud Orain, "François Véron de Forbonnais and the Invention of Antiphysiocracy," in Kaplan and Reinert, *Economic Turn*, 139–168.

33. Meek, *Economics of Physiocracy*, 46–50.

34. Meek, *Economics of Physiocracy*, 70.

35. Jean Ehrard, *Lumières et esclavage: L'esclavage colonial et l'opinion publique en France au XVIIIe siècle* (Brussels: André Versaille, 2008); Røge, *Economists and the Reinvention of Empire*, 176; David Allen Harvey, "Slavery on the Balance Sheet: Pierre-Samuel Dupont de Nemours and the Physiocratic Case for Free Labor," *Journal of the Western Society for French History* 42 (2014): 75–87, at 76.

CHAPTER 12: FREE MARKETS VERSUS NATURE

1. Erik S. Reinert and Fernanda A. Reinert, "33 Economic Bestsellers Published Before 1750," *European Journal of the History of Economic Thought* 25, no. 6 (2018): 1206–1263; Derek Beales, *Enlightenment and Reform in Eighteenth Century Europe* (London: I. B. Tauris, 2005), 64; Istvan Hont, *Jealousy of Trade: International Competition and the Nation-State in Historical Perspective* (Cambridge, MA: Harvard University Press, 2005), 45, 134; Sophus A. Reinert, *The Academy of Fisticuffs: Political Economy and Commercial Society in Enlightenment Italy* (Cambridge, MA: Harvard University Press, 2018), 7; John Robertson, *The Case for Enlightenment: Scotland and Naples, 1680–1760* (Cambridge: Cambridge University Press, 2005), 22; Koen Stapelbroek, "Commerce and Morality in Eighteenth-Century Italy," *History of European Ideas* 32, no. 4 (2006): 361–366, at 364; Antonio Muratori, *Della pubblica felicità: Oggetto de'buoni principi* (Lucca, 1749), p. 3 of "To the Reader."

2. Eric Cochrane, *Florence in the Forgotten Centuries, 1527–1800* (Chicago: University of Chicago Press, 1973), 461; Reinert, *Academy of Fisticuffs*, 299; Antonio Genovesi, *Delle lezioni di commercio, o s'ia d'economia civile*, 2 vols. (Naples: Fratelli di Simone, 1767), 2:77, 133; Robertson, *Case for Enlightenment*, 356–357.

3. Steven L. Kaplan and Sophus A. Reinert, eds., *The Economic Turn: Recasting Political Economy in Enlightenment Europe* (London: Anthem Press, 2019), 3–13; Pietro Verri, *Meditazioni sulla economia politica* (Venice: Giambatista Pasquale, 1771), 18, 33–34.

4. Ferdinando Galiani, *Dialogues sur le commerce des blés*, ed. Philip Stewart (Paris: SFEDS, 2018), 59.

5. Galiani, *Dialogues*, 115–116; Franco Venturi, "Galiani tra enciclopedisti e fisiocrati," *Rivista storica italiana* 72, no. 3 (1960): 45–64, at 53.

6. Jean-Claude Perrault, *Une histoire intellectuelle de l'économie politique (XVII–XVIIIe siècles)* (Paris: Éditions de l'EHESS, 1992), 238.

7. Perrault, *Une histoire intellectuelle*, 16–17.

8. Perrault, *Une histoire intellectuelle*, 19.

9. Meek, *The Economics of Physiocracy* (London: Allen and Unwin, 1963), 47–49.

10. Meek, *Economics of Physiocracy*, 51; Madeleine Dobie, *Trading Places: Colonization and Slavery in Eighteenth-Century French Culture* (Ithaca, NY: Cornell University Press, 2010), 14–15.

11. Benoit Malbranque, *Le libéralisme à l'essaie. Turgot intendant du Limousin (1761–1774)* (Paris: Institut Coppet, 2015), 44.

12. Emma Rothschild, *Economic Sentiments: Adam Smith, Condorcet, and the Enlightenment* (Cambridge, MA: Harvard University Press, 2001), 79; Malbranque, *Le libéralisme à l'essaie*, 58.

13. Cynthia A. Bouton, *The Flour War: Gender, Class, and Community in Late Ancien Régime French Society* (University Park: Penn State University Press, 1993), 81; Gilbert Foccarello, "Galiani, Necker, and Turgot: A Debate on Economic Reform and Policy in 18th Century France," *European Journal of the History of Economic Thought* 1, no. 3 (1994): 519–550.

14. Jacob Soll, "From Virtue to Surplus: Jacques Necker's *Compte Rendu* (1781) and the Origins of Modern Political Discourse," *Representations* 134, no. 1 (2016): 29–63; Jacques Necker, *Sur la législation et le commerce des grains* (Paris: Chez Pissot, 1775), 50–52.

15. Steven L. Kaplan, *Bread, Politics, and Political Economy in the Reign of Louis XV*, 2nd ed. (New York: Anthem Press, 2012), 589–595.

16. Kaplan, *Bread, Politics*, 247; Istvan Hont, *Politics in Commercial Society: Jean-Jacques Rousseau and Adam Smith*, ed. Béla Kapossy and Michael Sonensher (Cambridge, MA: Harvard University Press, 2015), 18–19.

17. Antoine Lilti, *The Invention of Celebrity* (Cambridge, UK: Polity, 2017), 117; Jean-Jacques Rousseau, *Du contrat social*, ed. Pierre Burgelin (Paris: Garnier-Flammarion, 1966), 41; Jean-Jacques Rousseau, *A Discourse on Inequality*, ed. Maurice Cranston (London: Penguin, 1984), 77.

18. Rousseau, *Discourse on Inequality*, 101, 109, 127, 137.

CHAPTER 13: ADAM SMITH AND THE BENEVOLENT FREE-TRADE SOCIETY

1. Friedrich Hayek, *The Road to Serfdom*, ed. Bruce Caldwell (Chicago: University of Chicago Press, 2007), 88, 100; Milton Friedman, *Free to Choose: A Personal Statement*, 3rd ed. (New York: Harcourt, 1990), 1–2.

2. Adam Smith, *An Inquiry into the Nature and Causes of the Wealth of Nations*, ed. Roy Harold Campbell and Andrew Skinner, 2 vols. (Indianapolis: Liberty Fund, 1981), vol. 1, bk. I, chap. vii, para. 12; vol. 2, bk. V, chap. iih, para. 12; vol. 2, bk. IV, chap. viii, para. 49; vol. 2, bk. IV, chap. 9, para. 3; Adam Smith, *The Theory of Moral Sentiments*, ed. D. D.

Raphael and A. L. Macfie (Indianapolis: Liberty Fund, 1984), pt. 6, sec. 2, chap. 2, para. 17.

3. Steven Pincus, *The Global British Empire to 1784*, unpublished manuscript; Paul Butel, "France, the Antilles, and Europe in the Seventeenth and Eighteenth Centuries: Renewals of Foreign Trade," in *The Rise of Merchant Empires*, ed. James D. Tracy (Cambridge: Cambridge University Press, 1990), 168–172; T. S. Ashton, *An Economic History of England: The Eighteenth Century* (London: Methuen, 1955), 104; François Crouzet, "Angleterre et France au XVIIIe siècle: Essaie d'analyse comparé de deux croissances économiques," *Annales. Économies, sociétés, civilisations* 21, no. 2 (1966): 254–291, at 268; Ralph Davis, "English Foreign Trade, 1700–1774," *Economic History Review*, n.s., 15, no. 2 (1962): 285–303, at 286; François Crouzet, *La guerre économique franco-anglaise au XVIIIe siècle* (Paris: Fayard, 2008), 367–370; Paul Cheney, *Revolutionary Commerce: Globalization and the French Monarchy* (Cambridge, MA: Harvard University Press, 2010), 101; François Crouzet, *Britain Ascendant: Comparative Studies in Franco-British Economic History*, trans. Martin Thom (Cambridge: Cambridge University Press, 1990), 216.

4. Dan Edelstein, *The Enlightenment: A Genealogy* (Chicago: University of Chicago Press, 2010), 9.

5. David Hume, *An Inquiry Concerning Human Understanding*, ed. Charles W. Hendel (Indianapolis: Library of the Liberal Arts, 1955), 1–11, 17; Dario Perinetti, "Hume at La Flèche: Skepticism and the French Connection," *Journal of the History of Philosophy* 56, no. 1 (2018): 45–74, at 57–58; Margaret Schabas and Carl Wennerlind, *A Philosopher's Economist: Hume and the Rise of Capitalism* (Chicago: University of Chicago Press, 2020), 33; Pedro Faria, "David Hume, the Académie des Inscriptions, and the Nature of Historical Evidence in the Eighteenth Century," *Modern Intellectual History* 18, no. 2 (2020): 288–322.

6. Perinetti, "Hume at La Flèche," 54; Hume, *Concerning Human Understanding*, 168.

7. Hume, *Concerning Human Understanding*, 172–173; James A. Harris, *Hume: An Intellectual Biography* (Cambridge: Cambridge University Press, 2015), 97.

8. Carl L. Becker, *The Heavenly City of the Eighteenth-Century Philosophers* (New Haven, CT: Yale University Press, 1932), 85, 102; Anthony Grafton, *The Footnote: A Curious History* (Cambridge, MA: Harvard University Press, 1997), 103; David Hume, *Selected Essays*, ed. Stephen

Copley and Andrew Edgar (Oxford: Oxford University Press, 1998), xiii, 56, 58, 61.

9. Hume, *Selected Essays*, 188–189, 193, 194.

10. Jesse Norman, *Adam Smith: The Father of Economics* (New York: Basic Books, 2018), 194.

11. Smith, *Theory of Moral Sentiments*, sec. 1, chap. 1, para. 1; sec. 3, chap. 2, para. 9; Adam Smith, "Letter to the *Edinburgh Review*," 1755, in Smith, *Essays on Philosophical Subjects*, with Dugald Stewart's "Account of Adam Smith," ed. W. P. D. Wightman, J. C. Bryce, and I. S. Ross (Indianapolis: Liberty Fund, 1982), 253.

12. Smith, *Theory of Moral Sentiments*, pt. 1, sec. 1, chap. 2, para. 5.

13. Epictetus, *The Discourses, The Handbook, Fragments*, ed. J. M. Dent (London: Orion Books, 1995), 42, 44, 58; Smith, *Theory of Moral Sentiments*, pt. 1, chap. 1, para. 5.

14. Smith, *Theory of Moral Sentiments*, pt. 3, chap. 5, paras. 6–7; pt. 7, sec. 2, chap. 1, para. 39; Adam Smith, *Essays on Philosophical Subjects*, ed. W. P. D. Wightman and J. C. Bryce (Indianapolis: Liberty Fund, 1980), 45, 49, 104; Emma Rothschild, "Adam Smith and the Invisible Hand," *American Economic Review* 84, no. 2 (1994): 319–322, at 319.

15. Smith, *Wealth of Nations*, vol. 1, bk. IV, chap. iiic, pt. 2, para. 9.

16. Smith, *Theory of Moral Sentiments*, sec. 2, chap. 3, para. 1; sec. 5, chap. 2, paras. 10–13; sec. 7, chap. 4, paras. 36–37; Donald Winch, *Riches and Poverty: An Intellectual History of Political Economy in Britain, 1750–1834* (Cambridge: Cambridge University Press 1996), 98–99; Fonna Forman-Barzilai, *Adam Smith and the Circles of Sympathy: Cosmopolitanism and Moral Theory* (Cambridge: Cambridge University Press, 2010), 226.

17. Smith, *Theory of Moral Sentiments*, pt. 6, sec. 2, chap. 2, para. 13.

18. Nicholas Phillipson, *Adam Smith: An Enlightened Life* (New Haven, CT: Yale University Press, 2010), 159–166.

19. Phillipson, *Adam Smith*, 166; Geoffrey Holmes and Daniel Szechi, *The Age of Oligarchy: Pre-Industrial Britain, 1722–1783* (London: Longman, 1993), 282.

20. Phillipson, *Adam Smith*, 182.

21. Harris, *Hume*, 409–415; Phillipson, *Adam Smith*, 188.

22. Phillipson, *Adam Smith*, 193.

23. Smith, *Wealth of Nations*, vol. 2, bk. IV, chap. ix, para. 38; vol. 1, bk. II, chap. v, para. 12.

24. Smith, *Wealth of Nations*, vol. 1, bk. I, chap. viii, paras. 15–22; vol. 1, bk. I, chap. x, paras. 19, 31.

25. Smith, *Wealth of Nations*, vol. 2, bk. IV, chap. ix, paras. 11–14, vol. 2, bk. IV, chap. ii, para. 9; vol. 1, bk. I, chap. viii, para. 35; vol. 1, bk. IV, chap. ii, para. 9; vol. 2, bk. IV, chap. ix, para. 9; vol. 2, bk. V, chap. iik, para. 7.

26. Smith, *Wealth of Nations*, vol. 1, bk. I, chap. ii, paras. 1–2.

27. Emma Rothschild, *Economic Sentiments: Adam Smith, Condorcet, and the Enlightenment* (Cambridge, MA: Harvard University Press, 2001), 127.

28. Smith, *Wealth of Nations*, vol. 1, bk. IV, chap. ii, para. 38; vol. 2, bk. IV, chap. ix, paras. 1–3; vol. 1, bk. IV, chap. ii, para. 30.

29. E. P. Thompson, "Eighteenth-Century English Society: Class Struggle Without Class?," *Social History* 3, no. 2 (1978): 133–165, at 135; Frank McLynne, *Crime and Punishment in Eighteenth-Century England* (London: Routledge, 1989); Smith, *Wealth of Nations*, vol. 1, bk. I, chap. xic, para. 7.

30. Smith, *Wealth of Nations*, vol. 2, bk. IV, chap. viib, para. 20; vol. 2, bk. IV, chap. viic, para. 103.

31. Smith, *Wealth of Nations*, vol. 1, "Introduction and Plan of the Work," para. 4; vol. 2, bk. IV, chap. viib, para. 54.

32. John Rae, *Life of Adam Smith: 1895*, ed. Jacob Viner (New York: Augustus M. Kelley Publishers, 1977), 71–72.

33. Rothschild, *Economic Sentiments*, 133; Dugald Stewart, *Account of the Life and Writings of Adam Smith*, in *Works*, ed. Dugald Stewart, 7 vols. (Cambridge, MA: Hilliard and Brown, 1829), 7:1–75, at 67.

34. Smith, *Wealth of Nations*, vol. 1, bk. III, chap. iv, para. 20.

35. Smith, *Wealth of Nations*, vol. 2, bk. IV, chap. ii, paras. 10–20.

36. Smith, *Wealth of Nations*, vol. 1, bk. IV, chap. iiic, paras. 9, 13.

37. Rothschild, *Economic Sentiments*, 133–136; Voltaire, *Candide*, ed. Philip Littell (New York: Boni and Liveright, 1918), 168; Jacob Soll, *The Reckoning: Financial Accountability and the Rise and Fall of Nations* (New York: Basic Books, 2014), 129–130.

CHAPTER 14: FREE MARKET EMPIRE

1. William J. Baumol, *Economic Dynamics: An Introduction* (New York: Macmillan, 1951); D. M. Nachane, "In the Tradition of 'Magnificent Dynamics,'" *Economic and Political Weekly*, June 9, 2007.

2. Jeremy Bentham, *The Principles of Morals and Legislation* (Amherst, NY: Prometheus Books, 1988), 1–3, 29, 40.

3. Jeremy Bentham, "Bentham on Population and Government," *Population and Development Review* 21, no. 2 (1995): 399–404.

4. Thomas Malthus, *An Essay on the Principle of Population and Other Writings*, ed. Robert J. Mayhew (London: Penguin, 2015), 19; Adam Smith, *An Inquiry into the Nature and Causes of the Wealth of Nations*, ed. Roy Harold Campbell and Andrew Skinner, 2 vols. (Indianapolis: Liberty Fund, 1981), vol. 1, bk. I, chap. viii, para. 36.

5. Malthus, *Essay on the Principle of Population*, 40, 65, 74, 155–163.

6. David Ricardo, *Works*, ed. John Ramsay McCulloch (London: John Murray, 1846), 50–55; Paul Samuelson, "The Canonical Classical Model of Political Economy," in *Paul Samuelson on the History of Economic Analysis: Selected Essays*, ed. Steven J. Medema and Anthony M. C. Waterman (Cambridge: Cambridge University Press, 2015), 89–116, at 102–105.

7. Ricardo, *Works*, 55.

8. Smith, *Wealth of Nations*, vol. 1, bk. I, chap. viii, para. 37; Joan Robinson, "What Are the Questions?" *Journal of Economic Literature* 15, no. 4 (1977): 1318–1339, at 1334; Andre Gunder Frank, *Dependent Accumulation and Underdevelopment* (New York: Monthly Review Press, 1979); Henk Ligthart, "Portugal's Semi-Peripheral Middleman Role in Its Relations with England, 1640–1760," *Political Geography Quarterly* 7, no. 4 (1988): 353–362, at 360–361; Matthew Watson, "Historicising Ricardo's Comparative Advantage Theory, Challenging the Normative Foundations of Liberal International Political Economy," *New Political Economy* 22, no. 3 (2017): 257–272, at 259; John Gallagher and Ronald Robinson, "The Imperialism of Free Trade," *Economic History Review* 6, no. 1 (1953): 1–15, at 5; D. C. M. Platt, "The Imperialism of Free Trade: Some Reservations," *Economic History Review* 21, no. 2 (1968): 296–306; Joan Robinson, *Contributions to Modern Economics* (New York: Academic Press, 1978), 213; Joan Robinson, *The Economics of Imperfect Competition*, 2nd ed. (London: Palgrave Macmillan, 1969).

9. Frank Trentmann, *Free Trade Nation: Commerce, Consumption, and Civil Society in Modern Britain* (Oxford: Oxford University Press, 2008), 1–8.

10. Anthony Howe, *Free Trade and Liberal England, 1846–1946* (Oxford: Oxford University Press, 1998), 4, 113; Eileen P. Sullivan, "J. S. Mill's Defense of the British Empire," *Journal of the History of Ideas* 44,

no. 4 (1983): 599–617, at 606; John Stuart Mill, *Principles of Political Economy and Chapters on Socialism*, ed. Jonathan Riley (Oxford: Oxford University Press, 1994), xxxix, 112–113.

11. Mill, *Principles of Political Economy*, 113.

12. John Stuart Mill, *Considerations on Representative Government* (Ontario: Batoche Books, 2001), 46; Gary Remer, "The Classical Orator as Political Representative: Cicero and the Modern Concept of Representation," *Journal of Politics* 72, no. 4 (2010): 1063–1082, at 1064; Mill, *Principles of Political Economy*, 86.

13. Mill, *Principles of Political Economy*, 124–125, 377.

14. Mill, *Principles of Political Economy*, 381.

15. Charles Darwin, *The Life and Letters of Charles Darwin*, ed. Francis Darwin, 3 vols. (London: John Murray, 1887), 3:178–179; Charles Darwin, *The Origin of Species by Means of Natural Selection of the Preservation of Favoured Races in the Struggle for Life* (New York: Signet Classics, 2003), 5; Charles Darwin, *The Descent of Man, and Selection in Relation to Sex* (New York: Appleton and Company, 1889), 44.

16. Geoffrey Martin Hodgson, *Economics in the Shadows of Darwin and Marx: Essays on Institutional and Evolutionary Themes* (Cheltenham, UK: Edward Elgar, 2006), 12; Karl Marx, "The Production Process of Capital: Theories of Surplus Value," in Karl Marx and Friedrich Engels, *Collected Works*, vol. 31, *Marx, 1861–1863* (London: Lawrence and Wishart, 1989), 551; Gareth Stedman-Jones, *Karl Marx: Greatness and Illusion* (Cambridge, MA: Belknap Press of Harvard University Press, 2016), 174–175, 382–383; Karl Marx, *Capital*, ed. Ernest Mandel, trans. David Fernbach, 3 vols. (London: Penguin, 1992), 2:218; Bela A. Balassa, "Karl Marx and John Stuart Mill," *Weltwirtschaftsliches Archiv* 83 (1959): 147–165, at 150.

17. Michael Hudson, *America's Protectionist Takeoff, 1815–1914: The Neglected American School of Political Economy* (New York: Garland, 1975).

18. Hudson, *America's Protectionist Takeoff*, 54.

19. Jack Rackove, *Original Meanings: Politics and Ideas in the Making of the Constitution* (New York: Vintage, 1997), 236; Alexander Hamilton, *Report on the Subject of Manufactures* (Philadelphia: William Brown, 1827), 20.

20. Maurice G. Baxter, *Henry Clay and the American System* (Lexington: University of Kentucky Press, 1995), 27–28; Brian Reinbold and

Yi Wen, "Historical U.S. Trade Deficits," Economic Research, Federal Reserve Bank, 2019, no. 13, https://research.stlouisfed.org/publications /economic-synopses/2019/05/17/historical-u-s-trade-deficits.

21. Cheryl Shonhardt-Bailey, *From the Corn Laws to Free Trade: Interests, Ideas, and Institutions in Historical Perspective* (Cambridge, MA: MIT Press, 2006), 285; Francis Wrigley Hirst, *Free Trade and Other Fundamental Doctrines of the Manchester School* (London: Harper and Brothers, 1903).

22. Richard Cobden, "Repeal of the Corn Laws," May 15, 1843, in Hirst, *Free Trade*, 143–190, at 190; Richard Cobden, "Free Trade and the Reduction of Armaments," December 18, 1849, in Hirst, *Free Trade*, 239–257, at 252.

23. Richard Cobden, "Armaments, Retrenchment, and Financial Reform," January 10, 1849, in Hirst, *Free Trade*, 291–308, at 305; David Todd, *Free Trade and Its Enemies in France, 1814–1851* (Cambridge: Cambridge University Press, 2015), 201.

24. Boyd Hilton, *The Age of Atonement: The Influence of Evangelicalism on Social and Economic Thought, 1785–1865* (Oxford: Clarendon Press, 1986), 7, 261.

25. William Stanley Jevons, "Brief Account of a General Mathematical Theory of Political Economy," *Journal of the Royal Statistical Society, London* 29 (June 1866): 282–287; William Stanley Jevons, *Political Economy* (New York: Appleton and Company, 1878), 7; Eric Hobsbawm, *Industry and Empire: The Birth of the Industrial Revolution* (London: Penguin, 1999), 17, 211.

26. Hobsbawm, *Industry and Empire*, 31–38.

27. Jevons, *Political Economy*, 62, 76, 77, 79, 81; Donald Winch, "The Problematic Status of the Consumer in Orthodox Economic Thought," in *The Making of the Consumer: Knowledge, Power, and Identity in the Modern World*, ed. Frank Trentmann (Oxford: Berg, 2006), 31–52.

28. William Stanley Jevons, *The Coal Question* (London: Macmillan, 1865).

29. Jennifer Siegel, *For Peace and Money: French and British Finance in the Service of the Tsars and Commissars* (Oxford: Oxford University Press, 2014).

30. Alfred Marshall, *Principles of Economics* (New York: Cosimo, 2006), 233.

31. Marshall, *Principles of Economics*, 30–31, 68–69, 273.

CHAPTER 15: THE END OF VIRTUE: LIBERALISM AND LIBERTARIANISM

1. William Cunningham, *The Rise and Decline of the Free Trade Movement* (Cambridge: Cambridge University Press, 1905), 5–9.

2. Cunningham, *Rise and Decline*; Frank Trentmann, *Free Trade Nation: Commerce, Consumption, and Civil Society in Modern Britain* (Oxford: Oxford University Press, 2008), 91–98, 243.

3. Cunningham, *Rise and Decline*, 37, 85.

4. Cunningham, *Rise and Decline*, 97.

5. Cunningham, *Rise and Decline*, 119, 121–123, 158, 160.

6. Cunningham, *Rise and Decline*, 191–194, 197–198.

7. Cunningham, *Rise and Decline*, 200, 210.

8. John Maynard Keynes, *Laissez-Faire and Communism* (New York: New Republic, 1926), 65.

9. Keynes, *Laissez-Faire*, 31, 164.

10. Joan Robinson, *The Economics of Imperfect Competition*, 2nd ed. (London: Palgrave Macmillan, 1969), 211–228.

11. Joan Robinson, *The Accumulation of Capital* (New York: Palgrave Macmillan, 2013), 248, 330.

12. Carl Menger, *Principles of Economics*, trans. James Dingwall and Bert F. Hoselitz (Auburn, AL: Ludwig von Mises Institute, 2007), 51, 72–73; Janek Wasserman, *The Marginal Revolutionaries: How Austrian Economists Fought the War of Ideas* (New Haven, CT: Yale University Press, 2019), 33; Wasserman, *Marginal Revolutionaries*, 73.

13. Ludwig von Mises, *Economic Calculation in the Socialist Commonwealth*, trans. S. Alder (Auburn, AL: Ludwig von Mises Institute, 1990), 1–10.

14. Von Mises, *Economic Calculation*, 9; Wasserman, *Marginal Revolutionaries*, 82.

15. Wasserman, *Marginal Revolutionaries*, 35, 134.

16. Stephan A. Marglin and Juliet B. Schor, eds., *The Golden Age of Capitalism: Reinterpreting the Postwar Experience*, 2nd ed. (Oxford: Oxford University Press, 2007), 41.

17. Henry Ashby Turner Jr., "Big Business and the Rise of Hitler," *American Historical Review* 75, no. 1 (1969): 56–70.

18. Friedrich Hayek, *The Road to Serfdom*, ed. Bruce Caldwell (Chicago: University of Chicago Press, 2007), 35, 76, 89, 100, 110.

19. Elisabetta Galeotti, "Individualism, Social Rules, Tradition: The Case of Friedrich A. Hayek," *Political Theory* 15, no. 2 (1987): 163–181, at 169.

20. David Levy, "Interview with Milton Friedman," Federal Reserve Bank of Minneapolis, June 1, 1992, www.minneapolisfed.org/article/1992/interview-with-milton-friedman.

21. Milton Friedman, "Market Mechanisms and Central Economic Planning," in Milton Friedman, Sidney Hook, Rose Friedman, and Roger Freeman, *Market Mechanisms and Central Economic Planning* (Washington, DC: American Enterprise Institute, 1981), 1–19, at 9.

22. Milton Friedman, *Free to Choose: A Personal Statement*, 3rd ed. (New York: Harcourt, 1990), 94–97, 129.

23. Milton Friedman, "Quantity of Money Theory: A Restatement," in Milton Friedman, ed., *Studies in the Quantity Theory of Money* (Chicago: University of Chicago Press, 1956), 3–21, at 12.

24. Milton Friedman and Anna Jacobson Schwartz, *A Monetary History of the United States, 1867–1960* (Princeton, NJ: Princeton University Press, 1963), 7, 11.

25. Milton Friedman, "The Demand for Money: Some Theoretical and Empirical Results," National Bureau of Economic Research, Occasional Paper 68, 1959, www.nber.org/system/files/chapters/c5857/c5857.pdf, 1–25, at 2.

26. Milton Friedman, *Capitalism and Freedom*, 3rd ed. (Chicago: University of Chicago Press, 2002), 137.

27. Milton Friedman, *An Economist's Protest: Columns in Political Economy* (Sun Lakes, AZ: Thomas Horon and Daughter, 1972), 6; Milton Friedman, "Say 'No' to Intolerance," *Liberty Magazine* 4, no. 6 (1991): 17–20.

28. Kim Phillips-Fein, *Invisible Hands: The Businessmen's Crusade Against the New Deal* (New York: Norton, 2009), 3.

29. Phillips-Fein, *Invisible Hands*, 4, 61 (du Pont quotation p. 4); Kevin M. Kruse, *One Nation Under God: How Corporate America Invented Christian America* (New York: Basic Books, 2015), 25.

30. Kruse, *One Nation Under God*, 61.

31. Kruse, *One Nation Under God*, 35; Phillips-Fein, *Invisible Hands*, 69, 77; Barry Goldwater, *The Conscience of a Conservative* (Shepherdsville, KY: Victor Publishing, 1960), 53.

32. Phillips-Fein, *Invisible Hands*, 228.

33. Jennifer Burns, "Godless Capitalism: Ayn Rand and the Conservative Movement," *Modern Intellectual History* 1, no. 3 (2004): 359–385; Brian Doherty, *Radicals for Capitalism: A Freewheeling History of the Modern Libertarian Movement* (New York: Public Affairs, 2008), 11.

34. Doug Bandow, "The West Fails to Social Engineer South Sudan," *American Conservative*, September 19, 2019, www.cato.org/commentary /west-fails-social-engineer-south-sudan.

35. Richard H. K. Vietor, *How Countries Compete: Strategy, Structure, and Government in the Global Economy* (Boston: Harvard Business School Press, 2007), 18.

CONCLUSION: AUTHORITARIAN CAPITALISM, DEMOCRACY, AND FREE MARKET THOUGHT

1. Isabella M. Weber, "The (Im-)Possibility of Rational Socialism: Mises in China's Market Reform Debate," 2021, University of Massachusetts, Amherst, Economics Department Working Paper Series, no. 2021-19, available at ScholarWorks@UMassAmherst, https://scholar works.umass.edu/econ_workingpaper/316; Isabella M. Weber, *How China Escaped Shock Therapy: The Market Reform Debate* (Abingdon, Oxon, UK: Routledge, 2021); Steven Mark Cohn, *Competing Economic Paradigms in China: The Co-Evolution of Economic Events, Economic Theory and Economics Education, 1976–2016* (Abingdon, Oxon, UK: Routledge, 2016), 26; Milton Friedman, *Friedman in China* (Hong Kong: Chinese University Press, 1990), 74; Milton Friedman, *Capitalism and Freedom*, 3rd ed. (Chicago: University of Chicago Press, 2002), 3–4; Milton Friedman, *Free to Choose: A Personal Statement*, 3rd ed. (New York: Harcourt, 1990), 57.

2. Cited in Weber, "The (Im-)Possibility of Rational Socialism."

3. Isabella Weber, "Origins of China's Contested Relation with Neoliberalism: Economics, the World Bank, and Milton Friedman at the Dawn of Reform," *Global Perspectives* 1, no 1 (2020): 1–14, at 7; Milton Friedman, "Market Mechanisms and Central Economic Planning," in Milton Friedman, Sidney Hook, Rose Friedman, and Roger Freeman, *Market Mechanisms and Central Economic Planning* (Washington, DC: American Enterprise Institute, 1981), 3; Weber, "The (Im-)Possibility of Rational Socialism."

4. Keith Bradsher and Li Yuan, "China's Economy Became No. 2 by Defying No. 1," *New York Times*, November 25, 2018.

5. Justin Yifu Lin, *Economic Development and Transition: Thought, Strategy, and Viability* (Cambridge: Cambridge University Press, 2009); Barry Naughton, *The Chinese Economy, Adaptation and Growth* (Cambridge, MA: MIT Press, 2018); Pankaj Mishra, "The Rise of China and the Fall of the 'Free Trade' Myth," *New York Times*, February 7, 2018; Keith Bradsher and Li Yuan, "The Chinese Thought They Had Little to Learn from Conventional Wisdom. Now It's the West That's Taking Notes," *New York Times*, November 25, 2018.

6. Jason Brennan, *Against Democracy* (Princeton, NJ: Princeton University Press, 2016), 192–193.

7. Karl Polanyi, *The Great Transformation: The Political and Economic Origins of Our Time* (Boston: Beacon Press, 1957).

8. Ellen Frankel Paul, "W. Stanley Jevons: Economic Revolutionary, Political Utilitarian," *Journal of the History of Ideas* 40, no. 2 (1979): 263–283, at 279.

INDEX

Index

Index

Index

Index

Index

Index

319

Index

Index

Index

Index

Index

Index

Jacob Soll is University Professor and a professor of philosophy, history, and accounting at the University of Southern California. The author of *The Reckoning* and *The Information Master*, he has been the recipient of many prestigious awards, including the MacArthur Fellowship, known as the "genius" grant. He lives in Los Angeles.